Spring 5 Design Patterns

Master efficient application development with patterns such as proxy, singleton, the template method, and more

Dinesh Rajput

BIRMINGHAM - MUMBAI

Spring 5 Design Patterns

First published: October 2017

Production reference: 1031017

Published by Packt Publishing Ltd.
Livery Place
35 Livery Street
Birmingham
B3 2PB, UK.

ISBN 978-1-78829-945-9

www.packtpub.com

Credits

Author
Dinesh Rajput

Reviewer
Rajeev Kumar Mohan

Commissioning Editor
Merint Mathew

Acquisition Editor
Karan Sadawana

Content Development Editor
Lawrence Veigas

Technical Editor
Supriya Thabe

Copy Editor
Sonia Mathur

Project Coordinator
Prajakta Naik

Proofreader
Safis Editing

Indexer
Rekha Nair

Graphics
Abhinash Sahu

Production Coordinator
Arvindkumar Gupta

About the Author

Dinesh Rajput is the chief editor of a website **Dineshonjava**, a technical blog dedicated to the Spring and Java technologies. It has a series of articles related to Java technologies. Dinesh has been a Spring enthusiast since 2008 and is a Pivotal Certified Spring Professional, an author, and a blogger. He has more than 10 years of experience with different aspects of Spring and Java design and development. His core expertise lies in the latest version of Spring Framework, Spring Boot, Spring Security, creating REST APIs, Microservice Architecture, Reactive Pattern, Spring AOP, Design Patterns, Struts, Hibernate, Web Services, Spring Batch, Cassandra, MongoDB, and Web Application Design and Architecture.

He is currently working as a technology manager at a leading product and web development company. He worked as a developer and tech lead at the Bennett, Coleman & Co. Ltd and was the first developer in his previous company, Paytm. Dinesh is passionate about the latest Java technologies and loves to write technical blogs related to it. He is a very active member of the Java and Spring community on different forums. When it comes to the Spring Framework and Java, Dinesh tops the list!

Through the course of writing this book, I contacted many people who helped me to clarify many dark corners of Reactive Patterns and GoF patterns. First of all, many thanks to the reviewer of this book, Rajeev Kumar Mohan, who is a technology consultant and trainer.

Special thanks go to Naveen Jain, who helped me create some real-world scenarios for all GoF design patterns, as mentioned in the examples.

And of course, my thanks to my lovely wife Anamika for encouraging me and supporting me in the writing of this book. Also thanks to my dear son Arnav for playing mobile games with me; it made me feel refreshed at the time of writing this book.

Finally, this book took shape from the work of Packt editors, Lawrence Veigas and Karan, who guided me through the writing process and Supriya, who joined at the last stage of the publishing process and brought many suggestions on how to make the book better and more useful for readers.

About the Reviewer

Rajeev Kumar Mohan has over 17 years of experience in IT, Software Development, and Corporate Training. He has worked for various IT majors like IBM, Pentasoft, Sapient, and Deft Infosystems. He started career as a programmer and managed various projects.

He is subject matter expert in Java, J2EE and related Frameworks, Android, and many UI Technologies. Besides SCJP and SCWCD, Rajeev has completed four masters.

He is Organic Chemistry and Computer Science master MCA and MBA. Rajeev is recruitment consultant and impaneled training consultant for HCL, Amdocs, Steria, TCS, Wipro, Oracle University, IBM, CSC, Genpact , Sapient Infosys and Capgemini.

Rajeev is the founder of Greater Noida based firm SNS Infotech. He also worked for the National Institute Of Fashion Technology [NIFT].

I would like to thank God to provide me opportunity to review the book. I would also like to thank my kids Sana and Saina and wife Nilam for their cooperation and for encouraging and allowing me to finish the review on time.

www.PacktPub.com

For support files and downloads related to your book, please visit www.PacktPub.com.

Did you know that Packt offers eBook versions of every book published, with PDF and ePub files available? You can upgrade to the eBook version at www.PacktPub.com and as a print book customer, you are entitled to a discount on the eBook copy. Get in touch with us at service@packtpub.com for more details.

At www.PacktPub.com, you can also read a collection of free technical articles, sign up for a range of free newsletters and receive exclusive discounts and offers on Packt books and eBooks.

https://www.packtpub.com/mapt

Get the most in-demand software skills with Mapt. Mapt gives you full access to all Packt books and video courses, as well as industry-leading tools to help you plan your personal development and advance your career.

Why subscribe?

- Fully searchable across every book published by Packt
- Copy and paste, print, and bookmark content
- On demand and accessible via a web browser

Customer Feedback

Thanks for purchasing this Packt book. At Packt, quality is at the heart of our editorial process. To help us improve, please leave us an honest review on this book's Amazon page at `https://www.amazon.com/dp/1788299450`.

If you'd like to join our team of regular reviewers, you can email us at `customerreviews@packtpub.com`. We award our regular reviewers with free eBooks and videos in exchange for their valuable feedback. Help us be relentless in improving our products!

I want to dedicate this book to my parents, my lovely wife, and my dear son Arnav.

Specially dedicated to my Grand Father Late Mr. Arjun Singh

Table of Contents

Preface

Spring 5 Design Patterns is for all Java developers who want to learn Spring for the enterprise application. Therefore, enterprise Java developers will find it particularly useful in the understanding of design patterns used by the Spring Framework and how it solves common design problems in the enterprise application, and they will fully appreciate the examples presented in this book. Before reading this book, readers should have basic knowledge of Core Java, JSP, Servlet, and XML.

Spring 5 Framework is newly launched by Pivotal with reactive programming. Spring 5 introduces many new features and enhancements from its previous version. We will discuss all this in the book. *Spring 5 Design Patterns* will give you in-depth insight about the Spring Framework.

The great part of today's Spring Framework is that all companies have already taken it as a primary framework for development of the enterprise application. For Spring, no external enterprise server is needed to start working with it.

The goals of writing this book are to discuss all design patterns used behind the Spring Framework and how they are implemented in the Spring Framework. Here, the author has also given you some best practices that must be used in the design and development of the application.

The book contains 12 chapters that cover everything from the basics to more complex design pattern such as reactive programming.

Spring 5 Design Patterns is divided into three sections. The first section introduces you to the essentials of the design patterns and the Spring Framework. The second section steps behind the front end and shows where Spring fits in the back end of an application. The third section expands on this by showing how to build web applications with Spring and introducing a new feature of the Spring 5 reactive programming. This part also shows how to handle concurrency in the enterprise application.

What this book covers

`Chapter 1`, *Getting Started with the Spring Framework 5.0 and Design Patterns,*gives an overview of the Spring 5 Framework and all new features of the Spring 5 Framework, including some basic examples of DI and AOP. You'll also get an overview of the great Spring portfolio.

`Chapter 2`, *Overview of GOF Design Patterns - Core Design Patterns,*gives an overview of the Core Design Pattern of the GoF Design Patterns family, including some best practices for an application design. You'll also get an overview of the common problems solving with design patterns.

`Chapter 3`, *Consideration of the Structural and the Behavioural Patterns*, gives an overview of the Structural and Behavioural Design Pattern of the GoF Design Patterns family, including some best practices for an application design. You'll also get an overview of the common problem solving with design patterns.

`Chapter 4`, *Wiring Beans using Dependency Injection Pattern*, explores dependency injection pattern and detail about the configuration of Spring in an application, showing you various ways of configurations in your application. This includes a configuration with XML, Annotation, Java, and Mix.

`Chapter 5`, *Understanding the Bean Life cycle and Used Patterns*, gives an overview of Spring Bean Life cycle managed by the Spring container, including an understanding of Spring containers and IoC. You'll also get an overview of the Spring bean life cycle callback handlers and post processors.

`Chapter 6`, *Spring Aspect Oriented Programming with Proxy and Decorator Pattern*, explores how to use Spring AOP to decouple cross-cutting concerns from the objects that they service. This chapter also sets the stage for later chapters where you'll use AOP to provide declarative services such as transactions, security, and caching.

`Chapter 7`, *Accessing Database with Spring and JDBC Template Pattern*, explores how to access the data with Spring and JDBC; here, you'll see how to use Spring's JDBC abstraction and JDBC Template to query relational databases in a way that is far simpler than native JDBC.

`Chapter 8`, *Accessing Database with Spring ORM and Transactions Implementing Patterns*, shows how Spring integrates with the ORM Frameworks, such as Hibernate and other implementations of the Java Persistence API (JPA) with Spring Transaction Management. Also, this contains magic provided by Spring Data JPA for on-the-fly queries generation.

`Chapter 9`, *Improving Performance of Application using Caching Patterns*, shows how to improve application performance by avoiding the database altogether if the data needed is readily available. So, I will show you how Spring provides support for caching data.

`Chapter 10`, *Implementing MVC Pattern in a Web Application using Spring*, gives a quick overview of developing a web application with the Spring MVC. You'll learn the MVC pattern, Front Controller pattern, Dispatcher Servlet with the basics of Spring MVC, a web framework built on the principles of the Spring Framework. You'll discover how to write controllers to handle web requests and see how to transparently bind request parameters and payload to your business objects while providing validation and error handling at the same time. This chapter also gives a brief introduction to view and view resolver in the Spring MVC.

`Chapter 11`, *Implementing Reactive Design Pattern*, explores the Reactive Programming Model, which is programming with asynchronous data streams. You'll see how the Reactive System is implemented in the Spring Web Module.

`Chapter 12`, *Implementing Concurrency Patterns*, takes a closer look at concurrency when handling multiple connections inside a web server. As outlined in our architectural model, request handling is decoupled from application logic.

What you need for this book

This book can be read without a computer or laptop at hand, in which case you need nothing more than the book itself. Although to follow the examples in the book, you need Java 8, which you can download from `http://www.oracle.com/technetwork/java/javase/downloads/jdk8-downloads-2133151.html`. You will also need your favorite IDE for the examples, but I have used the Software Spring Tool Suite; download the latest version of Spring Tool Suite (STS) from `https://spring.io/tools/sts/all` according to your system OS. The Java 8 and STS work on a variety of platforms--Windows, macOS, and Linux.

Who this book is for

Spring 5 Design Patterns is for all Java developers who want to learn Spring for the enterprise application. Therefore, enterprise Java developers will find it particularly useful in the understanding of design patterns used by Spring Framework and how it solves common design problems in the enterprise application, and they will fully appreciate the examples presented in this book. Before reading this book, readers should have basic knowledge of Core Java, JSP, Servlet, and XML.

Conventions

In this book, you will find a number of text styles that distinguish between different kinds of information. Here are some examples of these styles and an explanation of their meaning.

Code words in text, database table names, folder names, filenames, file extensions, pathnames, dummy URLs, and user input are shown as follows: "In our code, we have a `TransferServiceImpl` class, and its constructor takes two arguments:"

A block of code is set as follows:

```
public class JdbcTransferRepository implements TransferRepository{
  JdbcTemplate jdbcTemplate;
  public setDataSource(DataSource dataSource) {
    this.jdbcTemplate = new JdbcTemplate(dataSource);
}
 // ...
}
```

New terms and **important words** are shown in bold.

Warnings or important notes appear like this.

Tips and tricks appear like this.

Reader feedback

Feedback from our readers is always welcome. Let us know what you think about this book--what you liked or disliked. Reader feedback is important to us as it helps us develop titles that you will really get the most out of.

To send us general feedback, simply email `feedback@packtpub.com`, and mention the book's title in the subject of your message.

If there is a topic that you have expertise in and you are interested in either writing or contributing to a book, see our author guide at `www.packtpub.com/authors`.

Customer support

Now that you are the proud owner of a Packt book, we have a number of things to help you to get the most from your purchase.

Downloading the example code

You can download the example code files for this book from your account at http://www.packtpub.com. If you purchased this book elsewhere, you can visit http://www.packtpub.com/support and register to have the files emailed directly to you.

You can download the code files by following these steps:

1. Log in or register to our website using your email address and password.
2. Hover the mouse pointer on the **SUPPORT** tab at the top.
3. Click on **Code Downloads & Errata**.
4. Enter the name of the book in the **Search** box.
5. Select the book for which you're looking to download the code files.
6. Choose from the drop-down menu where you purchased this book from.
7. Click on **Code Download**.

Once the file is downloaded, please make sure that you unzip or extract the folder using the latest version of:

* WinRAR / 7-Zip for Windows
* Zipeg / iZip / UnRarX for Mac
* 7-Zip / PeaZip for Linux

The code bundle for the book is also hosted on GitHub at https://github.com/PacktPublishing/Spring5-Design-Patterns. We also have other code bundles from our rich catalog of books and videos available at https://github.com/PacktPublishing/. Check them out!

Errata

Although we have taken every care to ensure the accuracy of our content, mistakes do happen. If you find a mistake in one of our books--may be a mistake in the text or the code--we would be grateful if you could report this to us. By doing so, you can save other readers from frustration and help us improve subsequent versions of this book. If you find any errata, please report them by visiting http://www.packtpub.com/submit-errata, selecting your book, clicking on the **Errata Submission Form** link, and entering the details of your errata. Once your errata are verified, your submission will be accepted and the errata will be uploaded to our website or added to any list of existing errata under the Errata section of that title.

To view the previously submitted errata, go to https://www.packtpub.com/books/content/support and enter the name of the book in the search field. The required information will appear under the **Errata** section.

Piracy

Piracy of copyrighted material on the internet is an ongoing problem across all media. At Packt, we take the protection of our copyright and licenses very seriously. If you come across any illegal copies of our works in any form on the internet, please provide us with the location address or website name immediately so that we can pursue a remedy.

Please contact us at copyright@packtpub.com with a link to the suspected pirated material.

We appreciate your help in protecting our authors and our ability to bring you valuable content.

Questions

If you have a problem with any aspect of this book, you can contact us at questions@packtpub.com, and we will do our best to address the problem.

1
Getting Started with Spring Framework 5.0 and Design Patterns

This chapter will help you gain a better understanding of the Spring Framework with modules, and use the design patterns that are responsible for the success of Spring. This chapter will cover every major module of the Spring Framework. We begin with an introduction to the Spring Framework. We will have a look at the new features and enhancement introduced in Spring 5. We will also understand the design patterns used in the major modules of the Spring Framework.

At the end of this chapter, you will understand how Spring works, and how Spring solves the common problems of the design level of the enterprise application by using design patterns. You will know how to improve loose coupling between the components of applications and how to simplify application development by using Spring with design patterns.

This chapter will cover the following topics:

- Introduction of the Spring Framework
- Simplifying application development using Spring and its pattern
    - Using the power of the POJO pattern
    - Injecting dependencies
    - Applying aspects to address cross-cutting concerns
    - Applying a template pattern to eliminate boilerplate code

- Creating a Spring container for containing beans using the Factory pattern
    - Creating a container with an application context
    - The life of a bean in the container
- Spring modules
- New features in Spring Framework 5.0

Introducing Spring Framework

In the early days of Java, there were lots of heavier enterprise Java technologies for enterprise applications that provided enterprise solutions to programmers. However, it was not easy to maintain the applications because it was tightly coupled with the framework. A couple of years ago, apart from Spring, all Java technologies were heavier, like EJB. At the time, Spring was introduced as an alternative technology especially made for EJB because Spring provided a very simple, leaner, and lighter programming model compared with other existing Java technologies. Spring makes this possible by using many available design patterns, but it focused on the **Plain Old Java Object** (**POJO**) programming model. This model provided the simplicity to the Spring Framework. It also empowered ideas such as the **dependency injection** (**DI**) pattern and **Aspect-Oriented Programming** (**AOP**) by using the Proxy pattern and Decorator pattern.

The Spring Framework is an open source application framework and a Java-based platform that provides comprehensive infrastructure support for developing enterprise Java applications. So developers don't need to care about the infrastructure of the application; they should be focused on the business logic of the application rather than handling the configuration of the application. All infrastructure, configuration, and meta-configuration files, either Java-based configuration or XML-based configuration, both are handled by the Spring Framework. So this framework makes you more flexible in building an application with a POJOs programming model rather than a non-invasive programming model.

The Spring **Inversion of Control** (**IoC**) container is the heart of the entire framework. It helps glue together the different parts of the application, thus forming a coherent architecture. Spring MVC components can be used to build a very flexible web tier. The IOC container simplifies the development of the business layer with POJOs.

Spring simplifies the application development and removes a lot of the dependency on the other APIs. Let's see some examples of how you, as an application developer, can benefit from the Spring platform:

- All application classes are simple POJO classes--Spring is not invasive. It does not require you to extend framework classes or implement framework interfaces for most use cases.
- Spring applications do not require a Java EE application server, but they can be deployed on one.
- You can execute a method in a database transaction by using transaction management in Spring Framework without having any third-party transactional API.
- Using Spring, you can use a Java method as a request handler method or remote method, like a `service()` method of a servlet API, but without dealing with the servlet API of the servlet container.
- Spring enables you to use a local `java` method as a message handler method without using a **Java Message Service** (**JMS**) API in the application.
- Spring also enables you to use the local `java` method as a management operation without using a **Java Management Extensions** (**JMX**) API in the application.
- Spring serves as a container for your application objects. Your objects do not have to worry about finding and *establishing* connections with each other.
- Spring instantiates the beans and injects the dependencies of your objects into the application--it serves as a life cycle manager of the beans.

Simplifying application development using Spring and its pattern

Developing an enterprise application using the traditional Java platform has a lot of limitations when it comes to organizing the basic building blocks as individual components for reusability in your application. Creating reusable components for basic and common functionality is best design practice, so you cannot ignore it. To address the reusability problem in your application, you can use various design patterns, such as the Factory pattern, Abstract Factory pattern, Builder pattern, Decorator pattern, and Service Locator pattern, to compose the basic building blocks into a coherent whole, such as class and object instances, to promote the reusability of components. These patterns address the common and recursive application problems. Spring Framework simply implements these patterns internally, providing you with an infrastructure to use in a formalized way.

There are lots of complexities in enterprise application development, but Spring was created to address these, and makes it possible to simplify the process for developers. Spring isn't only limited to server-side development--it also helps simplifies things regarding building projects, testability, and loose coupling. Spring follows the POJO pattern, that is, a Spring component can be any type of POJO. A component is a self-contained piece of code that ideally could be reused in multiple applications.

Since this book is focused on all **design patterns** that are adopted by the Spring Framework to simplify Java development, we need to discuss or at least provide some basic implementation and consideration of design patterns and the best practices to design the infrastructure for enterprise application development. Spring uses the following strategies to make java development easy and testable:

- Spring uses the power of the *POJO pattern* for lightweight and minimally invasive development of enterprise applications
- It uses the power of the **dependency injection pattern** (**DI pattern**) for loose coupling and makes a system interface oriented
- It uses the power of the *Decorator and Proxy design pattern* for declarative programming through aspects and common conventions
- It uses the power of the *Template Design pattern* for eliminating boilerplate code with aspects and templates

In this chapter, I'll explain each of these ideas, and also show concrete examples of how Spring simplifies Java development. Let's start with exploring how Spring remains minimally invasive by encouraging POJO-oriented development by using the POJO pattern.

Using the power of the POJO pattern

There are many other frameworks for Java development that lock you in by forcing you to extend or implement one of their existing classes or interfaces; Struts, Tapestry, and earlier versions of EJB had this approach. The programming model of these frameworks is based on the invasive model. This makes it harder for your code to find bugs in the system, and sometimes it will render your code unintelligible. However, if you are working with Spring Framework, you don't need to implement or extend its existing classes and interfaces, so this is simply POJO-based implementation, following a non-invasive programming model. It makes it easier for your code to find bugs in the system, and keeps the code understandable.

Spring allows you to do programming with very simple non Spring classes, which means there is no need to implement Spring-specific classes or interfaces, so all classes in the Spring-based application are simply POJOs. That means you can compile and run these files without dependency on Spring libraries; you cannot even recognize that these classes are being used by the Spring Framework. In Java-based configuration, you will use Spring annotations, which is the worst case of the Spring-based application.

Let's look at this with the help of the following example:

```
package com.packt.chapter1.spring;
public class HelloWorld {
  public String hello() {
    return "Hello World";
  }
}
```

The preceding class is a simple POJO class with no special indication or implementation related to the framework to make it a Spring component. So this class could function equally well in a Spring application as it could in a non-Spring application. This is the beauty of Spring's non-invasive programming model. Another way that Spring empowers POJO is by collaborating with other POJOs using the DI pattern. Let's see how DI works to help decouple components.

Injecting dependencies between POJOs

The term *dependency injection* is not new-it is used by PicoContainer. Dependency injection is a design pattern that promotes loose coupling between the Spring components--that is, between the different collaborating POJOs. So by applying DI to your complex programming, your code will become simpler, easier to understand, and easier to test.

In your application, many objects are working together for a particular functionality as per your requirement. This collaboration between the objects is actually known as dependency injection. Injecting dependency between the working components helps you to unit test every component in your application without tight coupling.

In a working application, what the end user wants is to see the output. To create the output, a few objects in the application work together and are sometimes coupled. So when you are writing these complex application classes, consider the reusability of these classes and make these classes as independent as possible. This is a best practice of coding that will help you in unit testing these classes independently.

How DI works and makes things easy for development and testing

Let's look at DI pattern implementation in your application. It makes things easy to understand, loosely coupled, and testable across the application. Suppose we have a simple application (something more complex than a *Hello World* example that you might make in your college classes). Every class is working together to perform some business task and help build business needs and expectations. That means that each class in the application has its measure of responsibility for a business task, together with other collaborating objects (its dependencies). Let's look at the following image. This dependency between the objects can create complexity and tight coupling between the dependent objects:

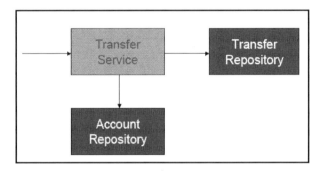

The TransferService component is traditionally dependent on two other components: TransferRepository and AccountRepository

A typical application system consists of several parts working together to carry out a use case. For example, consider the `TransferService` class, shown next.

`TransferService` using direct instantiation:

```
package com.packt.chapter1.bankapp.transfer;
public class TransferService {
  private AccountRepository accountRepository;
  public TransferService () {
    this.accountRepository = new AccountRepository();
  }
  public void transferMoney(Account a, Account b) {
    accountRepository.transfer(a, b);
  }
}
```

The `TransferService` object needs an `AccountRepository` object to make money transfer from account `a` to account `b`. Hence, it creates an instance of the `AccountRepository` object directly and uses it. But direct instantiation increases coupling and scatters the object creation code across the application, making it hard to maintain and difficult to write a unit test for `TransferService`, because, in this case, whenever you want to test the `transferMoney()` method of the `TransferService` class by using the `assert` to unit test, then the `transfer()` method of the `AccountRepository` class is also called unlikely by this test. But the developer is not aware about the dependency of `AccountRepository` on the `TransferService` class; at least, the developer is not able to test the `transferMoney()` method of the `TransferService` class using unit testing.

In enterprise applications, coupling is very dangerous, and it pushes you to a situation where you will not be able to do any enhancement in the application in the future, where any further changes in such an application can create a lot of bugs, and where fixing these bugs can create new bugs. Tightly coupled components are one of the reasons for major problems in these applications. Unnecessary tightly coupled code makes your application non-maintainable, and as time goes by, its code will not be reused, as it cannot be understood by other developers. But sometimes a certain amount of coupling is required for an enterprise application because completely uncoupled components are not possible in real-world cases. Each component in the application has some responsibility for a role and business requirement, to the extent that all components in the application have to be aware of the responsibility of the other components. That means coupling is necessary sometimes, but we have to manage the coupling between required components very carefully.

Using factory helper pattern for dependent components

Let's try another method for dependent objects using the Factory pattern. This design pattern is based on the GOF factory design pattern to create object instances by using a factory method. So this method actually centralizes the use of the new operator. It creates the object instances based on the information provided by the client code. This pattern is widely used in the dependency injection strategy.

`TransferService` using factory helper:

```
package com.packt.chapter1.bankapp.transfer;
public class TransferService {
  private AccountRepository accountRepository;
  public TransferService() {
    this.accountRepository =
      AccountRepositoryFactory.getInstance("jdbc");
  }
  public void transferMoney(Account a, Account b) {
    accountRepository.transfer(a, b);
  }
}
```

In the preceding code, we use the Factory pattern to create an object of
`AccountRepository`. In software engineering, one of the best practices of application
design and development is **program-to-interface** (**P2I**). According to this practice, concrete
classes must implement an interface that is used in the client code for the caller rather than
using a concrete class. By using P2I, you can improve the preceding code. Therefore, we can
easily replace it with a different implementation of the interface with little impact on the
client code. So programming-to-interface provides us with a method involving low
coupling. In other words, there is no direct dependency on a concrete implementation
leading to low coupling. Let's look at the following code. Here, `AccountRepository` is an
interface rather than a class:

```
public interface AccountRepository{
  void transfer();
  //other methods
}
```

So we can implement it as per our requirement, and it is dependent upon the client's
infrastructure. Suppose we want an `AccountRepository` during the development phase
with JDBC API. We can provide a `JdbcAccountRepositry` concrete implementation of the
`AccountRepositry` interface, as shown here:

```
public class JdbcAccountRepositry implements AccountRepositry{
  //...implementation of methods defined in AccountRepositry
  // ...implementation of other methods
}
```

In this pattern, objects are created by factory classes to make it easy to maintain, and this avoids scattering the code of object creation across other business components. With a factory helper, it is also possible to make object creation configurable. This technique provides a solution for tight coupling, but we are still adding factory classes to the business component for fetching collaborating components. So let's see the DI pattern in the next section and look at how to solve this problem.

Using DI pattern for dependent components

According to the DI pattern, dependent objects are given their dependencies at the time of the creation of the objects by some factory or third party. This factory coordinates each object in the system in such a way that each dependent object is not expected to create their dependencies. This means that we have to focus on defining the dependencies instead of resolving the dependencies of collaborating objects in the enterprise application. Let's look at the following image. You will learn that dependencies are injected into the objects that need them:

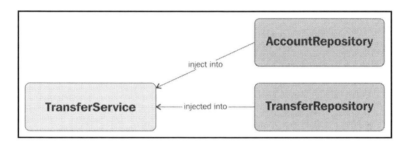

Dependency injection between the different collaborating components in the application

To illustrate this point, let's look at `TransferService` in the next section--a `TransferService` has dependency with `AccountRepository` and `TransferRepository`. Here, `TransferService` is capable of transferring money by any kind implementation of `TransferRepository`, that is, we can either use `JdbcTransferRepository` or `JpaTransferRepository`, depending on whichever comes along according to the deployment environment.

`TransferServiceImpl` is flexible enough to take on any `TransferRepository` it's given:

```
package com.packt.chapter1.bankapp;
public class TransferServiceImpl implements TransferService {
  private TransferRepository transferRepository;
  private AccountRepository  accountRepository;
  public TransferServiceImpl(TransferRepository transferRepository,
   AccountRepository  accountRepository) {
    this.transferRepository =
     transferRepository;//TransferRepository is injected
    this.accountRepository  = accountRepository;
    //AccountRepository is injected
  }
  public void transferMoney(Long a, Long b, Amount amount) {
    Account accountA = accountRepository.findByAccountId(a);
    Account accountB = accountRepository.findByAccountId(b);
    transferRepository.transfer(accountA, accountB, amount);
  }
}
```

Here you can see that `TransferServiceImpl` doesn't create its own repositories implementation. Instead, we have given the implementation of repositories at the time of construction as a constructor argument. This is a type of DI known as *constructor injection*. Here we have passed the repository interface type as an argument of the constructor. Now `TransferServiceImpl` could use any implementation of repositories, either JDBC, JPA, or mock objects. The point is that `TransferServiceImpl` isn't coupled to any specific implementation of repositories. It doesn't matter what kind of repository is used to transfer an amount from one account to another account, as long as it implements the repositories interfaces. If you are using the DI pattern of the Spring Framework, loose coupling is one of the key benefits. The DI pattern always promotes P2I, so each object knows about its dependencies by their associated interface rather than associated implementation, so the dependency can easily be swapped out with another implementation of that interface instead of changing to its dependent class implementation.

Spring provides support for assembling such an application system from its parts:

- Parts do not worry about finding each other
- Any part can easily be swapped out

The method for assembling an application system by creating associations between application parts or components is known as **wiring**. In Spring, there are many ways to wire collaborating components together to make an application system. For instance, we could use either an XML configuration file or a Java configuration file.

Now let's look at how to inject the dependencies of `TransferRepository` and `AccountRepository` into a `TransferService` with Spring:

```xml
<?xml version="1.0" encoding="UTF-8"?>
<beans xmlns="http://www.springframework.org/schema/beans"
xmlns:xsi="http://www.w3.org/2001/XMLSchema-instance"
xsi:schemaLocation="http://www.springframework.org/schema/beans
http://www.springframework.org/schema/beans/spring-beans.xsd">
<bean id="transferService"
 class="com.packt.chapter1.bankapp.service.TransferServiceImpl">
     <constructor-arg ref="accountRepository"/>
     <constructor-arg ref="transferRepository"/>
</bean>
<bean id="accountRepository" class="com.
 packt.chapter1.bankapp.repository.JdbcAccountRepository"/>
<bean id="transferRepository" class="com.
 packt.chapter1.bankapp.repository.JdbcTransferRepository"/>
</beans>
```

Here, `TransferServiceImpl`, `JdbcAccountRepository`, and `JdbcTransferRepository` are declared as beans in Spring. In the case of the `TransferServiceImpl` bean, it's constructed, passing a reference to the `AccountRepository` and `TransferRepository` beans as constructor arguments. You might like to know that Spring also allows you to express the same configuration using Java.

Spring offers Java-based configuration as an alternative to XML:

```java
package com.packt.chapter1.bankapp.config;

import org.springframework.context.annotation.Bean;
import org.springframework.context.annotation.Configuration;

import com.packt.chapter1.bankapp.repository.AccountRepository;
import com.packt.chapter1.bankapp.repository.TransferRepository;
import
 com.packt.chapter1.bankapp.repository.jdbc.JdbcAccountRepository;
import
 com.packt.chapter1.bankapp.repository.jdbc.JdbcTransferRepository;
import com.packt.chapter1.bankapp.service.TransferService;
import com.packt.chapter1.bankapp.service.TransferServiceImpl;

@Configuration
public class AppConfig {
 @Bean
 public TransferService transferService(){
   return new TransferServiceImpl(accountRepository(),
```

```
      transferRepository());
  }
  @Bean
  public AccountRepository accountRepository() {
    return new JdbcAccountRepository();
  }
  @Bean
  public TransferRepository transferRepository() {
    return new JdbcTransferRepository();
  }
}
```

The benefits of the dependency injection pattern are the same whether you are using an XML-based or a Java-based configuration:

- Dependency injection promotes loose coupling. You can remove hard-coded dependencies with best practice P2I, and you could provide dependencies from outside the application by using the Factory pattern and its built-in swappable and pluggable implementation
- The DI pattern promotes the composition design of object-oriented programming rather than inheritance programming

Although `TransferService` depends on an `AccountRepository` and `TransferRepository`, it doesn't care about what type (JDBC or JPA) of implementations of `AccountRepository` and `TransferRepository` are used in the application. Only Spring, through its configuration (XML- or Java-based), knows how all the components come together and are instantiated with their required dependencies using the DI pattern. DI makes it possible to change those dependencies with no changes to the dependent classes--that is, we could use either a JDBC implementation or a JPA implementation without changing the implementation of `AccountService`.

In a Spring application, an implementation of the application context (Spring offers `AnnotationConfigApplicationContext` for Java-based and `ClassPathXmlApplicationContext` for XML-based implementations) loads bean definitions and wires them together into a Spring container. The application context in Spring creates and wires the Spring beans for the application at startup. Look into the implementation of the Spring application context with Java-based configuration--It loads the Spring configuration files (`AppConfig.java` for Java and `Sprig.xml` for XML) located in the application's classpath. In the following code, the `main()` method of the `TransferMain` class uses a `AnnotationConfigApplicationContext` class to load the configuration class `AppConfig.java` and get an object of the `AccountService` class.

Spring offers Java-based configuration as an alternative to XML:

```
package com.packt.chapter1.bankapp;

import org.springframework.context.ConfigurableApplicationContext;
import
 org.springframework.context.annotation
 .AnnotationConfigApplicationContext;

import com.packt.chapter1.bankapp.config.AppConfig;
import com.packt.chapter1.bankapp.model.Amount;
import com.packt.chapter1.bankapp.service.TransferService;

public class TransferMain {

  public static void main(String[] args) {
    //Load Spring context
    ConfigurableApplicationContext applicationContext =
      new AnnotationConfigApplicationContext(AppConfig.class);
    //Get TransferService bean
    TransferService transferService =
     applicationContext.getBean(TransferService.class);
      //Use transfer method
    transferService.transferAmmount(1001, 2001,
     new Amount(2000.0));
    applicationContext.close();
  }

}
```

Here we have a quick introduction to the dependency injection pattern. You'll learn a lot more about the DI pattern in the coming chapters of this book. Now let's look at another way of simplifying Java development using Spring's declarative programming model through aspects and proxy patterns.

Applying aspects for cross cutting concerns

In a Spring application, the DI pattern provides us with loose coupling between collaborating software components, but **Aspect-Oriented Programming** in Spring (Spring **AOP**) enables you to capture common functionalities that are repetitive throughout your application. So we can say that Spring AOP promotes loose coupling and allows cross-cutting concerns, listed as follows, to be separated in a most elegant fashion. It allows these services to be applied transparently through declaration. With Spring AOP, it is possible to write custom aspects and configure them declaratively.

The generic functionalities that are needed in many places in your application are:

- Logging and tracing
- Transaction management
- Security
- Caching
- Error handling
- Performance monitoring
- Custom business rules

The components listed here are not part of your core application, but these components have some additional responsibilities, commonly referred to as cross-cutting concerns because they tend to cut across multiple components in a system beyond their core responsibilities. If you put these components with your core functionalities, thereby implementing cross-cutting concerns without modularization, it will have two major problems:

- **Code tangling**: A coupling of concerns means that a cross-cutting concern code, such as a security concern, a transaction concern, and a logging concern, is coupled with the code for business objects in your application.
- **Code scattering**: Code scattering refers to the same concern being spread across modules. This means that your concern code of security, transaction, and logging is spread across all modules of the system. In other words, you can say there is a duplicity of the same concern code across the system.

The following diagramillustrates this complexity. The business objects are too intimately involved with the cross-cutting concerns. Not only does each object know that it's being logged, secured, and involved in a transactional context, but each object is also responsible for performing those services assigned only to it:

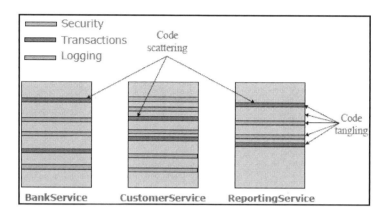

Cross-cutting concerns, such as logging, security and transaction, are often scattered about in modules where those tasks are not their primary concern

Spring AOP enables the modularization of cross-cutting concerns to avoid tangling and scattering. You can apply these modularized concerns to the core business components of the application declaratively without affecting the aforementioned the above components. The aspects ensure that the POJOs remain plain. Spring AOP makes this magic possible by using the Proxy Design Pattern. We will discuss the Proxy Design pattern more in the coming chapters of this book.

How Spring AOP works

The following points describe the work of Spring AOP:

- **Implement your mainline application logic**: Focusing on the core problem means that, when you are writing the application business logic, you don't need to worry about adding additional functionalities, such as logging, security, and transaction, between the business codes-Spring AOP takes care of it.

- **Write aspects to implement your cross-cutting concerns**: Spring provides many aspects out of the box, which means you can write additional functionalities in the form of the aspect as independent units in Spring AOP. These aspects have additional responsibilities as cross-cutting concerns beyond the application logic codes.

- **Weave the aspects into your application**: Adding the cross-cutting behaviors to the right places, that is, after writing the aspects for additional responsibilities, you could declaratively inject them into the right places in the application logic codes.

Let's look at an illustration of AOP in Spring:

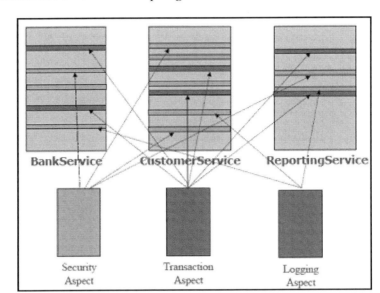

AOP-based system evolution--this leaves the application components to focus on their specific business functionalities

In the preceding diagram, Spring AOP separates the cross-cutting concerns, for example, security, transaction, and logging, from the business modules, that is, `BankService`, `CustomerService`, and `ReportingService`. These cross-cutting concerns are applied to predefined points (stripes in the preceding diagram) of the business modules at the running time of the application.

Suppose that you want to log the messages before and after calling the `transferAmmount()` method of `TransferService` using the services of a `LoggingAspect`. The following listing shows the `LoggingAspect` class you might use.

`LoggingAspect` call is used for logging the system for `TransferService`:

```
package com.packt.chapter1.bankapp.aspect;

import org.aspectj.lang.annotation.After;
import org.aspectj.lang.annotation.Aspect;
import org.aspectj.lang.annotation.Before;

@Aspect
public class LoggingAspect {
  @Before("execution(* *.transferAmount(..))")
  public void logBeforeTransfer(){
```

```
    System.out.println("####LoggingAspect.logBeforeTransfer()
    method called before transfer amount####");
  }
  @After("execution(* *.transferAmount(..))")
  public void logAfterTransfer(){
    System.out.println("####LoggingAspect.logAfterTransfer() method
    called after transfer amount####");
  }
}
```

To turn LoggingAspect into an aspect bean, all you need to do is declare it as one in the Spring configuration file. Also, to make it an aspect, you have to add the @Aspect annotation to this class. Here's the updated AppConfig.java file, revised to declare LoggingAspect as an aspect.

Declaring LoggingAspect as an aspect and enabling the Apsect proxy feature of Spring AOP:

```
package com.packt.chapter1.bankapp.config;

import org.springframework.context.annotation.Bean;
import org.springframework.context.annotation.Configuration;
import
  org.springframework.context.annotation.EnableAspectJAutoProxy;

import com.packt.chapter1.bankapp.aspect.LoggingAspect;
import com.packt.chapter1.bankapp.repository.AccountRepository;
import com.packt.chapter1.bankapp.repository.TransferRepository;
import
  com.packt.chapter1.bankapp.repository.jdbc.JdbcAccountRepository;
import
  com.packt.chapter1.bankapp.repository.jdbc.JdbcTransferRepository;
import com.packt.chapter1.bankapp.service.TransferService;
import com.packt.chapter1.bankapp.service.TransferServiceImpl;

@Configuration
@EnableAspectJAutoProxy
public class AppConfig {
  @Bean
  public TransferService transferService(){
    return new TransferServiceImpl(accountRepository(),
    transferRepository());
  }
  @Bean
  public AccountRepository accountRepository() {
    return new JdbcAccountRepository();
  }
```

```
    @Bean
    public TransferRepository transferRepository() {
      return new JdbcTransferRepository();
    }
    @Bean
    public LoggingAspect loggingAspect() {
      return new LoggingAspect();
    }
}
```

Here, we're using Spring's AOP configuration based on Java to declare the `LoggingAspect` bean as an aspect. First, we declare `LoggingAspect` as a bean. Then we annotate that bean with the `@Aspect` annotation.

We annotate `logBeforeTransfer()` of `LoggingAspect` with the `@Before` annotation so that this method is called before the `transferAmount()` is executed. This is called **before advice**. Then, we annotate another method of `LoggingAspect` with the `@After` annotation to declare that the `logAfterTransfer()` method should be called after `transferAmount()` has executed. This is known as **after advice**.

`@EnableAspectJAutoProxy` is used to enable Spring AOP features in the application. This annotation actually forces you to apply proxy to some of the components that are defined in the spring configuration file. We'll talk more about Spring AOP later, in Chapter 6, *Spring Aspect Oriented Programming with Proxy and Decorator Pattern*. For now, it's enough to know that you've asked Spring to call `logBeforeTransfer()` and `logAferTransfer()` of `LoggingAspect` before and after the `transferAmount()` method of the `TransferService` class. For now, there are two important points to take away from this example:

- `LoggingAspect` is still a POJO (if you ignore the `@Aspect` annotation or are using XML-based configuration)--nothing about it indicates that it's to be used as an aspect.
- It is important to remember that `LoggingAspect` can be applied to `TransferService` without `TransferService` needing to explicitly call it. In fact, `TransferService` remains completely unaware of the existence of `LoggingAspect`.

Let's move to another way that Spring simplifies Java development.

Applying the template pattern to eliminate boilerplate code

At one point in the enterprise application, we saw some code that looked like code we had already written before in the same application. That is actually boilerplate code. It is code that we often have to write again and again in the same application to accomplish common requirements in different parts of the application. Unfortunately, there are a lot of places where Java APIs involve a bunch of boilerplate code. A common example of boilerplate code can be seen when working with JDBC to query data from a database. If you've ever worked with JDBC, you've probably written something in code that deals with the following:

- Retrieving a connection from the connection pool
- Creating a `PreparedStatement` object
- Binding SQL parameters
- Executing the `PreparedStatement` object
- Retrieving data from the `ResultSet` object and populating data container objects
- Releasing all database resources

Let's look at the following code, it contains boilerplate code with the JDBC API of the Java:

```java
public Account getAccountById(long id) {
  Connection conn = null;
  PreparedStatement stmt = null;
  ResultSet rs = null;
  try {
    conn = dataSource.getConnection();
    stmt = conn.prepareStatement(
      "select id, name, amount from " +
      "account where id=?");
    stmt.setLong(1, id);
    rs = stmt.executeQuery();
    Account account = null;
    if (rs.next()) {
      account = new Account();
      account.setId(rs.getLong("id"));
      account.setName(rs.getString("name"));
      account.setAmount(rs.getString("amount"));
    }
    return account;
  } catch (SQLException e) {
  } finally {
      if(rs != null) {
```

```
        try {
           rs.close();
        } catch(SQLException e) {}
      }
      if(stmt != null) {
        try {
           stmt.close();
        } catch(SQLException e) {}
      }
      if(conn != null) {
        try {
           conn.close();
        } catch(SQLException e) {}
      }
    }
  return null;
}
```

In the preceding code, we can see that the JDBC code queries the database for an account name and amount. For this simple task, we have to create a connection, then create a statement, and finally query for the results. We also have to catch SQLException, a checked exception, even though there's not a lot you can do if it's thrown. Lastly, we have to clean up the mess, closing down the connection statement and result set. This could also force it to handle JDBC's exception, so you must catch SQLException here as well. This kind of boilerplate code seriously hurts reusability.

Spring JDBC solves the problem of boilerplate code by using the Template Design pattern, and it makes life very easy by removing the common code in templates. This makes the data access code very clean and prevents nagging problems, such as connection leaks, because the Spring Framework ensures that all database resources are released properly.

The Template Design pattern in Spring

Let's see how to go about using the Template Design pattern in spring:

- Define the outline or skeleton of an algorithm

1. Leave the details for specific implementations until later.
2. Hide away large amounts of boilerplate code.

- Spring provides many template classes:
- JdbcTemplate
- JmsTemplate

- RestTemplate
- WebServiceTemplate
- Most hide low-level resource management

Let's look at the same code that we used earlier with Spring's JdbcTemplate and how it removes the boilerplate code.

Use JdbcTemplates to let your code the focus on the task:

```
public Account getAccountById(long id) {
   return jdbcTemplate.queryForObject(
     "select id, name, amoount" +
     "from account where id=?",
      new RowMapper<Account>() {
         public Account mapRow(ResultSet rs,
          int rowNum) throws SQLException {
            account = new Account();
            account.setId(rs.getLong("id"));
            account.setName(rs.getString("name"));
            account.setAmount(rs.getString("amount"));
            return account;
         }
      },
    id);
}
```

As you can see in the preceding code, this new version of getAccountById() is much simpler as compared to the boiler plate code, and here the method is focused on selecting an account from the database rather than creating a database connection, creating a statement, executing the query, handling the SQL exception, and finally closing the connection as well. With the template, you have to provide the SQL query and a RowMapper used for mapping the resulting set data to the domain object in the template's queryForObject() method. The template is responsible for doing everything for this operation, such as database connection and so on. It also hides a lot of boilerplate code behind the framework.

We have seen in this section how Spring attacks the complexities of Java development with the power of POJO-oriented development and patterns such as the DI pattern, the Aspect-using Proxy pattern, and the Template method design pattern.

In the next section, we will look at how to use a Spring container to create and manage the Spring beans in the application.

Using a Spring container to manage beans with the Factory pattern

Spring provides us with a container, and our application objects live in this Spring container. As shown in the following diagram, this container is responsible for creating and managing the objects:

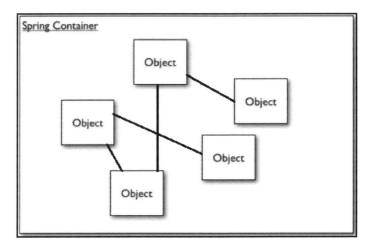

In a Spring application, our application objects live in this Spring container

The **Spring Container** also wires the many **Object** together according to its configuration. It is configured with some initialized parameters, and manages their complete life cycle from start to finish.

Basically, there are two distinct types of Spring container:

- Bean factory
- Application contexts

Bean factory

In the Spring Framework, the `org.springframework.beans.factory.BeanFactory` interface provides the bean factory, which is a Spring IoC container. `XmlBeanFactory` is an implementation class for this interface. This container reads the configuration metadata from an XML file. It is based on the GOF factory method design pattern--it creates, manages, caches, and wires the application objects in a sophisticated manner. The bean factory is merely an object pool where objects are created and managed by configuration. For small applications, this is sufficient, but enterprise applications demand more, so spring provides another version of the spring container with more features.

In the next section, we will learn about the application context and how Spring creates it in the application.

Application contexts

In the Spring Framework, the `org.springframework.context.ApplicationContext` interface also provides Spring's IoC container. It is simply a wrapper of the bean factory, providing some extra application context services, such as support for AOP and, hence, declarative transaction, security, and instrumentation support such as support for message resources required for internationalization, and the ability to publish application events to interested event listeners.

Creating a container with an application context

Spring provides several flavors of application context as a bean container. There are multiple core implementations of the `ApplicationContext` interface, as shown here:

- `FileSystemXmlApplicationContext`: This class is an implementation of `ApplicationContext` that loads application context bean definitions from the configuration files (XML) located in the file system.
- `ClassPathXmlApplicationContext`: This class is an implementation of `ApplicationContext` that loads application context bean definitions from the configuration files (XML) located in the classpath of the application.
- `AnnotationConfigApplicationContext`: This class is an implementation of `ApplicationContext` that loads application context bean definitions from the configuration classes (Java based) from the class path of the application.

Spring provides you with a web-aware implementation of the `ApplicationContext` interface, as shown here:

- `XmlWebApplicationContext`: This class is a web-aware implementation of `ApplicationContext` that loads application context bean definitions from the configuration files (XML) contained in a web application.
- `AnnotationConfigWebApplicationContext`: This class is a web-aware implementation of `ApplicationContext` that loads Spring web application context bean definitions from one or more Java-based configuration classes.

We can use either one of these implementations to load beans into a bean factory. It depends upon our application configuration file locations. For example, if you want to load your configuration file `spring.xml` from the file system in a specific location, Spring provides you with a `FileSystemXmlApplicationContext`, class that looks for the configuration file `spring.xml` in a specific location within the file system:

```
ApplicationContext context = new
  FileSystemXmlApplicationContext("d:/spring.xml");
```

In the same way, you can also load your application configuration file `spring.xml` from the classpath of your application by using a `ClassPathXmlApplicationContext` class provided by Spring. It looks for the configuration file `spring.xml` anywhere in the classpath (including JAR files):

```
ApplicationContext context = new
  ClassPathXmlApplicationContext("spring.xml");
```

If you are using a Java configuration instead of an XML configuration, you can use `AnnotationConfigApplicationContext`:

```
ApplicationContext context = new
  AnnotationConfigApplicationContext(AppConfig.class);
```

After loading the configuration files and getting an application context, we can fetch beans from the Spring container by calling the `getBean()` method of the application context:

```
TransferService transferService =
  context.getBean(TransferService.class);
```

In the following section, we will learn about the Spring bean life cycle, and how a Spring container reacts to the Spring bean to create and manage it.

Life of a bean in the container

The Spring application context uses the Factory method design pattern to create Spring beans in the container in the correct order according to the given configuration. So the Spring container has the responsibility of managing the life cycle of the bean from creation to destruction. In the normal java application, Java's `new` keyword is used to instantiate the bean, and it's ready to use. Once the bean is no longer in use, it's eligible for garbage collection. But in the Spring container, the life cycle of the bean is more elaborate. The following image shows the life cycle of a typical Spring bean:

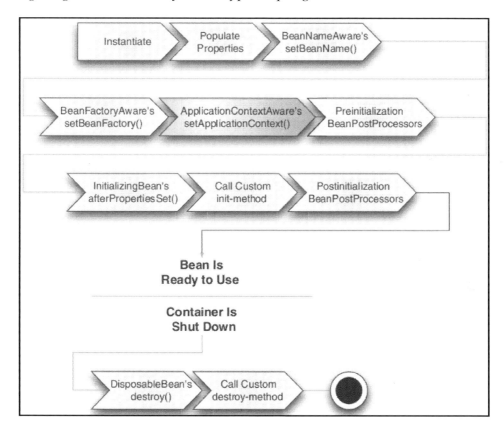

The life cycle of a Spring bean in the Spring container is as follows:

1. Load all bean definitions, creating an ordered graph.
2. Instantiate and run `BeanFactoryPostProcessors` (you can update bean definitions here).
3. Instantiate each bean.

4. Spring injects the values and bean references into the beans' properties.

5. Spring passes the ID of the bean to the `setBeanName()` method of the `BeanNameAware` interface if any bean implements it.

6. Spring passes the reference of the bean factory itself to the `setBeanFactory()` method of `BeanFactoryAware` if any bean implements it.

7. Spring passes the reference of the application context itself to the `setApplicationContext()` method of `ApplicationContextAware` if any bean implements it.

8. `BeanPostProcessor` is an interface, and Spring allows you to implement it with your bean, and modifies the instance of the bean before the initializer is invoked in the Spring bean container by calling its `postProcessBeforeInitialization()`.

9. If your bean implements the `InitializingBean` interface, Spring calls its `afterPropertiesSet()` method to initialize any process or loading resource for your application. It's dependent on your specified initialization method. There are other methods to achieve this step, for example, you can use the `init-method` of the `<bean>` tag, the `initMethod` attribute of the `@Bean` annotation, and JSR 250's `@PostConstruct` annotation.

10. `BeanPostProcessor` is an interface, and spring allows you to implement it with your bean. It modifies the instance of the bean after the initializer is invoked in the spring bean container by calling its `postProcessAfterInitialization()`.

11. Now your bean is ready to use in the step, and your application can access this bean by using the `getBean()` method of the application context. Your beans remain live in the application context until it is closed by calling the `close()` method of the application context.

12. If your bean implements the `DisposibleBean` interface, Spring calls its `destroy()` method to destroy any process or clean up the resources of your application. There are other methods to achieve this step-for example, you can use the `destroy-method` of the `<bean>` tag, the `destroyMethod` attribute of the `@Bean` annotation, and JSR 250's `@PreDestroy` annotation.

13. These steps show the life cycle of Spring beans in the container.

14. The next section describes the modules that are provided by the Spring Framework.

Spring modules

Spring Framework has several distinct modules for a specific set of functionalities, and they work more or less independently of the others. This system is very flexible, so the developer can choose only those required for the enterprise application. For example, a developer can just use the Spring DI module and build the rest of the application with non-Spring components. So, Spring provides integration points to work with other frameworks and APIs--for example, you can use the Spring Core DI pattern only with the Struts application. In case the development team is more proficient in using Struts, it can be used instead of Spring MVC while the rest of the application uses Spring components and features, such as JDBC and transactions. So while the developers need to deploy the required dependencies with the Struts application, there is no need to add a whole Spring Framework.

Here is an overview of the entire module structure:

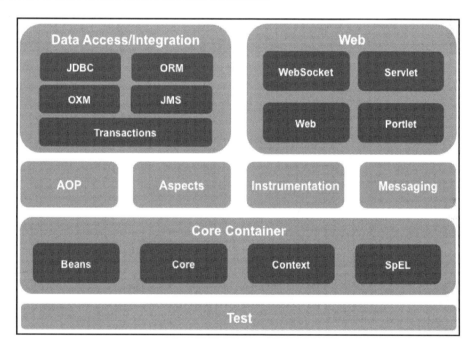

The various modules of the Spring Framework

Let's look at each of Spring's modules and see how each fits in to the bigger picture.

Core Spring container

This module of the Spring Framework uses lot of the design pattern such as the Factory method design pattern, DI pattern, Abstract Factory Design pattern, Singleton Design pattern, Prototype Design pattern, and so on. All other Spring modules are dependent on this module. You'll implicitly use these classes when you configure your application. It is also called the IoC container and is central to Spring's support for dependency injection, which manages how the beans in a Spring application are created, configured, and managed. You can create Spring container either by using the implementations of `BeanFactory` or the implementations of the `ApplicationContext`. This module contains the Spring bean factory, which is the portion of Spring that provides the DI.

Spring's AOP module

Spring AOP is a Java-based AOP Framework with AspectJ integration. It uses dynamic proxies for aspect weaving and focuses on using AOP to solve enterprise problems. This module is based on Proxy and Decorator Design patterns. This module enables the modularization of cross-cutting concerns to avoid tangling and eliminate scattering. Like DI, it supports loose coupling between the core business service and cross-cutting concerns. You can implement your custom aspects and configure them declaratively in your application without impacting on the code of business objects. It provides much flexibility in the code; you could remove or change the aspect logic without touching the code of the business objects. This is a very important module of the spring framework, so I will discuss it in detail in `Chapter 6`, *Spring Aspect Oriented Programming with Proxy and Decorator Pattern* of this book.

Spring DAO - data access and integration

Spring DAO and Spring JDBC make life very easy by using templates to remove the common code. The templates implement the GOF template method design pattern and provide suitable extension points to plug in custom code. If you are working with a traditional JDBC application, you have to write lots of boilerplate code to, for example, create a database connection, create a statement, find a result set, handle SQLException, and finally close the connection. If you are working with a Spring JDBC Framework with a DAO layer, then you do not have to write boilerplate code, unlike a traditional JDBC application. That means that Spring allows you to keep your application code clean and simple.

Spring's ORM

Spring also provides support to ORM solutions, and it provides integration with ORM tools for easy persistence of POJO objects in relational databases. This module actually provides an extension to the Spring DAO module. Like JDBC-based templates, Spring provides ORM templates to work with leading ORM products, such as Hibernate, JPA, OpenJPA, TopLink, iBATIS, and so on.

Spring web MVC

Spring provides a web and remote module for the enterprise web application. This module helps build highly flexible web applications, leveraging the complete benefits of the Spring IOC container. This module of Spring uses the patterns such as the MVC architectural pattern, Front Controller pattern, and the DispatcherServlet Pattern, and it seamlessly integrates with the servlet API. The Spring web module is very pluggable and flexible. We can add any of the view technologies, such as JSP, FreeMarker, Velocity, and so on. We can also integrate it with other frameworks, such as Struts, Webwork, and JSF, using spring IOC and DI.

New features in Spring Framework 5.0

Spring 5.0 is the freshest release of Spring available. There are a lot of exciting new features in Spring 5.0, including the following:

- Support for JDK 8 + 9 and Java EE 7 Baseline:

  Spring 5 supports Java 8 as a minimum requirement, as the entire framework codebase is based on Java 8.

  Spring Framework required at least Java EE 7 to run Spring Framework 5.0 applications. That means it requires Servlet 3.1, JMS 2.0, JPA 2.1.

- Deprecated and removed packages, classes, and methods:

  In Spring 5.0, some packages have been either removed or deprecated. It has had a package called `mock.static` removed from the spring-aspects module, and hence there is no support for `AnnotationDrivenStaticEntityMockingControl`.

Packages such as `web.view.tiles2` and `orm.hibernate3/hibernate4` have also been removed as of Spring 5.0. Now, in the latest spring framework, Tiles 3 and Hibernate 5 are being used.

The Spring 5.0 framework doesn't support Portlet, Velocity, JasperReports, XMLBeans, JDO, Guava (and so on) anymore.

Some deprecated classes and methods of earlier versions of Spring have been removed as of Spring 5.0.

- Adding the new reactive programming model:

    This model of programming has been introduced in the Spring 5.0 Framework. Let's look at the following listed point about the reactive programming model.

    Spring 5 introduced the Spring-core module `DataBuffer` and encoder/decoder abstractions with non-blocking semantics into the reactive programming model.

    Using the reactive model, Spring 5.0 provides the Spring-web module for HTTP message codec implementations with **JSON (Jackson)** and **XML (JAXB)** support.

    The Spring reactive programming model added a new `spring-web-reactive` module with reactive support for the `@Controller` programming model, adapting reactive streams to Servlet 3.1 containers, as well as non-Servlet runtimes, such as Netty and Undertow.

    Spring 5.0 also introduced a new `WebClient` with reactive support on the client side to access services.

As listed here, you can see that there are a lot of exciting new features and enhancements in the Spring Framework 5. So in this book, we will look at many of these new features with examples and their adopted design patterns.

Summary

After reading this chapter, you should now have a good overview of the Spring Framework and its most-used design patterns. I highlighted the problem with the J2EE traditional application, and how Spring solves these problems and simplifies Java development by using lots of design patterns and good practices to create an application. Spring aims to make enterprise Java development easier and to promote loosely coupled code. We have also discussed Spring AOP for cross-cutting concerns and the DI pattern for use with loose coupling and pluggable Spring components so that the objects don't need to know where their dependencies come from or how they're implemented. Spring Framework is an enabler for best practices and effective object design. Spring Framework has two important features--First it has a Spring container to create and manage the life of beans and second it provides support to several modules and integration to help simplify Java development.

2
Overview of GOF Design Patterns - Core Design Patterns

In this chapter, you'll be given an overview of GOF Design Patterns, including some best practices for making an application design. You'll also get an overview of common problem--solving with design patterns.

I will explain the design patterns that are commonly used by the Spring Framework for better design and architecture. We are all in a global world, which means that if we have services in the market, they can be accessed across the Globe. Simply put, now is the age of the distributed computing system. So first, what is a distributed system? It's an application that is divided into smaller parts that run simultaneously on different computers and the smaller parts communicate over the network, generally using protocols. These smaller parts are called **tiers**. So if we want to create a distributed application, *n*-tier architecture is a better choice for that type of application. But developing an *n*-tier distributed application is a complex and challenging job. Distributing the processing into separate tiers leads to better resource utilization. It also support the allocation of tasks to experts who are best suited to work and develop a particular tier. Many challenges exist in developing distributed applications, some of which are detailed here:

- Integration between the tiers
- Transaction management
- Concurrency handling of enterprise data
- Security of the application and so on

So my focus in this book is on simplifying Java EE application design and development by applying patterns and best practices with the Spring Framework. In this book, I will cover some common GOF Design Patterns, and how Spring adopted these for providing the best solutions to the aforementioned listed problems of enterprise application because the design of distributed objects is an immensely complicated task, even for experienced professionals. You need to consider critical issues, such as scalability, performance, transactions, and so on, before drafting a final solution. That solution is described as a pattern.

At the end of this chapter, you will understand how design patterns provide the best solution to address any design-related and development-related issues, and how to start development with the best practices. Here, you will get more ideas about GOF Design Patterns, with real-life examples. You will get information about how the Spring Framework implements these design patterns internally to provide the best enterprise solution.

This chapter will cover the following points:

- Introducing the power of design patterns
- Common GOF Design Patterns overview
  - Core design patterns
    - Creational design patterns
    - Structural design patterns
    - Behavioral design patterns
  - J2EE design patterns
    - Design patterns at presentation layer
    - Design patterns at business layer
    - Design patterns at integration layer
- Some best practices for Spring application development

Introducing the power of design patterns

So what is a design pattern? Actually, the phrase design pattern is not associated with any programming language, and also it doesn't provide language-specific solutions to problems. A design pattern is associated with the solution to repetitive problems. For example, if any problem occurs frequently, a solution to that problem has been used effectively. Any non-reusable solution to a problem can't be considered a pattern, but the problem must occur frequently in order to have a reusable solution, and to be considered as a pattern. So a design pattern is a software engineering concept describing recurring solutions to common problems in software design. Design patterns also represent the best practices used by experienced object-oriented software developers.

When you make a design for an application, you should consider all the solutions to common problems, and these solutions are called **design patterns**. The understanding of design patterns must be good across the developer team so that the staff can communicate with each other effectively. In fact, you may be familiar with some design patterns; however, you may not have used well-known names to describe them. This book will take you through a step-by-step approach and show you examples that use Java while you learn design pattern concepts.

A design pattern has three main characteristics:

- A Design pattern is *specific to a particular scenario* rather than a specific platform. So its context is the surrounding condition under which the problem exists. The context must be documented within the pattern.
- Design patterns have been *evolved to provide the best solutions* to certain problems faced during software development. So this should be limited by the context in which it is being considered.
- Design patterns are *the remedy for the problems under consideration.*

For example, if a developer is referring to the GOF Singleton design pattern and signifies the use of a single object, then all developers involved should understand that you need to design an object that will only have a single instance in the application. So the Singleton design pattern will be composed of a single object and the developers can tell each other that the program is following a Singleton pattern.

Common GoF Design Pattern overview

The authors Erich Gamma, Richard Helm, Ralph Johnson, and John Vlissides are often referred to as the GoF, or Gang of Four. They published a book titled *Design Patterns: Elements of Reusable Object-Oriented Software*, which initiated the concept of design patterns in software development.

In this chapter, you will learn what GOF patterns are and how they help solve common problems encountered in object-oriented design.

The **Gang of Four** (**GoF**) patterns are 23 classic software design patterns providing recurring solutions to common problems in software design. The patterns are defined in the book *Design Patterns: Elements of Reusable Object-Oriented Software*. These patterns are categorized into two main categories:

- Core Design Patterns
- J2EE Design Patterns

Furthermore, **Core Design Patterns** are also subdivided into three main categories of design pattern, as follows:

- **Creational Design Pattern**: Patterns under this category provide a way to construct objects when constructors will not serve your purpose. The creation logic of objects is hidden. The programs based on these patterns are more flexible in deciding object creation according to your demands and your use cases for the application.
- **Structural Design Pattern**: Patterns under this category deal with the composition of classes or objects. In the enterprise application, there are two commonly used techniques for reusing functionality in object-oriented systems: one is class Inheritance and the other is the Object Composition Concept of inheritance. The Object Composition Concept of inheritance is used to compose interfaces and define ways to compose objects to obtain new functionalities.
- **Behavioral Design Pattern**: Patterns under this category, characterize the ways in which classes or objects interact and distribute responsibility. These design patterns are specifically concerned with communication between objects. The behavioral design pattern is used to control and reduce complicated application flow in the enterprise application.

Now, let's look at the other category, the **JEE Design patterns**. This is the other main category of design patterns. Application design can be immensely simplified by applying Java EE design patterns. Java EE design patterns have been documented in Sun's Java Blueprints. These Java EE Design patterns provide time-tested solution guidelines and best practices for object interaction in the different layers of a Java EE application. These design patterns are specifically concerned with the following listed layers:

- Design pattern at the presentation layer
- Design pattern at the business layer
- Design pattern at the integration layer

Let's explore creational design patterns in the upcoming section.

Creational design patterns

Let's look at the underlying design patterns of this category and how Spring Framework adopts them to provide loose coupling between components and create and manage the lifecycle of Spring components. Creational design patterns are associated with the method of object creation. The creation logic of the object is hidden to the caller of this object.

We are all aware of how to create an object using the `new` keyword in Java, as follows:

```
Account account = new Account();
```

But this way is not suitable for some cases, because it is a hardcoded way of creating an object. It is also not a best practice to create an object because the object might be changed according to the nature of the program. Here, the creational design pattern provides the flexibility to create an object according to the nature of the program.

Now let's look at the different design patterns under this category.

Factory design pattern

Define an interface for creating an object, but let subclasses decide which class to instantiate. Factory Method lets a class defer instantiation to subclasses.
- GOF Design Pattern

The Factory design pattern is a creational design pattern. The Factory design pattern is also known as the Factory method design pattern. According to this design pattern, you get an object of a class without exposing the underlying logic to the client. It assigns a new object to the caller by using a common interface or abstract class. This means that the design pattern hides the actual logic of the implementation of an object, how to create it, and which class to instantiate it in. So the client shouldn't worry about creating, managing, and destroying an object-the Factory pattern takes responsibility for these tasks. The Factory pattern is one of the most-used design patterns in Java.

Let's look at the benefits of the Factory pattern:

- The Factory pattern promotes loose coupling between collaborating components or classes by using interfaces rather than binding application-specific classes into the application code
- Using this pattern, you can get an implementation of an object of classes that implement an interface, at runtime
- The object life cycle is managed by the factory implemented by this pattern

Now let's discuss some common problems where you should apply the Factory design pattern:

- This pattern removes the burden on the developer to create and manage the objects
- This pattern removes the tight coupling between collaboration components because a component doesn't know what subclasses it will be required to create
- Avoid hard code to create an object of the class

Implementing the Factory design pattern in Spring Framework

Spring Framework transparently uses this Factory design pattern to implement Spring containers using `BeanFactory` and `ApplicationContext` interfaces. Spring's container works based on the Factory pattern to create spring beans for the Spring application and also manages the life cycle of every Spring bean. `BeanFactory` and `ApplicationContext` are factory interfaces, and Spring has lots of implementing classes. The `getBean()` method is the factory method that gives you Spring beans accordingly.

Let's see a sample implementation of the Factory design pattern.

Sample implementation of the Factory design pattern

There are two classes `SavingAccount` and `CurrentAccount` implementing an interface `Account`. So, you can create a `Factory` class with a method that takes one or more arguments and its return type is `Account`. This method is known as the Factory method because it creates the instances of either `CurrentAccount` or `SavingAccount`. The `Account` interface is used for loose coupling. So, according to the passed arguments in the factory method, it chooses which subclass to instantiate. This factory method will have the superclass as its return type:

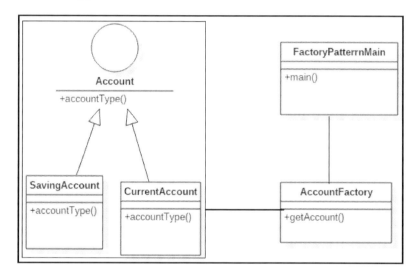

UML Diagram for the Factory design pattern

Let's look at this design pattern in the following example. Here, I am going to create an `Account` interface and some concrete classes that implement the `Account` interface:

```
package com.packt.patterninspring.chapter2.factory;
public interface Account {
  void accountType();
}
```

Now let's create `SavingAccount.java`, which will implement the `Account` interface:

```
package com.packt.patterninspring.chapter2.factory;
public class SavingAccount implements Account{
  @Override
  public void accountType() {
    System.out.println("SAVING ACCOUNT");
  }
}
```

Same with `CurrentAccount.java`, it will also implement the `Account` interface:

```
package com.packt.patterninspring.chapter2.factory;
public class CurrentAccount implements Account {
  @Override
  public void accountType() {
    System.out.println("CURRENT ACCOUNT");
  }
}
```

A Factory class `AccountFactory` is now going to be defined. `AccountFactory` generates an object of the concrete class, either `SavingAccount` or `CurrentAccount`, based on the account type given as an argument to the Factory method:

`AccountFactory.java` is a Factory to produce the `Account` type object:

```
package com.packt.patterninspring.chapter2.factory.pattern;
import com.packt.patterninspring.chapter2.factory.Account;
import com.packt.patterninspring.chapter2.factory.CurrentAccount;
import com.packt.patterninspring.chapter2.factory.SavingAccount;
public class AccountFactory {
  final String CURRENT_ACCOUNT = "CURRENT";
  final String SAVING_ACCOUNT  = "SAVING";
  //use getAccount method to get object of type Account
  //It is factory method for object of type Account
  public Account getAccount(String accountType){
    if(CURRENT_ACCOUNT.equals(accountType)) {
        return new CurrentAccount();
    }
    else if(SAVING_ACCOUNT.equals(accountType)){
        return new SavingAccount();
    }
    return null;
  }
}
```

`FactoryPatternMain` is the main calling class of `AccountFactory` to get an `Account` object. It will pass an argument to the factory method that contains information of the account type, such as `SAVING` and `CURRENT`. `AccountFactory` returns the object of the type that you passed to the factory method.

Let's create a demo class `FactoryPatterMain.java` to test the factory method design pattern:

```
package com.packt.patterninspring.chapter2.factory.pattern;
import com.packt.patterninspring.chapter2.factory.Account;
public class FactoryPatterMain {
  public static void main(String[] args) {
     AccountFactory accountFactory = new AccountFactory();
     //get an object of SavingAccount and call its accountType()
     method.
     Account savingAccount = accountFactory.getAccount("SAVING");
     //call accountType method of SavingAccount
     savingAccount.accountType();
     //get an object of CurrentAccount and call its accountType()
     method.
     Account currentAccount = accountFactory.getAccount("CURRENT");
     //call accountType method of CurrentAccount
     currentAccount.accountType();
   }
 }
```

You can test this file and see the output on the console, which should look like this:

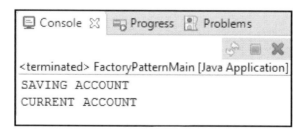

Now that we've seen the Factory design pattern, let's turn to a different variant of it-the Abstract factory design pattern.

Abstract factory design pattern

Provide an interface for creating families of related or dependent objects without specifying their concrete classes. - GOF Design Patterns

The Abstract Factory pattern comes under the creational design pattern. It is a high-level design pattern compared to the factory method design pattern. According to this design pattern, you just define an interface or abstract class to create a related dependent object without specifying its concrete subclass. So here, the abstract factory returns a factory of classes. Let me simplify it for you. You have a set of factory method design patterns, and you just put these factories under a factory using the factory design pattern, which means that it is simply a factory of factories. And there is no need to take the knowledge about all of the factories into the factory--you can make your program using a top-level factory.

In the Abstract Factory pattern, an interface is responsible for creating a factory of related objects without explicitly specifying their classes. Each generated factory can give the objects as per the Factory pattern.

The benefits of the Abstract Factory pattern are as follows:

- The Abstract Factory Design provides loose coupling between the component families. It also isolates the client code from concrete classes.
- This design pattern is a higher-level design than the Factory pattern.
- This pattern provides better consistency at construction time of objects across the application.
- This pattern easily swaps component families.

Common problems where you should apply the Abstract factory design pattern

When you design a Factory pattern for object creation in your application, there are times when you want a particular set of related objects to be created with certain constraints and apply the desired logic across the related objects in your application. You can achieve this design by creating another factory inside the factory for a set of related objects and apply the required constraints. You can also program the logic to a set of related objects.

When you want to customize the instantiation logic of related objects, then you could use this design pattern.

Implementing the Abstract factory design pattern in the Spring Framework

In the Spring Framework, the `FactoryBean` interface is based on the Abstract Factory design pattern. Spring provides a lot of implementation of this interface, such as `ProxyFactoryBean`, `JndiFactoryBean`, `LocalSessionFactoryBean`, `LocalContainerEntityManagerFactoryBean`, and so on. A `FactoryBean` is also useful to help Spring construct objects that it couldn't easily construct itself. Often this is used to construct complex objects that have many dependencies. It might also be used when the construction logic itself is highly volatile and depends on the configuration.

For example, in Spring Framework, one of the `FactoryBean` implementations is `LocalSessionFactoryBean`, which is used to get a reference of a bean that was associated with the hibernate configuration. It is a specific configuration concerning the data source. It should be applied before you get an object of `SessionFactory`. You can use the `LocalSessionFactoryBean` to apply the specific data source configuration in a consistent way. You may inject the result of a FactoryBean's `getObject()` method into any other property.

Let's create a sample implementation of the Abstract Factory design pattern.

Sample implementation of the Abstract Factory design pattern

I am going to create a `Bank` and `Account` interface and some concrete classes implementing these interfaces. Here, I also create an abstract factory class, `AbstractFactory`. I have some factory classes, `BankFactory` and `AccountFactory`; these classes extend the `AbstractFactory` class. I will also create a `FactoryProducer` class to create the factories.

Let's see this design pattern in the following image:

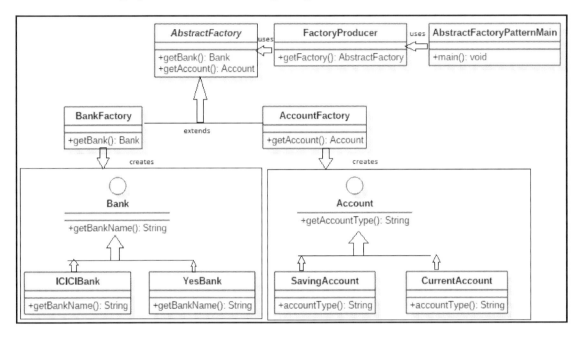

UML diagram for the Abstract Factory design pattern

Create a demo class, `AbstractFactoryPatternMain`; it uses `FactoryProducer` to get an `AbstractFactory` object. Here, I pass information such as `ICICI`, `YES` to `AbstractFactory` to get an object of `Bank`, and I also pass information such as `SAVING`, `CURRENT` to `AbstractFactory` to get an `Account` type.

Here is the code for `Bank.java`, which is an interface:

```
package com.packt.patterninspring.chapter2.model;
public interface Bank {
  void bankName();
}
```

Now let's create `ICICIBank.java`, which implements the `Bank` interface:

```java
package com.packt.patterninspring.chapter2.model;
public class ICICIBank implements Bank {
  @Override
  public void bankName() {
    System.out.println("ICICI Bank Ltd.");
  }
}
```

Let's create another `YesBank.java`, an implementing `Bank` interface:

```java
package com.packt.patterninspring.chapter2.model;
public class YesBank implements Bank{
  @Override
  public void bankName() {
      System.out.println("Yes Bank Pvt. Ltd.");
  }
}
```

In this example, I am using the same interface and implementing classes of `Account` as I used in the Factory pattern example in this book.

`AbstractFactory.java` is an abstract class that is used to get factories for `Bank` and `Account` objects:

```java
package com.packt.patterninspring.chapter2.abstractfactory.pattern;
import com.packt.patterninspring.chapter2.model.Account;
import com.packt.patterninspring.chapter2.model.Bank;
public abstract class AbstractFactory {
  abstract Bank getBank(String bankName);
  abstract Account getAccount(String accountType);
}
```

`BankFactory.java` is a factory class extending `AbstractFactory` to generate an object of the concrete class based on the given information:

```java
package com.packt.patterninspring.chapter2.abstractfactory.pattern;
import com.packt.patterninspring.chapter2.model.Account;
import com.packt.patterninspring.chapter2.model.Bank;
import com.packt.patterninspring.chapter2.model.ICICIBank;
import com.packt.patterninspring.chapter2.model.YesBank;
public class BankFactory extends AbstractFactory {
  final String ICICI_BANK = "ICICI";
  final String YES_BANK   = "YES";
  //use getBank method to get object of name bank
  //It is factory method for object of name bank
  @Override
```

```
     Bank getBank(String bankName) {
        if(ICICI_BANK.equalsIgnoreCase(bankName)){
             return new ICICIBank();
        }
        else if(YES_BANK.equalsIgnoreCase(bankName)){
             return new YesBank();
        }
        return null;
     }
     @Override
     Account getAccount(String accountType) {
        return null;
     }
  }
```

AccountFactory.java is a factory class that extends AbstractFactory.java to generate an object of the concrete class based on the given information:

```java
package com.packt.patterninspring.chapter2.abstractfactory.pattern;
import com.packt.patterninspring.chapter2.model.Account;
import com.packt.patterninspring.chapter2.model.Bank;
import com.packt.patterninspring.chapter2.model.CurrentAccount;
import com.packt.patterninspring.chapter2.model.SavingAccount;
public class AccountFactory extends AbstractFactory {
   final String CURRENT_ACCOUNT = "CURRENT";
   final String SAVING_ACCOUNT  = "SAVING";
   @Override
   Bank getBank(String bankName) {
      return null;
   }
   //use getAccount method to get object of type Account
   //It is factory method for object of type Account
   @Override
   public Account getAccount(String accountType){
     if(CURRENT_ACCOUNT.equals(accountType)) {
           return new CurrentAccount();
     }
     else if(SAVING_ACCOUNT.equals(accountType)){
           return new SavingAccount();
     }
     return null;
   }
}
```

`FactoryProducer.java` is a class that creates a Factory generator class to get factories by passing a piece of information, such as `Bank` or `Account`:

```
package com.packt.patterninspring.chapter2.abstractfactory.pattern;
public class FactoryProducer {
   final static String BANK    = "BANK";
   final static String ACCOUNT = "ACCOUNT";
   public static AbstractFactory getFactory(String factory){
      if(BANK.equalsIgnoreCase(factory)){
            return new BankFactory();
      }
      else if(ACCOUNT.equalsIgnoreCase(factory)){
            return new AccountFactory();
      }
      return null;
    }
 }
```

`FactoryPatterMain.java` is a demo class for the Abstract Factory design pattern. `FactoryProducer` is a class to get `AbstractFactory` in order to get the factories of concrete classes by passing a piece of information, such as the type:

```
package com.packt.patterninspring.chapter2.factory.pattern;
import com.packt.patterninspring.chapter2.model.Account;
public class FactoryPatterMain {
  public static void main(String[] args) {
     AccountFactory accountFactory = new AccountFactory();
     //get an object of SavingAccount and call its accountType()
     method.
     Account savingAccount = accountFactory.getAccount("SAVING");
     //call accountType method of SavingAccount
     savingAccount.accountType();
     //get an object of CurrentAccount and call its accountType()
     method.
     Account currentAccount = accountFactory.getAccount("CURRENT");
     //call accountType method of CurrentAccount
     currentAccount.accountType();
  }
 }
```

You can test this file and see the output on the console:

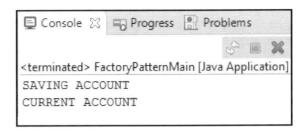

Now that we've seen the abstract Factory design pattern, let's turn to a different variant of it-the singleton design pattern.

Singleton design pattern

Ensure a class has only one instance and provide a global point of access to it - GOF Design Patterns

The Singleton pattern is a creational design pattern, it is one of the simplest design patterns in Java. According to the singleton design pattern, the class provides the same single object for each call--that is, it is restricting the instantiation of a class to one object and provides a global point of access to that class. So the class is responsible for creating an object and also ensures that only a single object should be created for each client call for this object. This class doesn't allow a direct instantiation of an object of this class. It allows you to get an object instance only by an exposed static method.

This is useful when exactly one object is needed to coordinate actions across the system. You can create a single pattern using two forms, as listed here:

- **Early instantiation**: Creation of instance at load time
- **Lazy instantiation**: Creation of instance when required

Benefits of the Singleton pattern:

- It provides controller access to crucial (usually heavy object) classes, such as the connection class for DB and the `SessionFactory` class in hibernate
- It saves heaps of memory
- It is a very efficient design for multithreaded environments
- It is more flexible because the class controls the instantiation process, and the class has the flexibility to change the instantiation process
- It has low latency

Common problems where you should apply Singleton pattern

The Singleton pattern solves only one problem--if you have a resource that can only have a single instance, and you need to manage that single instance, then you need a singleton. Normally, if you want to create a database connection with the given configuration in the distributed and multithread environment, it might be the case that every thread can create a new database connection with a different configuration object, if you don't follow the singleton design. With the Singleton pattern, each thread gets the same database connection object with the same configuration object across the system. It is mostly used in multithreaded and database applications. It is used in logging, caching, thread pools, configuration settings, and so on.

Singleton design pattern implementation in the Spring Framework

The Spring Framework provides a Singleton scoped bean as a singleton pattern. It is similar to the singleton pattern, but it's not exactly the same as the Singleton pattern in Java. According to the Singleton pattern, a scoped bean in the Spring Framework means a single bean instance per container and per bean. If you define one bean for a particular class in a single Spring container, then the Spring container creates one and only one instance of the class defined by that bean definition.

Let's create a sample application of the singleton design pattern.

Sample implementation of the Singleton design pattern

In the following code example, I will be creating a class with a method to create an instance of this class if one does not exist. If the instance is already present, then it will simply return the reference of that object. I have also taken thread safety into consideration, and so I have used a synchronized block here before creating the object of that class.

Let's check out the UML diagram for the Singleton design pattern:

```
package com.packt.patterninspring.chapter2.singleton.pattern;
public class SingletonClass {
  private static SingletonClass instance = null;
  private SingletonClass() {
  }
  public static SingletonClass getInstance() {
    if (instance == null) {
      synchronized(SingletonClass.class){
          if (instance == null) {
              instance = new SingletonClass();
          }
      }
    }
    return instance;
  }
}
```

One thing to be noted in the preceding code is that I have written a private constructor of the `SingletonClass` class to make sure that there is no way to create the object of that class. This example is based on lazy initialization, which means that the program creates an instance on demand the first time. So you could also eagerly instantiate the object to improve the runtime performance of your application. Let's see the same `SingletonClass` with eager initialization:

```
package com.packt.patterninspring.chapter2.singleton.pattern;
public class SingletonClass {
  private static final SingletonClass INSTANCE =
      new SingletonClass();
  private SingletonClass() {}
  public static SingletonClass getInstance() {
    return INSTANCE;
  }
}
```

Now that we've seen the singleton design pattern, let's turn to a different variant of it--the Prototype design pattern.

Prototype design pattern

Specify the kind of objects to create using a prototypical instance, and create new objects by copying this prototype. - GOF Design Patterns

The Prototype pattern comes under the creational design pattern family of GOF patterns in software development. This pattern is used to create the objects by using a clone method of objects. It is determined by a prototypical instance. In the enterprise application, object creation is costly in terms of creating and initializing the initial properties of objects. If such a type of object is already in your hand, then you go for the prototype pattern; you just copy an existing similar object instead of creating it, which is time-consuming.

This pattern involves implementing a prototype interface, it creates a clone of the current object. This pattern is used when the direct creation of the object is costly. For example, say that an object is to be created after a costly database operation. We can cache the object, returns its clone on the next request, and update the database as and when it is needed, thus reducing database calls.

Benefits of the Prototype design pattern

The following list shows the benefits of using the Prototype pattern:

- Reduces the time to create the time-consuming objects by using the prototype pattern
- This pattern reduces subclassing
- This pattern adds and removes objects at runtime
- This pattern configures the application with classes dynamically

Let's see the UML class structure of the Prototype design pattern.

UML class structure

The following UML diagram shows all the components of the Prototype design pattern:

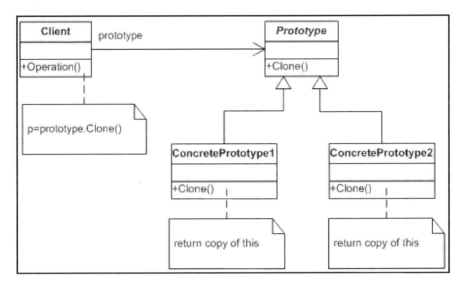

UML diagram for Prototype design pattern

Let's see these components as listed in following points:

- **Prototype**: The Prototype is an interface. It is uses the clone method to create instances of this interface type.

- **ConcretePrototype**: This is a concrete class of the Prototype interface to implement an operation to clone itself.

- **Client**: This is a `caller` class to create a new object of a Prototype interface by calling a `clone` method of the prototype interface.

Let's see a sample implementation of the prototype design pattern.

Sample implementation of the Prototype design pattern

I am going to create an abstract `Account` class and concrete classes extending the `Account` class. An `AccountCache` class is defined as a next step, which stores account objects in a `HashMap` and returns their clone when requested. Create an abstract class implementing the `Clonable` interface.

```
package com.packt.patterninspring.chapter2.prototype.pattern;
public abstract class Account implements Cloneable{
  abstract public void accountType();
  public Object clone() {
    Object clone = null;
    try {
      clone = super.clone();
    }
    catch (CloneNotSupportedException e) {
      e.printStackTrace();
    }
    return clone;
  }
}
```

Now let's create concrete classes extending the preceding class:

Here's the `CurrentAccount.java` file:

```
package com.packt.patterninspring.chapter2.prototype.pattern;
public class CurrentAccount extends Account {
  @Override
  public void accountType() {
    System.out.println("CURRENT ACCOUNT");
  }
}
```

Here's how `SavingAccount.java` should look:

```
package com.packt.patterninspring.chapter2.prototype.pattern;
public class SavingAccount extends Account{
  @Override
  public void accountType() {
    System.out.println("SAVING ACCOUNT");
  }
}
```

Let's create a class to get concrete classes in the `AccountCache.java` file:

```
package com.packt.patterninspring.chapter2.prototype.pattern;
import java.util.HashMap;
import java.util.Map;
public class AccountCache {
    public static Map<String, Account> accountCacheMap =
        new HashMap<>();
    static{
        Account currentAccount = new CurrentAccount();
        Account savingAccount = new SavingAccount();
        accountCacheMap.put("SAVING", savingAccount);
        accountCacheMap.put("CURRENT", currentAccount);
    }
}
```

`PrototypePatternMain.java` is a demo class that we will use to test the design pattern `AccountCache` to get the `Account` object by passing a piece of information, such as the type, and then call the `clone()` method:

```
package com.packt.patterninspring.chapter2.prototype
    .pattern;
public class PrototypePatternMain {
  public static void main(String[] args) {
    Account currentAccount = (Account)
      AccountCache.accountCacheMap.get("CURRENT").clone();
    currentAccount.accountType();
    Account savingAccount = (Account)
      AccountCache.accountCacheMap.get("SAVING") .clone();
    savingAccount.accountType();
  }
}
```

We've covered this so far and it's good. Now let's look at the next design pattern.

Builder design pattern

Separate the construction of a complex object from its representation so that the same construction process can create different representations. - GOF Design Patterns

The Builder design pattern is used to construct a complex object step by step, and finally it will return the complete object. The logic and process of object creation should be generic so that you can use it to create different concrete implementations of the same object type. This pattern simplifies the construction of complex objects and it hides the details of the object's construction from the client caller code. When you are using this pattern, remember you have to build it one step at a time, which means you have to break the object construction login into multiple phases, unlike other patterns, such as the abstract factory and the factory method pattern, which the object in a single step.

Benefits of the Builder pattern:

- This pattern provides you with complete isolation between the construction and representation of an object
- This pattern allows you to construct the object in multiple phases, so you have greater control over the construction process
- This pattern provides the flexibility to vary an object's internal representation

UML class structure

The following UML diagram shows all the components of the Builder design pattern:

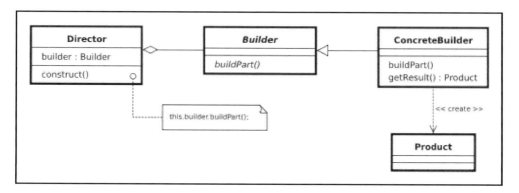

UML diagram for the Builder design pattern:

- **Builder** (AccountBuilder): This is an abstract class or interface for creating the details of an Account object.

- **ConcreteBuilder**: This is an implementation to construct and assemble details of the account by implementing the Builder interface.

- **Director**: This constructs an object using the Builder interface.

- **Product** (Account): This represents the complex object under construction. `AccountBuilder` builds the account's internal representation and defines the process by which it's assembled.

Implementing the Builder pattern in the Spring Framework

The Spring Framework implements the Builder design pattern transparently in some functionalities. The following classes are based on the Builder design pattern in the Spring Framework:

- `EmbeddedDatabaseBuilder`
- `AuthenticationManagerBuilder`
- `UriComponentsBuilder`
- `BeanDefinitionBuilder`
- `MockMvcWebClientBuilder`

Common problems where you should apply Builder pattern

In an enterprise application, you can apply the Builder pattern where the object creation has been done by using multiple steps. In each step, you do a portion of the process. In this process, you set some required parameters and some optional parameters, and after the final step, you will get a complex object.

The Builder pattern is an object creation software design pattern. The intention is to abstract the steps of construction so that different implementations of these steps can construct different representations of objects. Often, the Builder pattern is used to build products in accordance with the composite pattern.

Sample implementation of the Builder design pattern

In the following code example, I am going to create an `Account` class that has `AccountBuilder` as an inner class. The `AccountBuilder` class has a method to create an instance of this class:

```
package com.packt.patterninspring.chapter2.builder.pattern;
public class Account {
  private String accountName;
  private Long accountNumber;
  private String accountHolder;
  private double balance;
  private String type;
  private double interest;
  private Account(AccountBuilder accountBuilder) {
      super();
      this.accountName = accountBuilder.accountName;
      this.accountNumber = accountBuilder.accountNumber;
      this.accountHolder = accountBuilder.accountHolder;
      this.balance = accountBuilder.balance;
      this.type = accountBuilder.type;
      this.interest = accountBuilder.interest;
  }
  //setters and getters
   public static class AccountBuilder {
      private final String accountName;
      private final Long accountNumber;
      private final String accountHolder;
      private double balance;
      private String type;
      private double interest;
      public AccountBuilder(String accountName,
          String accountHolder, Long accountNumber) {
          this.accountName = accountName;
          this.accountHolder = accountHolder;
          this.accountNumber = accountNumber;
      }
      public AccountBuilder balance(double balance) {
          this.balance = balance;
          return this;
      }
      public AccountBuilder type(String type) {
          this.type = type;
          return this;
      }
      public AccountBuilder interest(double interest) {
          this.interest = interest;
          return this;
```

```
        }
        public Account build() {
            Account user = new Account(this);
            return user;
        }
    }
    public String toString() {
    return "Account [accountName=" + accountName + ",
        accountNumber=" + accountNumber + ", accountHolder="
        + accountHolder + ", balance=" + balance + ", type="
        + type + ", interest=" + interest + "]";
    }
}
```

`AccountBuilderTest.java` is a demo class that we will use to test the design pattern. Let's look at how to build an `Account` object by passing the initial information to the object:

```
package com.packt.patterninspring.chapter2.builder.pattern;
public class AccountBuilderTest {
  public static void main(String[] args) {
    Account account = new Account.AccountBuilder("Saving
        Account", "Dinesh Rajput", 11111)
            .balance(38458.32)
            .interest(4.5)
            .type("SAVING")
            .build();
    System.out.println(account);
  }
}
```

You can test this file and see the output on the console:

```
<terminated> AccountBuilderTest [Java Application] C:\Program Files\Java\jre1.8.0_131\bin\javaw.exe (27-Jun-2017, 2:10:21 AM)
Account [accountName=Saving Account, accountNumber=1111, accountHolder=Dinesh Rajput, balance=38458.32, type=SAVING, interest=4.5]
```

Now, we've seen the Builder design pattern. In the upcoming Chapter 3, *Consideration of Structural and Behavioural Patterns,* I will explore another part of the GOF Design Patterns family.

Summary

After reading this chapter, the reader should now have a good idea about the overview of GOF creational design patterns and its best practices. I highlighted the problems that come from not using design patterns in enterprise application development, and how Spring solves these problems by using the creational design patterns and good practices in the application. In this chapter, I have mentioned only one of the Creational Design pattern categories out of the three main categories of the GOF Design Patterns. The Creational design pattern is used for the creation of object instances, and also applies constraints at the creation time in the enterprise application in a specific manner using the Factory, Abstract Factory, Builder, Prototype, and Singleton patterns. In the next chapter, we will look at the other categories of the GOF Design Patterns-the structural design pattern and the behavioral design pattern. The structural design pattern is used to design the structure of an enterprise application by dealing with the composition of classes or objects so that it reduces the application's complexity and improves the reusability and performance of the application. The Adapter Pattern, Bridge Pattern, Composite Pattern, Decorator Pattern, Facade Pattern, and Flyweight Pattern come under this category of the pattern. The Behavioral design pattern characterizes the ways in which classes or objects interact and distribute responsibility. The patterns that come under this category are specifically concerned with communication between objects. Let's move to complete the remaining GOF patterns in the next chapter.

3
Consideration of Structural and Behavioral Patterns

You have seen implementations and examples of the creational design pattern from the GOF pattern family in Chapter 2, *Overview of GOF Design Patterns - Core Design Patterns*. Now, in this chapter, you'll be given an overview of other parts of GOF Design Patterns, they are the structural and behavioral design patterns, including some best practices for application design. You'll also get an overview of common problem solving with these design patterns.

At the end of this chapter, you will understand how these design patterns provide the best solution to address the design and development related issues in the object composition and delegating responsibilities between the working objects in the application. You will get information about how the Spring Framework implements the structural and behavioral designs pattern internally to provide best enterprise solutions.

This chapter will cover the following points:

- Implementing the structural design patterns
- Implementing the behavioral design patterns
- J2EE design patterns

Examining the core design patterns

Let's continue our journey into the core design patterns:

- **Structural design pattern**: Patterns under this category deal with the composition of classes or objects. In the enterprise application, there are two common techniques for reusing functionality in object-oriented systems as follows:
  - **Inheritance**: It is used to inherit commonly used states and behaviors from other classes.
  - **Composition**: It is used to compose the other objects as instance variables of classes. It defines ways to compose objects to obtain new functionalities.
- **Behavioral design pattern**: Patterns under this category characterize the ways in which classes or objects interact with and distribute responsibility. These patterns define the methods of communication between the objects in the enterprise application. So here, you will learn how to use behavioral patterns to reduce complicated flow control. Furthermore, you will use behavioral patterns to encapsulate algorithms and dynamically select them at runtime.

Structural design patterns

In the previous section, we discussed creational design patterns and how they provide the best solutions for object creation according to business demands. Creational design patterns only provide a solution for creating objects in the application with how these objects merge with each other in the application for a specific business goal, the structural design pattern comes into the picture. In this chapter, we will be exploring structural patterns, and how these patterns are useful to define the relationship between the objects either using inheritance or composition for larger structures of an application. Structural patterns allow you to solve many problems related to structuring the relationship between the objects. They show you how to glue different parts of a system together in a flexible and extensible fashion. Structural patterns help you guarantee that when one of the parts changes, the entire structure does not need to change; in a car you could replace the tyres with different vendors without impacting the other parts of that car. They also show you how to recast parts of the system that do not fit (but that you need to use) into parts that do fit.

The adapter design pattern

Convert the interface of a class into another interface clients expect. Adapter lets classes work together that couldn't otherwise because of incompatible interfaces.
-GoF Design Patterns: Elements of Reusable Object-Oriented Software

Adapter design patterns come under the structural design pattern, according to this design pattern two incompatible classes work together that couldn't otherwise because of incompatible interfaces. This pattern works as a bridge between two incompatible interfaces. This pattern is used when two inferences of the application are incompatible in their functionalities, but these functionalities need to be integrated as a business requirement.

There are many real-life examples where we can use the adapter pattern. Suppose you have different types of electric plugs such as cylindrical and rectangular plugs, as shown in the following figure. You can use an adapter in between to fit a rectangular plug in a cylindrical socket assuming voltage requirements are met:

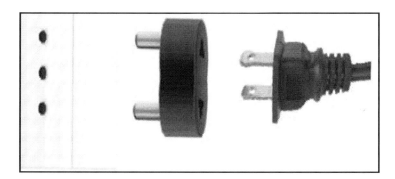

Benefits of the adapter pattern

Let's look at the following benefits of using the adapter design pattern in the application.

- The adapter pattern allows you to communicate and interact with two or more incompatible objects
- This pattern promotes the reusability of older existing functionalities in your application

Common requirements for the adapter pattern

The following are the common requirements for this design pattern to addresses the design problems:

- If you are to use this pattern in your application, there is a need to use an existing class with an incompatible interface.
- Another use of this pattern in your application is when you want to create a reusable class that collaborates with classes that have incompatible interfaces.
- There are several existing subclasses to be used, but it's impractical to adapt their interface by sub classing each one. An object adapter can adapt the interface of its parent class.

Let's see how Spring implements the adapter design pattern internally.

Implementation of the adapter design pattern in the Spring Framework

Spring Framework uses the adapter design pattern to implement a lot of functionality across the framework transparently. The following are some listed classes based on the adapter design pattern in the Spring Framework:

- JpaVendorAdapter
- HibernateJpaVendorAdapter
- HandlerInterceptorAdapter
- MessageListenerAdapter
- SpringContextResourceAdapter
- ClassPreProcessorAgentAdapter
- RequestMappingHandlerAdapter
- AnnotationMethodHandlerAdapter
- WebMvcConfigurerAdapter

The UML diagram for the adapter pattern

Let's understand the preceding UML diagram that illustrates the components of the adapter design pattern:

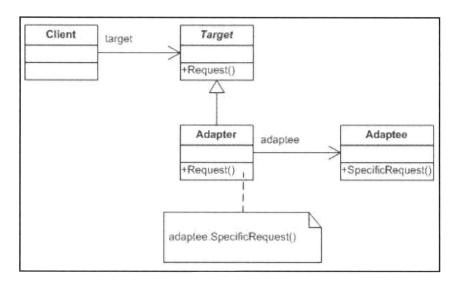

- **The Target Interface**: This is the desired interface class that will be used by the clients
- **The Adapter class**: This class is a wrapper class that implements the desired target interface and modifies the specific request available from the Adaptee class
- **The Adaptee class**: This is the class that is used by the Adapter class to reuse the existing functionalities and modify them for desired use
- **Client**: This class will interact with the Adapter class

Let's look at the following sample implementation of the adapter design pattern.

Sample implementation of the adapter design pattern

I am going to create an example that shows the actual demonstration of the adapter design pattern, so let's discuss this example, I am creating this example based on making payment through a payment gateway. Suppose I have one old payment gateway and also have the latest advanced payment gateway, and both gateways are unrelated to each other, so my requirement is, I want to migrate from the old payment gateway to an advanced payment gateway while changing my existing source code. I am creating an adapter class to solve this problem. This adapter class is working as a bridge between two different payment gateways, let's look at the following code:

Let's now create an interface for the old payment gateway:

```
package com.packt.patterninspring.chapter3.adapter.pattern;
import com.packt.patterninspring.chapter3.model.Account;
public interface PaymentGateway {
  void doPayment(Account account1, Account account2);
}
```

Let's now create an implementation class for the old payment gateway
`PaymentGateway.java`:

```
package com.packt.patterninspring.chapter3.adapter.pattern;
import com.packt.patterninspring.chapter3.model.Account;
public class PaymentGatewayImpl implements PaymentGateway{
  @Override
  public void doPayment(Account account1, Account account2){
    System.out.println("Do payment using Payment Gateway");
  }
}
```

The following interface and its implementation have new and advanced functionalities for
the payment gateway:

```
package com.packt.patterninspring.chapter3.adapter.pattern;
public interface AdvancedPayGateway {
  void makePayment(String mobile1, String mobile2);
}
```

Let's now create an implementation class for the advance payment gateway interface:

```
package com.packt.patterninspring.chapter3.adapter.pattern;
import com.packt.patterninspring.chapter3.model.Account;
public class AdvancedPaymentGatewayAdapter implements
   AdvancedPayGateway{
  private PaymentGateway paymentGateway;
  public AdvancedPaymentGatewayAdapter(PaymentGateway
     paymentGateway) {
    this.paymentGateway = paymentGateway;
  }
  public void makePayment(String mobile1, String mobile2) {
    Account account1 = null;//get account number by
       mobile number mobile
    Account account2 = null;//get account number by
       mobile number mobile
    paymentGateway.doPayment(account1, account2);
  }
}
```

Let's see a demo class for this pattern as follows:

```
package com.packt.patterninspring.chapter3.adapter.pattern;
public class AdapterPatternMain {
  public static void main(String[] args) {
    PaymentGateway paymentGateway = new PaymentGatewayImpl();
    AdvancedPayGateway advancedPayGateway = new
      AdvancedPaymentGatewayAdapter(paymentGateway);
    String mobile1 = null;
    String mobile2 = null;
    advancedPayGateway.makePayment(mobile1, mobile2);
  }
}
```

In the preceding class, we have the old payment gateway object as the `PaymentGateway` interface, but we convert this old payment gateway implementation to the advanced form of the payment gateway by using the `AdvancedPaymentGatewayAdapter` adapter class. Let's run this demo class and see the output as follows:

Now that we've seen the adapter design pattern, let's turn to a different variant of it--the Bridge design pattern.

The Bridge design pattern

> *Decouple an abstraction from its implementation so that the two can vary independently*
> *- GoF Design Patterns: Elements of Reusable Object-Oriented Software*

In software engineering, one of the most popular notions is preferred composition over inheritance. Bridge design pattern promotes this popular notion. Similar to the adapter pattern, this pattern also comes under the structural design pattern family of the GoF Design Pattern. The approach of the Bridge pattern is to decouple an abstraction used by the client code from its implementation; that means it separates the abstraction and its implementation in to separate class hierarchies. And also, Bridge pattern prefers composition over inheritance because inheritance isn't always flexible and it breaks the encapsulation, so any change made in the implementer affects the abstraction used by the client code.

The bridge provides a way to communicate between two different independent components in software development, and a bridge structure provides you with a way to decouple the abstract class and the implementer class. So any change made in either the implementation class or the implementer (that is, the interface) doesn't affect the abstract class or its refined abstraction class. It makes this possible by using composition between the interface and the abstraction. Bridge pattern uses an interface as a bridge between the concrete classes of an abstract class and implementing classes of that interface. You can make changes in both types of class without any impact on the client code.

Benefits of the Bridge pattern

Following are the benefits of the Bridge design pattern:

- The Bridge design pattern allows you to separate the implementation and the abstraction
- This design pattern provides the flexibility to change both types of classes without side effects in the client code
- This design pattern allows the hiding of actual implementation details from the client by using abstraction between them

Common problems solved by the Bridge design pattern

Following are the common problems addressed by the Bridge design pattern:

- Removes a permanent binding between the functional abstraction and its implementation
- You can make changes to the implementing classes without affecting the abstraction and client code
- You can extend the abstraction and its implementation using subclasses

Implementing the Bridge design pattern in the Spring Framework

The following Spring modules are based on the Bridge design pattern:

- `ViewRendererServlet`: It is a bridge servlet, mainly for Portlet MVC support
- **The Bridge design pattern**: The Bridge design pattern is used in the Spring logging process

Let's see a sample implementation of the Bridge design pattern.

Sample implementation of the Bridge design pattern

Let's look at the following example, where we will demonstrate the use of the Bridge design pattern. Suppose you want to open two types of accounts, one is a Savings Account and the other is a Current Account in the banking system.

System without using the Bridge design pattern

Let's look at an example without using the Bridge design pattern. In the following figure, you can see the relationship between the Bank and Account interfaces:

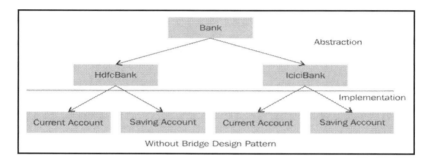

System without using the Bridge design pattern

Let's create a design without using the Bridge design pattern. First create an interface or an abstract class, **Bank**. And then create its derived classes: **IciciBank** and **HdfcBank**. To open an account in the bank, first decide on the types of account classes--**Saving Account** and **Current Account**, these classes extend the specific banks classes (**HdfcBank** and **IciciBank**). There is a simple deep inheritance hierarchy in this application. So what is wrong with this design as compared to the preceding figure? You will notice that in this design, there are two parts, one is the abstraction part and the other is the implementation part. Client code interacts with the abstraction part. Client code can only access new changes or new functionalities of the implementation part when you will update the abstraction part, meaning the parts, the abstraction, and the implementation, are tightly coupled with each other.

Now let's see how to improve this example using the Bridge design pattern:

System with the Bridge design pattern

In the following figure, we create a relation between the `Bank` and `Account` interface by using the Bridge design pattern:

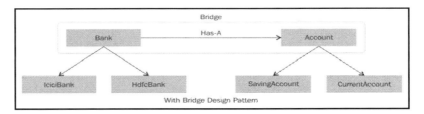

System using Bridge Design Pattern

UML structure for the Bridge design pattern

Let's look at the following figure of how the Bridge design pattern solves these design issues, as seen in the example where we did not use the Bridge design pattern. Bridge pattern separates the abstraction and implementation into two class hierarchies:

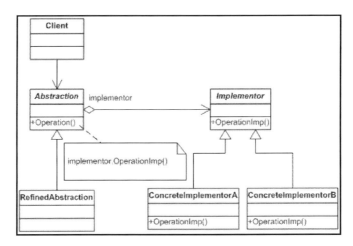

UML for Bridge design pattern

We have an `Account` interface that is acting as a bridge implementer and the concrete classes `SavingAccount`, and `CurrentAccount` implementing the Account interface. The `Bank` is an abstract class and it will use object of Account.

Let's create a bridge implementer interface.

Following is the `Account.java` file:

```
package com.packt.patterninspring.chapter3.bridge.pattern;
public interface Account {
  Account openAccount();
  void accountType();
}
```

Create concrete bridge implementer classes to implement the `implementer` interface. Let's create a `SavingAccount` class as an implementation of `Account`.

Following is the `SavingAccount.java` file:

```
package com.packt.patterninspring.chapter3.bridge.pattern;
public class SavingAccount implements Account {
  @Override
  public Account openAccount() {
    System.out.println("OPENED: SAVING ACCOUNT ");
    return new SavingAccount();
  }
  @Override
  public void accountType() {
    System.out.println("##It is a SAVING Account##");
  }
}
```

Create a `CurrentAccount` class that implements the `Account` interface.

Following is the `CurrentAccount.java` file:

```
package com.packt.patterninspring.chapter3.bridge.pattern;
public class CurrentAccount implements Account {
  @Override
  public Account openAccount() {
    System.out.println("OPENED: CURRENT ACCOUNT ");
    return new CurrentAccount();
  }
  @Override
  public void accountType() {
    System.out.println("##It is a CURRENT Account##");
  }
}
```

Create abstraction in the Bridge design pattern, but first, create the interface **Bank**.

Following is the Bank.java file:

```
package com.packt.patterninspring.chapter3.bridge.pattern;
public abstract class Bank {
  //Composition with implementor
  protected Account account;
  public Bank(Account account){
     this.account = account;
  }
  abstract Account openAccount();
}
```

Let's implement the first abstraction for the Bank interface and see the following implementation class for the Bank interface.

Following is the IciciBank.java file:

```
package com.packt.patterninspring.chapter3.bridge.pattern;
public class IciciBank extends Bank {
  public IciciBank(Account account) {
    super(account);
  }
  @Override
  Account openAccount() {
    System.out.print("Open your account with ICICI Bank");
    return account;
  }
}
```

Let's implement the second abstraction for the Bank interface and look at the following implementation class for the Bank interface.

Following is the HdfcBank.java file:

```
package com.packt.patterninspring.chapter3.bridge.pattern;
  public class HdfcBank extends Bank {
    public HdfcBank(Account account) {
      super(account);
    }
    @Override
    Account openAccount() {
      System.out.print("Open your account with HDFC Bank");
      return account;
    }
  }
```

Create a demonstration class of the Bridge design pattern.

Following is the `BridgePatternMain.java` file:

```
package com.packt.patterninspring.chapter3.bridge.pattern;
public class BridgePatternMain {
    public static void main(String[] args) {
        Bank icici = new IciciBank(new CurrentAccount());
        Account current = icici.openAccount();
        current.accountType();
        Bank hdfc = new HdfcBank(new SavingAccount());
        Account saving = hdfc.openAccount();
        saving.accountType();
    }
}
```

Let's run this demo class and see the following output in the console:

Now that we've seen the Bridge design pattern, let's turn to a different variant of it--the composite design pattern.

Composite design pattern

Compose objects into tree structures to represent part-whole hierarchies. Composite lets clients treat individual objects and compositions of objects uniformly.
-GoF Design Patterns

In software engineering, the composite pattern comes under the structural design pattern. According to this pattern, a group of objects of the same type are treated as a single object by the client. The idea behind the Composite design pattern is to compose a set of objects into a tree structure to represent a module of a larger structural application. And this structure for clients is a single unit or instance uniformly.

The motivation behind the Composite design pattern is that objects in the system are grouped into the tree structure, and a tree structure is a combination of the node-leaf and branches. In the tree structure, nodes have a number of leaves and other nodes. Leaf doesn't have anything, which means there is no child of leaf in the tree. Leaf is treated as the end point of tree-structured data.

Let's look at the following figure, which represents data in the tree structure in the form of node and leaf:

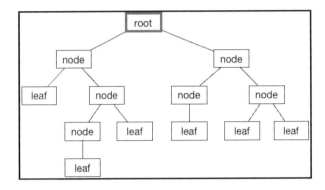

Tree structured data using nodes and leaves

Common problems solved by the composite pattern

As a developer, it is more difficult to design an application so that the client can access your objects uniformly across the application, even if that object was a composition of objects or an individual object. This design pattern resolves difficulties and allows you to design objects in such a way that you can use that object as a composition of objects and a single individual object.

This pattern solves the challenges faced when creating hierarchical tree structures to provide clients with a uniform way to access and manipulate objects in the tree. The composite pattern is a good choice; it is less complex in this situation to treat primitives and composites as homogeneous.

UML structure of the Composite design pattern

Composite design pattern is based on the composition of similar types of objects into the tree structure, as you know that each tree has three main parts branch, node, and leaf. So let's have a look at the following terms used in this design pattern.

Component: It is basically a branch of the tree and the branch has other branches, nodes, and leaves. Component provides the abstraction for all components, including composite objects. In the composition pattern, component **is** basically declared as an interface for objects.

Leaf: It is an object that implements all component methods.

Composite: It is represented as a node in the tree structure, it has other nodes and leaves, and it represents a composite component. It has methods to add the children, that is, it represents a collection of the same type of objects. It has other component methods for its children.

Let's look at the following UML diagram for this design pattern:

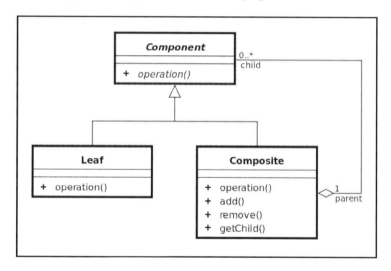

UML diagram for the Composite Design Pattern

Benefits of the Composite design pattern

- This pattern provides the flexibility to add new component to process dynamically, with change in the existing components
- This pattern allows you to create a class hierarchy that contains individual and composite objects

Sample implementation of the Composite design pattern

In the following example, I am implementing an Account interface, which can be either a SavingAccount and CurrentAccount or a composition of several accounts. I have a CompositeBankAccount class, which acts as a composite pattern actor class. Let's look at the following code for this example.

Create an Account interface that will be treated as a component:

```
public interface Account {
  void accountType();
}
```

Create a SavingAccount class and CurrentAccount class as an implementation of the component and that will also be treated as a leaf:

Following is the SavingAccount.java file:

```
public class SavingAccount implements Account{
  @Override
  public void accountType() {
    System.out.println("SAVING ACCOUNT");
  }
}
```

Following is the CurrentAccount.java file:

```
public class CurrentAccount implements Account {
  @Override
  public void accountType() {
    System.out.println("CURRENT ACCOUNT");
  }
}
```

Create a CompositeBankAccount class that will be treated as a Composite and implements the Account interface:

Following is the CompositeBankAccount.java file:

```
package com.packt.patterninspring.chapter3.composite.pattern;
import java.util.ArrayList;
import java.util.List;
import com.packt.patterninspring.chapter3.model.Account;
public class CompositeBankAccount implements Account {
  //Collection of child accounts.
  private List<Account> childAccounts = new ArrayList<Account>();
  @Override
```

```
    public void accountType() {
      for (Account account : childAccounts) {
          account.accountType();
      }
    }
    //Adds the account to the composition.
      public void add(Account account) {
        childAccounts.add(account);
      }
      //Removes the account from the composition.
      public void remove(Account account) {
        childAccounts.remove(account);
      }
    }
```

Create a CompositePatternMain class that will also be treated as a Client:

Following is the CompositePatternMain.java file:

```
package com.packt.patterninspring.chapter3.composite.pattern;
import com.packt.patterninspring.chapter3.model.CurrentAccount;
import com.packt.patterninspring.chapter3.model.SavingAccount;
public class CompositePatternMain {
  public static void main(String[] args) {
    //Saving Accounts
    SavingAccount savingAccount1 = new SavingAccount();
    SavingAccount savingAccount2 = new SavingAccount();
    //Current Account
    CurrentAccount currentAccount1 = new CurrentAccount();
    CurrentAccount currentAccount2 = new CurrentAccount();
    //Composite Bank Account
    CompositeBankAccount compositeBankAccount1 = new
    CompositeBankAccount();
    CompositeBankAccount compositeBankAccount2 = new
    CompositeBankAccount();
    CompositeBankAccount compositeBankAccount = new
    CompositeBankAccount();
    //Composing the bank accounts
    compositeBankAccount1.add(savingAccount1);
    compositeBankAccount1.add(currentAccount1);
    compositeBankAccount2.add(currentAccount2);
    compositeBankAccount2.add(savingAccount2);
    compositeBankAccount.add(compositeBankAccount2);
    compositeBankAccount.add(compositeBankAccount1);
    compositeBankAccount.accountType();
  }
}
```

Let's run this demo class and see the following output at the console:

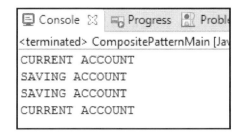

Now that we have discussed the composite design pattern, let's turn to the decorator design pattern.

Decorator design pattern

Attach additional responsibilities to an object dynamically. Decorators provide a flexible alternative to sub classing for extending functionality.
- GOF Design Pattern

In software engineering, the common intent of all GOF structural patterns is to simplify the complex relationship between objects and classes in a flexible enterprise application. The decorator pattern is a special type of design pattern among these that comes under the structural design pattern, which allows you to add and remove behaviors for an individual object at runtime dynamically or statically, without changing the existing behavior of other associated objects from the same class. This design pattern does this without violating the Single Responsibility Principle or the SOLID principle of object-oriented programming.

This design pattern uses the compositions over the inheritance for objects associations; it allows you to divide the functionality into different concrete classes with a unique area of concern.

Benefits of the Decorator design pattern

- This pattern allows you to extend functionality dynamically and statically without altering the structure of existing objects
- By using this pattern, you could add a new responsibility to an object dynamically
- This pattern is also known as **Wrapper**

- This pattern uses the compositions for object relationships to maintain SOLID principles
- This pattern simplifies coding by writing new classes for every new specific functionality rather than changing the existing code of your application

Common problems solved by the Decorator pattern

In an enterprise application, there is a business requirement or there might be a future plan to extend the behavior of the product by adding new functionalities. To achieve this, you could use inheritance to extend the behavior of an object. But inheritance should be done at compile time and methods are also available for other instances of that class. Because of the code modification, there is a violation of the Open Closed Principle. To avoid this violation of the SOLID principle, you can attach new responsibility to an object dynamically. This is the situation where the decorator design pattern comes into the picture and addresses this issue in a very flexible way. Let's look at the following example of how to implement this design pattern into a real case study.

Consider that a bank offers multiple accounts with different benefits to customers. It divides the customers into three categories--senior citizens, privileged, and young. The bank launches a scheme on the savings account for senior citizens--if they open a savings account in this bank, they will be provided medical insurance of up to $1,000. Similarly, the bank also provides a scheme for the privileged customers as an accident insurance of up to $1,600 and an overdraft facility of $84. There is no scheme for the young.

To address the new requirement, we can add new subclasses of `SavingAccount`; one each to represent a saving account with additional benefits as decoration, and this is what our design looks like now:

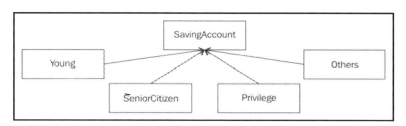

Application design with inheritance without using the Decorator Design Pattern

This design will be very complex as I will add more benefit schemes to the **SavingAccount**, but what would happen when the bank launches the same scheme for **CurrentAccount**? Clearly, this design is flawed, but this is an ideal use case for the decorator pattern. This pattern allows you to add runtime dynamic behavior. In this case, I will create an abstract **AccountDecorator** class to implement **Account**. And furthermore, I will create the **SeniorCitizen** class and **Privilege** class, which extends **AccountDecorator** because young does not have any extra benefits, so the SavingAccount class does not extend **AccountDecorator**. This is how the design will be:

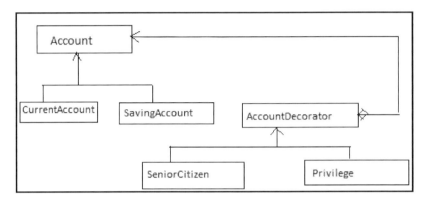

Application design with composition using the decorator design pattern

The preceding figure follows the Decorator design pattern by creating **AccountDecorator** as a **Decorator** in this pattern, and focuses on important things to observe the relationship between **Account** and **AccountDecorator**. This relationship is as follows:

- **Is-a** relationship between the `AccountDecorator` and `Account`, that is, inheritance for the correct type
- **Has-a** relationship between the `AccountDecorator` and `Account`, that is, composition in order to add new behavior without changing the existing code

Let's look at the UML structure:

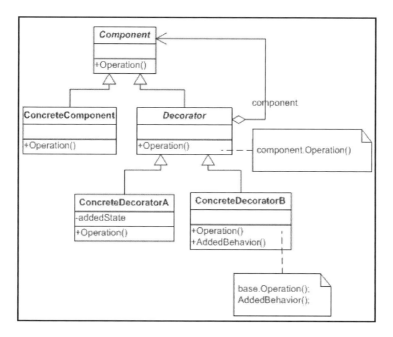

UML for the Decorator design pattern

The classes and objects participating in this pattern are:

- **Component (Account):** It is an interface for objects that can have responsibilities added to them dynamically
- **ConcreteComponent (SavingAccount):** It is a concrete class of component interface and it defines an object to which additional responsibilities can be attached
- **Decorator (AccountDecorator):** It has a reference to a **Component** object and defines an interface that conforms to the interface of the component
- **ConcreteDecorator (SeniorCitizen and Privilege):** It is a concrete implementation of **Decorator** and it adds responsibilities to the component

Implementing the Decorator pattern

Let's look at the following code to demonstrate the Decorator design pattern.

Create a component class:

Following is the `Account.java` file:

```
package com.packt.patterninspring.chapter3.decorator.pattern;
public interface Account {
    String getTotalBenefits();
}
```

Create concrete components classes:

Following is the `SavingAccount.java` file:

```
package com.packt.patterninspring.chapter3.decorator.pattern;
public class SavingAccount implements Account {
    @Override
    public String getTotalBenefits() {
        return "This account has 4% interest rate with per day
          $5000 withdrawal limit";
    }
}
```

Let's create another concrete class for Account component:

Following is the `CurrentAccount.java` file:

```
package com.packt.patterninspring.chapter3.decorator.pattern;
public class CurrentAccount implements Account {
    @Override
    public String getTotalBenefits() {
        return "There is no withdrawal limit for current account";
    }
}
```

Let's create a `Decorator` class for Account component. This decorator class apply other run time behavior to the Account component classes.

Following is the `AccountDecorator.java` file:

```
package com.packt.patterninspring.chapter3.decorator.pattern;
public abstract class AccountDecorator implements Account {
    abstract String applyOtherBenefits();
}
```

Let's create a `ConcreteDecorator` class to implement the AccountDecorator class. Following class `SeniorCitizen` is extended `AccountDecorator` class to access other run time behavior such as `applyOtherBenefits()`.

Following is the `SeniorCitizen.java` file:

```
package com.packt.patterninspring.chapter3.decorator.pattern;
public class SeniorCitizen extends AccountDecorator {
  Account account;
  public SeniorCitizen(Account account) {
     super();
     this.account = account;
  }
  public String getTotalBenefits() {
     return account.getTotalBenefits() + " other benefits are
        "+applyOtherBenefits();
  }
  String applyOtherBenefits() {
     return " an medical insurance of up to $1,000 for Senior
     Citizen";
  }
}
```

Let's create another `ConcreteDecorator` class to implement the `AccountDecorator` class. Following class `Privilege` is extended `AccountDecorator` class to access other run time behavior such as `applyOtherBenefits()`.

Following is the `Privilege.java` file:

```
package com.packt.patterninspring.chapter3.decorator.pattern;
public class Privilege extends AccountDecorator {
  Account account;
  public Privilege(Account account) {
     this.account = account;
  }
  public String getTotalBenefits() {
     return account.getTotalBenefits() + " other benefits are
        "+applyOtherBenefits();
  }
  String applyOtherBenefits() {
    return " an accident insurance of up to $1,600 and
       an overdraft facility of $84";
  }
}
```

Let's now write some test code to see how the Decorator pattern works at runtime:

Following is the `DecoratorPatternMain.java` file:

```
package com.packt.patterninspring.chapter3.decorator.pattern;
public class DecoratorPatternMain {
  public static void main(String[] args) {
     /*Saving account with no decoration*/
     Account basicSavingAccount = new SavingAccount();
     System.out.println(basicSavingAccount.getTotalBenefits());
     /*Saving account with senior citizen benefits decoration*/
     Account seniorCitizenSavingAccount = new SavingAccount();
     seniorCitizenSavingAccount = new
        SeniorCitizen(seniorCitizenSavingAccount);
     System.out.println
     (seniorCitizenSavingAccount.getTotalBenefits());
     /*Saving account with privilege decoration*/
     Account privilegeCitizenSavingAccount = new SavingAccount();
     privilegeCitizenSavingAccount = new
        Privilege(privilegeCitizenSavingAccount);
     System.out.println
     (privilegeCitizenSavingAccount.getTotalBenefits());
  }
}
```

Let's run this demo class and see the following output at the console:

Decorator design pattern in the Spring Framework

The Spring Framework uses the Decorator design pattern to build important functionalities such as transactions, cache synchronization, and security-related tasks. Let's look at some functionalities where Spring implements this pattern transparently:

- Weaving the advice into the Spring application. It uses the Decorator pattern via the CGLib proxy. It works by generating a subclass of the target class at runtime.
- `BeanDefinitionDecorator` : It is used to decorate the bean definition via applied custom attributes.
- `WebSocketHandlerDecorator`: It is used to decorate a WebSocketHandler with additional behaviors.

Now let's turn to another GOF Design Pattern - Facade design pattern.

Facade Design Pattern

Provide a unified interface to a set of interfaces in a subsystem. Facade defines a higher-level interface that makes the subsystem easier to use.
- GOF Design Patterns

The Facade design pattern is nothing but an interface of interfaces to simplify interactions between the client code and subsystem classes. This design comes under the GOF structural design pattern.

Benefits of Facade Pattern:

- This pattern reduces the complexities for clients to interact with subsystems
- This pattern consolidates all the business services as single interfaces to make them more understandable
- This pattern reduces dependencies of client code on the inner workings of a system

Knowing when to use the Facade Pattern

Suppose you are designing a system, and this system has a very large number of independent classes and also has a set of services to be implemented. This system is going to be very complex, so the Facade pattern comes into the picture and reduces the complexities of the larger system and simplifies interactions of the client code with a set of classes from a subsystem of the large complex system.

Suppose you want to develop a bank enterprise application with a large number of services to perform a task, for example, `AccountService` for getting the `Account` by `accountId`, `PaymentService` for payment gateway services, and `TransferService` for the amount transfer from one account to another account. A client code of the application interacts with all these services to transfer money from one account to another account. This is how different clients interact with the amount transfer process of the bank system. As shown in the following figure, here you can see client code that directly interacts with the subsystem classes and client also should aware about the internal working of subsystem classes, so it is simply a violation of the SOLID design principles because client code is tightly coupled with the classes of subsystem of your banking application:

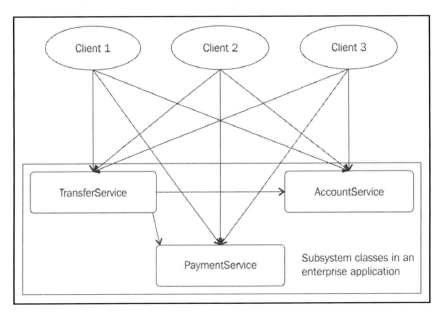

Banking Application Subsystem without Facade Design Pattern

Rather than client code directly interacting with the classes of a subsystem, you could introduce one more interface, which makes the subsystems easier to use, as shown in the following figure. This interface is known as a `Facade` interface, it is based on the Facade pattern, and it is a simple way to interact with the subsystems:

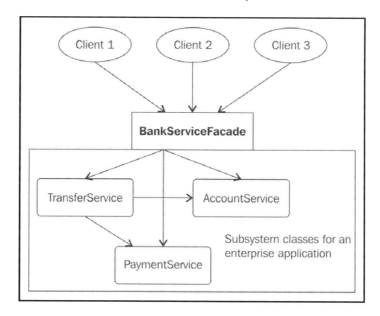

Banking Application Subsystem with Facade design pattern

Implementing the Facade design pattern

Let's look into the following listings to demonstrate the Facade design pattern.

Create subsystem service classes for your Bank application: Let's see the following PaymentService class for the subsystem.

Following is the `PaymentService.java` file:

```
package com.packt.patterninspring.chapter3.facade.pattern;
public class PaymentService {
  public static boolean doPayment(){
    return true;
  }
}
```

Let's create another service class AccountService for the subsystem.

Following is the `AccountService.java` file:

```
package com.packt.patterninspring.chapter3.facade.pattern;
import com.packt.patterninspring.chapter3.model.Account;
import com.packt.patterninspring.chapter3.model.SavingAccount;
public class AccountService {
  public static Account getAccount(String accountId) {
    return new SavingAccount();
  }
}
```

Let's create another service class TransferService for the subsystem.

Following is the `TransferService.java` file:

```
package com.packt.patterninspring.chapter3.facade.pattern;
import com.packt.patterninspring.chapter3.model.Account;
public class TransferService {
  public static void transfer(int amount, Account fromAccount,
      Account toAccount) {
    System.out.println("Transfering Money");
  }
}
```

Create a Facade Service class to interact with the subsystem: Let's see the following Facade interface for the subsystem and then implement this Facade interface as a global banking service in the application.

Following is the `BankingServiceFacade.java` file:

```
package com.packt.patterninspring.chapter3.facade.pattern;
public interface BankingServiceFacade {
    void moneyTransfer();
}
```

Following is the `BankingServiceFacadeImpl.java` file:

```
package com.packt.patterninspring.chapter3.facade.pattern;
import com.packt.patterninspring.chapter3.model.Account;
public class BankingServiceFacadeImpl implements
    BankingServiceFacade{
  @Override
  public void moneyTransfer() {
    if(PaymentService.doPayment()){
        Account fromAccount = AccountService.getAccount("1");
        Account toAccount   = AccountService.getAccount("2");
        TransferService.transfer(1000, fromAccount, toAccount);
    }
  }
}
```

Create the client of the Facade:

Following is the `FacadePatternClient.java` file:

```
package com.packt.patterninspring.chapter3.facade.pattern;
public class FacadePatternClient {
  public static void main(String[] args) {
    BankingServiceFacade serviceFacade = new
      BankingServiceFacadeImpl();
    serviceFacade.moneyTransfer();
  }
}
```

The UML structure for the Facade design pattern

The classes and objects participating in this pattern are:

- Facade (`BankingServiceFacade`)

This is a Facade interface that knows which subsystem classes are responsible for a request. This interface is responsible for delegating client requests to appropriate subsystem objects.

- Subsystem classes (`AccountService`, `TransferService`, `PaymentService`)

These interfaces are actually subsystem functionalities of the banking process system application. These are responsible for handling processes assigned by the Facade object. No interfaces in this category have a reference to the Facade object; they don't have implementation details of Facade. These are totally independent of Facade objects.

Let's see the following UML diagram for this pattern:

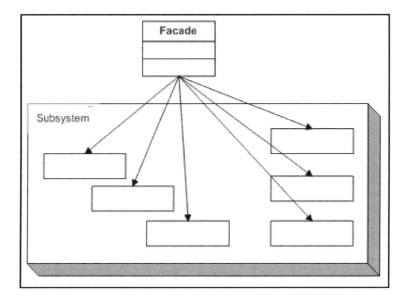

UML diagram for Facade design pattern

Facade Pattern in the Spring Framework

In the enterprise application, if you are working in Spring applications, the facade pattern is used commonly in the business service layer of the application to consolidate all services. And you could also apply this pattern on DAOs on the persistent layer.

Now that we've seen the Facade design pattern, let's turn to a different variant of it--Proxy design pattern.

Proxy design pattern

Provide a surrogate or placeholder for another object to control access to it.
-GOF Design Patterns

Proxy design pattern provides an object of a class with the functionality of another class with having it. This pattern comes under the structural design pattern of GOF Design Patterns. The intent of this design pattern is to provide an alternate class for another class , along with its functionality, to the outside world.

Purpose of the Proxy pattern

Let's look at the following points:

- This pattern hides the actual object from the outside world.
- This pattern can improve the performance because it is creating an object on demand.

UML structure for the Proxy design pattern

Let's see the following UML diagram for this pattern:

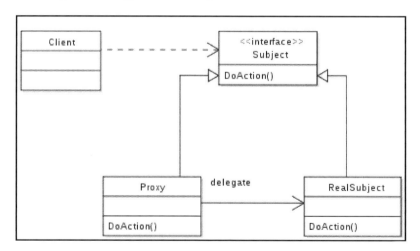

UML diagram for Proxy design pattern

Now let's look at the different components of this UML diagram:

- **Subject**: Actual interface to be implemented by Proxy and RealSubject.
- **RealSubject**: Real implementation of **Subject**. It is a real object that represented by the proxy.
- **Proxy**: It is a proxy object and it is also the implementation of the real object **Subject**. It maintains the references to the real object.

Implementing the Proxy design pattern

Let's look into following code to demonstrate the Proxy pattern.

Create a Subject.

Following is the `Account.java` file:

```
public interface Account {
    void accountType();
}
```

Create a RealSubject class that implements Subject, let's see the following class as RealSubject class for the Proxy design pattern.

Following is the `SavingAccount.java` file:

```
public class SavingAccount implements Account{
    public void accountType() {
        System.out.println("SAVING ACCOUNT");
    }
}
```

Create a Proxy class which implements Subject and having the Real Subject

Following is the `ProxySavingAccount.java` file:

```
package com.packt.patterninspring.chapter2.proxy.pattern;
import com.packt.patterninspring.chapter2.model.Account;
import com.packt.patterninspring.chapter2.model.SavingAccount;
public class ProxySavingAccount implements Account{
   private Account savingAccount;
   public void accountType() {
      if(savingAccount == null){
           savingAccount = new SavingAccount();
      }
      savingAccount.accountType();
   }
}
```

Proxy pattern in the Spring Framework

Spring Framework uses the Proxy design pattern in the Spring AOP module transparently. As I have discussed in Chapter 1, *Getting Started with Spring Framework 5.0 and Design Patterns*. In Spring AOP, you create proxies of the object to apply cross cutting concern across the point cut in the Spring application. In the Spring, other modules also implement the Proxy pattern, such as RMI, Spring's HTTP Invoker, Hessian, and Burlap.

Let's see the next section about Behavioral design pattern with its underlying patterns and example.

Behavioral design patterns

The intent of Behavioral design pattern is the interaction and cooperation between a set of objects to perform a task that no single object can carry out by itself. The interaction between the objects should be such that they should be loosely coupled. Patterns under this category, characterize the ways in which classes or objects interact and distribute responsibility. Let's see in the next sections, different variants of the Behavioral design patterns.

Chain of Responsibility design pattern

Avoid coupling the sender of a request to its receiver by giving more than one object a chance to handle the request. Chain the receiving objects and pass the request along the chain until an object handles it.
-GOF Design Patterns

Chain of responsibility design pattern comes under the Behavioral design pattern of GOF patterns family. According to this pattern, sender and receiver of a request are decoupled. The sender sends a request to the chain of receivers and any one of receivers in the chain can handle the request. In this pattern, the receiver object has the reference of another receiver object so that if it does not handle the request then it passes the same request to the other receiver object.

For example, in a banking System, you could use any ATM to withdraw the money in any place, so it is one of the live examples of the Chain of Responsibility design pattern.

There are following benefits of this pattern:

- This pattern reduces the coupling between sender and receiver objects in the system to handle a request.
- This pattern is more flexible to assign the responsibility to another referenced object.
- This pattern makes a chain of objects using composition, and this set of objects work as a single unit.

Let's see the following UML diagram showing all components of a chain of responsibility design pattern:

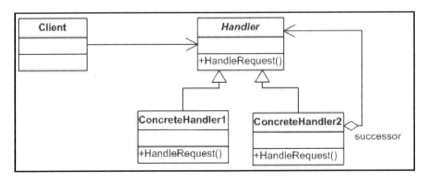

UML Diagram for Chain of Responsibility design pattern

- **Handler**: This is an abstract class or interface in the system to handle request.
- **ConcreteHandler**: These are concrete classes which implement **Handler** to handle the request, or it passes same request to the next successor of the handler chain.
- **Client**: It is main application class to initiate the request to the handler objects on the chain.

Chain of Responsibility pattern in the Spring Framework

Spring Security project implemented the Chain of Responsibility pattern in the Spring Framework. Spring Security allows you to implement authentication and authorization functionality in your application by using chains of security filters. This is a highly configurable framework. You can add your custom filter with this chain of filters to customize the functionality because of Chain of Responsibility design pattern.

Now that we've seen the Chain of responsibility design pattern, let's turn to a different variant of it--Command design pattern.

Command design pattern

> *Encapsulate a request as an object, thereby letting you parameterize clients with different requests, queue or log requests, and support undoable operations*
> *-GOF Design Patterns*

The Command design pattern falls under the Behavioral pattern family of the GOF patterns, this pattern is a very simple data-driven pattern which allows you to encapsulate your request data into an object and pass that object as a command to the invoker method, and it return the command as another object to the caller.

The following lists the benefits of using the Command pattern:

- This pattern enables you to transfer data as an object between the system components sender and receiver.
- This pattern allows you to parameterize objects by an action to perform.
- You could easily add new commands in the system without changing existing classes.

Let's look at the following UML diagram showing all components of Command design pattern:

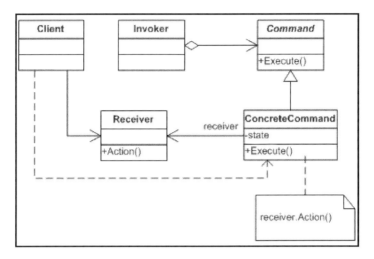

UML Diagram for Command Design Pattern

- **Command**: It is an interface or abstract class having an action to perform in the system.

- **ConcreteCommand**: It is a concrete implementation of the `Command` interface and defining an action will be performed.

- **Client**: This is a main class, it creates a `ConcreteCommand` object and sets its receiver.

- **Invoker**: It is a caller to invoke the request to carry the command object.

- **Receiver**: It is simple handler method which performs the actual operation by `ConcreteCommand`.

Command design pattern in the Spring Framework

Spring MVC has implemented the Command design pattern in the Spring Framework. In your enterprise applications using the Spring Framework, you often see the concepts of the Command pattern applied through the use of Command objects.

Now that we've seen Command design pattern, let's turn to a different variant of it-- Interpreter design pattern.

Interpreter Design pattern

Given a language, define a representation for its grammar along with an interpreter that uses the representation to interpret sentences in the language.
-GOF Design Pattern

Interpreter design pattern allows you to interpret an expression language in the programming to define a representation for its grammar. This type of a pattern comes under the Behavioral design pattern family of GOF patterns.

The following lists the benefits of using the Interpreter pattern:

- This pattern allows you to change and extend the grammar easily.
- Using the expression language is very easy

Let's see the following UML diagram is showing all components of Interpreter design pattern:

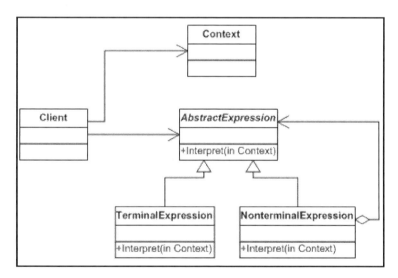

UML diagram for Interpreter design pattern

- **AbstractExpression:** It is an interface to execute a task by using `interpret()` operation.
- **TerminalExpression:** It is an implementation of above interface and it implements `interpret()` operation for terminal expressions.

- **NonterminalExpression:** It is also an implementation of above interface and it implements `interpret()` operation for non-terminal expressions.
- **Context:** It is a `String` expression and contains information that is global to the interpreter.
- **Client:** It is the main class to invoke the Interpret operation.

Interpreter design pattern in the Spring Framework

In the Spring Framework, Interpreter pattern is used with the **Spring Expression Language** (**SpEL**). Spring added this new feature from Spring 3.0, you can use it in your enterprise application using the Spring Framework.

Now that we've seen Interpreter design pattern, let's turn to a different variant of it--Iterator design pattern.

Iterator Design Pattern

> *Provide a way to access the elements of an aggregate object sequentially without Exposing its underlying representation.*
> *-GOF Design Pattern*

This is a very commonly used design pattern in the programming language as like in Java. This pattern comes from the Behavioral Design Pattern family of GOF pattern. This pattern allows you to access the items from the collection object in sequence without information its internal representation.

These are following benefits of the Iterator pattern:

- Easily access the items of the collection.
- You can use multiple to access the item from the collection because it support lot of variations in the traversal.
- It provides a uniform interface for traversing different structures in a collection.

Let's see the following UML diagram is showing all components of Iterator design pattern:

UML Diagram for Iterator Design Pattern

- **Iterator:** It is an interface or abstract class for accessing and traversing items of the collections.
- **ConcreteIterator:** It is an implementation of the **Iterator** interface.
- **Aggregate:** It is an interface to create an Iterator object.
- **ConcreteAggregate:** It is the implementation of the **Aggregate** interface, it implements the **Iterator** creation interface to return an instance of the proper **ConcreteIterator**.

Iterator design pattern in the Spring Framework

The Spring Framework also extends the Iterator pattern through the **CompositeIterator** class. Mainly this pattern used in the Collection Framework of Java for iterating the elements in sequence.

Now that we've seen Iterator design pattern, let's turn to a different variant of it--Observer design pattern.

Observer Design Pattern

Define a one-to-many dependency between objects so that when one object changes state,
all its dependents are notified and updated automatically
-GOF Design Pattern

Observer pattern is one of very common design pattern, This pattern is a part of the Behavioral design pattern family of GOF pattern that addresses responsibilities of objects in an application and how they communicate between them at runtime. According to this pattern, sometimes objects make a one-to-many relationship between the objects in your application, such that if one object is modified, it's notified to other dependent objects automatically.

For example, Facebook post comments are one of the examples of the observer design pattern. If you comment on a post of your friend then you are always notified by this post whenever anyone else comments on the same post again.

The Observer pattern provides communication between decoupled objects. It makes a relationship between objects mostly a one-to-many relationship. In this pattern, there is an object which is known as the subject. Whenever there is any change in the state of this subject, it will be notified to its list of dependents accordingly. This list of dependents is known as observers. The following figure illustrates the Observer pattern:

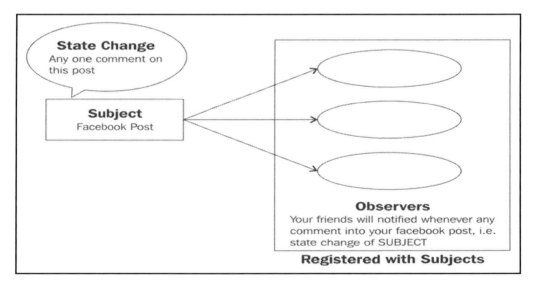

Use case of the Observer design pattern

There are following lists of the benefits of using the Observer pattern:

- This pattern provides decoupled relationship between the subject and observer
- It provides support for broadcasting

Let's see the following UML diagram is showing all components of Observer design pattern:

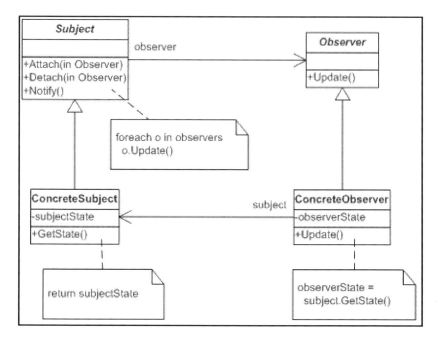

UML Diagram for Observer Design Pattern

- **Subject**: It is an interface. It has information about its observers.
- **ConcreteSubject**: It is a concrete implementation of **Subject**, it has information about all its observers to be notified when its state changes.
- **Observer**: It is an interface to be notified of changes in a subject.
- **ConcreteObserver**: It is a concrete implementation of Observer, it keeps its state consistent with the subject's state.

Observer pattern in the Spring Framework

In the Spring Framework, the Observer design pattern is used to implement event handling function of `ApplicationContext`. Spring provides us the `ApplicationEvent` class and `ApplicationListener` interface to enable event handling in Spring `ApplicationContext`. Any bean in your Spring application implements the `ApplicationListener` interface, it will receive an `ApplicationEvent` every time the `ApplicationEvent` is published by an event publisher. Here, the event publisher is the subject and the bean that implements ApplicationListener is the observer.

Now that we've seen Observer design pattern, let's turn to a different variant of it-- Template design pattern.

Template Design Pattern

Define the skeleton of an algorithm in an operation, deferring some steps to subclasses. Template Method lets subclasses redefine certain steps of an algorithm without changing the algorithm's structure.
60; -GOF Design Patterns

In Template design pattern, an abstract class wraps some defined ways to its method. That method allows you to override parts of the method without rewriting it. You could use its concrete class to your application to perform similar type actions. This design pattern comes under the Behavior design pattern family of GOF pattern.

There are following lists the benefits of using the Template pattern:

- It reduces the boilerplate codes in the application by reusing code.
- This pattern creates a template or way to reuse multiple similar algorithms to perform some business requirements.

Let's see the following UML diagram is showing the components of Template design pattern:

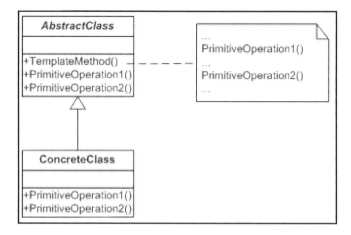

UML Diagram for Template design pattern

- **AbstractClass**: This is an abstract class that contains a template method defining the skeleton of an algorithm.
- **ConcreteClass:** This is a concrete subclass of **AbstractClass** that implements the operations to carry out the algorithm-specific primitive steps.

Let's see the next section about J2EE design patterns in the enterprise distributed applications

JEE design patterns

It is other main category of design patterns. Application design can be immensely simplified by applying Java EE design patterns. Java EE design patterns have been documented in Sun's Java Blueprints. These Java EE design patterns provide time-tested solution guidelines and best practices for object interaction in the different layer of a Java EE application. These design patterns are specifically concerned with the following listed layers:

- Design pattern at presentation layer
- Design pattern at business layer
- Design pattern at integration layer

These design patterns are specifically concerned with the following listed layers.

- **Design pattern at presentation layer**:
    - **View Helper**: It separates views from the business logic of an enterprise J2EE application.
    - **Front Controller**: It provides a single point of action to handle the all coming requests to the J2EE web application, it forwards the request to specific application controller to access model and view for presentation tier resources.
    - **Application Controller**-The request actually handled by the Application Controller, it acts as a front controller helper. It responsible for the coordination with the business models and view components.
    - **Dispatcher View**-It is related to the view only and it executes without business logic to prepare a response to the next view.
    - **Intercepting filters** -In the J2EE web application, you could configure multiple interceptors for pre and post processing an user's request such as tracking and auditing user's requests.
- **Design pattern at business layer**:
    - **Business Delegate**-It acts as a bridge between application controllers and business logic
    - **Application Service**-It provides business logics to implement the model as simple Java objects for presentation layer

- **Design pattern at integration layer**:
    - **Data Access Object**-It is implemented for accessing business data and it separates data access logic from business logic in the enterprise application.
    - **Web Service Broker**-It encapsulates the logic to access the external application's resources and it is exposed as web services.

Summary

After reading this chapter, the reader should now have a good idea about GOF Design Patterns and their best practices. I highlighted the problems that come if you don't implement design patterns in your enterprise application and how Spring solves these problems by using lots of design patterns and good practices to create an application. In the preceding chapter too, I have mentioned the three main categories of GOF Design Patterns such as Creational Design Pattern; it is useful for creation of object instances and also to apply some constraints at the creation time of the enterprise application by specific manner by Factory, Abstract Factory, Builder, Prototype and Singleton pattern. The second main category is the Structural design pattern, it is used for design structure of the enterprise application by dealing with the composition of classes or objects so that it reduces application complexity and improve the reusability and performance of the application. They are Adapter pattern, Bridge pattern, Composite pattern, Decorator pattern, and Facade pattern come under this category of patterns. Finally, one more main category of the pattern is Behavioral design pattern, it characterizes the ways in which classes or objects interact and distribute responsibility. Patterns come under this category are specifically concerned with communication between objects.

4

Wiring Beans using the Dependency Injection Pattern

In the previous chapter, you learned about the **Gang of Four** (**GOF**) design patterns with examples and use cases of each. Now, we will go into more detail about injecting beans and the configuration of dependencies in a Spring application, where you will see the various ways of configuring dependencies in a Spring application. This includes configuration with XML, Annotation, Java, and Mix.

Everyone loves movies, right? Well, if not movies, how about plays, or dramas, or theatre? Ever wondered what would happen if the different team members didn't speak to each other? By team I don't just mean the actors, but the sets team, make-up personnel, audio-visual guys, sound system guys, and so on. It is needless to say that every member has an important contribution towards the end product, and an immense amount of coordination is required between these teams.

A blockbuster movie is a product of hundreds of people working together toward a common goal. Similarly, great software is an application where several objects work together to meet some business target. As a team, every object must be aware of the other, and communicate with each other to get their jobs done.

In a banking system, the money transfer service must be aware of the account service, and the account service must be aware of the accounts repository, and so on. All these components work together to make the banking system workable. In Chapter 1, *Getting Started with Framework 5.0 and Design Patterns*, you saw the same banking example created with the traditional approach, that is, creating objects using construction and direct object initiation. This traditional approach leads to complicated code, is difficult to reuse and unit test, and is also highly coupled to one another.

But in Spring, objects have a responsibility to do their jobs without the need to find and create the other dependent objects that are required in their jobs. The Spring container takes the responsibility to find or create the other dependent objects, and to collaborate with their dependencies. In the previous example of the banking system, the transfer service depends on the account service, but it doesn't have to create the account service, so the dependency is created by the container, and is handed over to the dependent objects in the application.

In this chapter, we will discuss the behind-the-scenes story of the Spring-based application with reference to the **dependency injection (DI)** pattern, and how it works. By the end of this chapter, you will understand how the objects of your Spring-based application create associations between them, and how Spring wires these objects for a job done. You will also learn many ways to wire beans in Spring.

This chapter will cover the following topics:

- The dependency injection pattern
- Types of dependency injection patterns
- Resolving dependency using the Abstract Factory pattern
- Lookup-method injection pattern
- Configuring beans using the Factory pattern
- Configuring dependencies
- Common best practices for configuring dependencies in an application

The dependency injection pattern

In any enterprise application, coordination between the working objects is very important for a business goal. The relationship between objects in an application represents the dependency of an object, so each object would get the job done with coordination of the dependent objects in the application. Such required dependencies between the objects tend to be complicated and with tight-coupled programming in the application. Spring provides a solution to the tight-coupling code of an application by using the dependency injection pattern. Dependency injection is a design pattern, which promotes the loosely coupled classes in the application. This means that the classes in the system depend on the behavior of others, and do not depend on instantiation of object of the classes. The dependency injection pattern also promotes programming to interface instead of programming to implementation. Object dependencies should be on an interface, and not on concrete classes, because a loosely coupled structure offers you greater reusability, maintainability, and testability.

Solving problems using the dependencies injection pattern

In any enterprise application, a common problem to handle is how to configure and wire together the different elements to achieve a business goal--for example, how to bind together the controllers at the web layer with the services and repository interfaces written by different members of the team without knowing about the controllers of the web layers. So, there are a number frameworks that provide a solution for this problem by using lightweight containers to assemble the components from different layers. Examples of such types of frameworks are PicoContainer and Spring Framework.

The containers of PicoContainer and Spring use a number of design patterns to solve the problem of assembling the different components of different layers. Here, I am going to discuss one of these design patterns--the dependency injection pattern. Dependency injection provides us with a decoupled and loosely coupled system. It ensures construction of the dependent object. In the following example, we'll demonstrate how the dependency injection pattern solves the common problems related to collaboration between the various layered components.

Without dependency injection

In the following Java example, first of all, let's see what is a dependency between two classes? Take a look at the following class diagram:

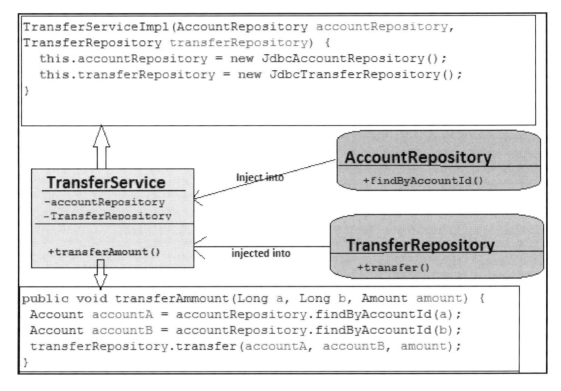

TransferService has dependencies with AccountRepository and TransferRepository for transferAmount() method with Direct Instantiation of repositories classes.

As seen in the preceding diagram, the **TransferService** class contains two member variables, **AccountRepository** and **TransferRepository.** These are initialized by the **TransferService** constructor. **TransferService** controls which implementation of the repositories is used. It also controls their construction. In this situation, **TransferService** is said to have a hard-coded dependency on the following example:

Following is the `TransferServiceImpl.java` file:

```java
public class TransferServiceImpl implements TransferService {
  AccountRepository accountRepository;
  TransferRepository transferRepository;
  public TransferServiceImpl(AccountRepository accountRepository,
  TransferRepository transferRepository) {
    super();
    // Specify a specific implementation in the constructor
    instead of using dependency injection
    this.accountRepository = new JdbcAccountRepository();
    this.transferRepository = new JdbcTransferRepository();
  }
  // Method within this service that uses the accountRepository and
  transferRepository
  @Override
  public void transferAmmount(Long a, Long b, Amount amount) {
    Account accountA = accountRepository.findByAccountId(a);
    Account accountB = accountRepository.findByAccountId(b);
    transferRepository.transfer(accountA, accountB, amount);
  }
}
```

In the preceding example, the `TransferServiceImpl` class has dependencies of two classes, that is `AccountRepository` and `TransferRepository`. The `TransferServiceImpl` class has two member variables of the dependent classes, and initializes them through its constructor by using the JDBC implementation of repositories such as `JdbcAccountRepository` and `JdbcTransferRepository`. The `TransferServiceImpl` class is tightly coupled with the JDBC implementation of repositories; in case the JDBC implementation is changed to a JPA implementation, you have to change your `TransferServiceImpl` class as well.

According to the SOLID (Single Responsibility Principle, Open Closed Principle, Liskov's Substitution Principle, Interface Segregation Principle, Dependency Inversion Principle) principles, a class should have a single responsibility in the application, but in the preceding example, the `TransferServiceImpl` class is also responsible for constructing the objects of `JdbcAccountRepository` and `JdbcTransferRepository` classes. We can't use direction instantiation of objects in the class.

In our first attempt to avoid the direct instantiation logic in the `TransferServiceImpl` class, we can use a `Factory` class that creates instances of `TransferServiceImpl`. According to this idea, `TransferServiceImpl` minimizes the dependency from `AccountRepository` and `TransferRepository`--earlier we had a tightly coupled implementation of the repositories, but now it refers only to the interface, as shown in the following diagram:

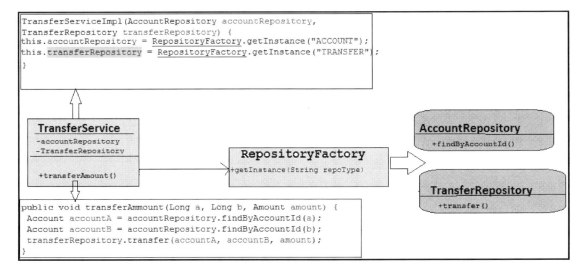

TransferService has dependencies with AccountRepository and TransferRepository for transferAmount() method with Factory of repositories classes.

But the `TransferServiceImpl` class is, again, tightly coupled with the implementation of the `RepositoryFactory` class. Moreover, this process is not suitable for cases where we have more number of dependencies, which increases either the `Factory` classes or the complexity of the `Factory` class. The repository classes can also have other dependencies.

The following code uses the `Factory` class to get the `AccountRepository` and `TransferRepository` classes:

Following is the `TransferServiceImpl.java` file:

```
package com.packt.patterninspring.chapter4.bankapp.service;
public class TransferServiceImpl implements TransferService {
    AccountRepository accountRepository;
    TransferRepository transferRepository;
    public TransferServiceImpl(AccountRepository accountRepository,
    TransferRepository transferRepository) {
        this.accountRepository = RepositoryFactory.getInstance();
        this.transferRepository = RepositoryFactory.getInstance();
```

```
    }
    @Override
    public void transferAmount(Long a, Long b, Amount amount) {
        Account accountA = accountRepository.findByAccountId(a);
        Account accountB = accountRepository.findByAccountId(b);
        transferRepository.transfer(accountA, accountB, amount);
    }
}
```

In the preceding code example, we have minimized tight coupling, and removed direction object instantiation from the `TransferServiceImpl` class, but this is not the optimal solution.

With dependency injection pattern

The Factory idea avoids direct instantiation of an object of a class, and we also have to create another module that is responsible for wiring the dependencies between classes. This module is known as a **dependency injector**, and is based on the **Inversion of Control (IoC)** pattern. According to the IoC Framework, the Container it is responsible for object instantiation, and to resolve the dependencies among classes in the application. This module has its own life cycle of construction and destruction for the object defined under its scope.

In the following diagram, we have used the dependency injection pattern to resolve the dependencies of the `TransferServiceImpl` class:

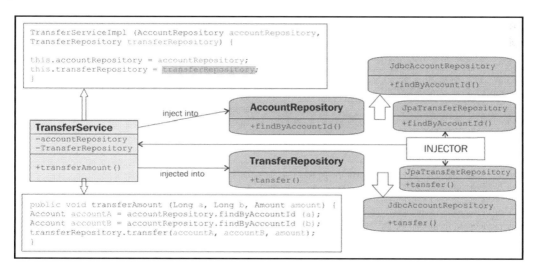

Using dependency injection design pattern to resolve dependencies for TransferService.

In the following example, we have used an interface to resolve the dependencies:

Following is the `TransferServiceImpl.java` file:

```
package com.packt.patterninspring.chapter4.bankapp.service;
public class TransferServiceImpl implements TransferService {
  AccountRepository accountRepository;
  TransferRepository transferRepository;
  public TransferServiceImpl(AccountRepository accountRepository,
  TransferRepository transferRepository) {
    this.accountRepository = accountRepository;
    this.transferRepository = transferRepository;
  }
  @Override
  public void transferAmmount(Long a, Long b, Amount amount) {
    Account accountA = accountRepository.findByAccountId(a);
    Account accountB = accountRepository.findByAccountId(b);
    transferRepository.transfer(accountA, accountB, amount);
  }
}
```

In the `TransferServiceImpl` class, we passed references of the `AccountRepository` and `TransferRepository` interfaces to the constructor. Now the `TransferServiceImpl` class is loosely coupled with the implementation repository class (use any flavor, either JDBC or JPA implementation of repository interfaces), and the framework is responsible for wiring the dependencies with the involved dependent class. Loose coupling offers us greater reusability, maintainability, and testability.

The Spring Framework implements the dependency injection pattern to resolve dependencies among the classes in a Spring application. Spring DI is based on the IoC concept, that is, the Spring Framework has a container where it creates, manages, and destructs the objects; it is known as a Spring IoC container. The objects lying within the Spring container are known as **Spring beans**. There are many ways to wire beans in a Spring application. Let's take a look at the three most common approaches for configuring the Spring container.

In the following section, we'll look at the types of the dependency injection pattern; you can configure the dependencies by using either one of them.

Types of dependency injection patterns

The following are the types of dependency injections that could be injected into your application:

- Constructor-based dependency injection
- Setter-based dependency injection

Constructor-based dependency injection pattern

Dependency injection is a design pattern to resolve the dependencies of dependent classes, and dependencies are nothing but object attributes. The injector has to be constructed for the dependent objects by using one of the ways constructor injection or setter injection. A constructor injection is one of the ways of fulfilling these object attributes at the time of creation to instantiate the object. An object has a public constructor that takes dependent classes as constructor arguments to inject the dependencies. You can declare more than one constructor into the dependent class. Earlier, only the PicoContainer Framework is used a constructor-based dependency injection to resolve dependencies. Currently, the Spring Framework also supports constructor injections to resolve dependencies.

Advantages of the constructor injection pattern

The following are the advantages if you use a constructor injection in your Spring application:

- Constructor-based dependency injection is more suitable for mandatory dependencies, and it makes a strong dependency contract
- Constructor-based dependency injection provides a more compact code structure than others
- It supports testing by using the dependencies passed as constructor arguments to the dependent class
- It favors the use of immutable objects, and does not break the information hiding principle

Disadvantages of constructor injection pattern

The following is the only drawback of this constructor-based injection pattern:

- It may cause circular dependency. (Circular dependency means that the dependent and the dependency class are also dependents on each other, for example, class A depends on Class B and Class B depends on Class A)

Example of constructor-based dependency injection pattern

Let's see the following example for constructor-based dependency injection. In the following code, we have a `TransferServiceImpl` class, and its constructor takes two arguments:

```
public class TransferServiceImpl implements TransferService {
  AccountRepository accountRepository;
  TransferRepository transferRepository;
  public TransferServiceImpl(AccountRepository accountRepository,
  TransferRepository transferRepository) {
    this.accountRepository = accountRepository;
    this.transferRepository = transferRepository;
  }
  // ...
}
```

The repositories will also be managed by the Spring container, and, as such, will have the `datasource` object for database configuration injected into them by the container, as follows:

Following is the `JdbcAccountRepository.java` file:

```
public class JdbcAccountRepository implements AccountRepository{
  JdbcTemplate jdbcTemplate;
  public JdbcAccountRepository(DataSource dataSource) {
    this.jdbcTemplate = new JdbcTemplate(dataSource);
  }
  // ...
}
```

Following is the `JdbcTransferRepository.java` file:

```
public class JdbcTransferRepository implements TransferRepository{
  JdbcTemplate jdbcTemplate;
  public JdbcTransferRepository(DataSource dataSource) {
    this.jdbcTemplate = new JdbcTemplate(dataSource);
  }
  // ...
}
```

You can see in the preceding code the JDBC implementation of the repositories as `AccountRepository` and `TransferRepository`. These classes also have one argument constructor to inject the dependency with the `DataSource` class.

Let's see another way of implementing a dependency injection in the enterprise application, which is setter injection.

Setter-based dependency injection

The injector of the container has another way to wire the dependency of the dependent object. In setter injection, one of the ways to fulfil these dependencies is by providing a setter method in the dependent class. Object has a public setter methods that takes dependent classes as method arguments to inject dependencies. For setter-based dependency injection, the constructor of the dependent class is not required. There are no changes required if you change the dependencies of the dependent class. Spring Framework and PicoContainer Framework support setter injection to resolve the dependencies.

Advantages of setter injection

The following are the advantages if you use the setter injection pattern in your Spring application:

- Setter injection is more readable than the constructor injection
- Setter injection solves the circular dependency problem in the application
- Setter injection allows costly resources or services to be created as late as possible, and only when required
- Setter injection does not require the constructor to be changed, but dependencies are passed through public properties that are exposed

Disadvantage of the setter injection

The following are the drawbacks of the setter injection pattern:

- Security is lesser in the setter injection pattern, because it can be overridden
- A setter-based dependency injection does not provide a code structure as compact as the constructor injection
- Be careful whenever you use setter injection, because it is not a required dependency

Example of a setter-based dependency injection

Let's see the following example for setter-based dependency injection. The following `TransferServiceImpl` class, has setter methods with one argument of the repository type:

Following is the `TransferServiceImpl.java` file:

```
public class TransferServiceImpl implements TransferService {
  AccountRepository accountRepository;
  TransferRepository transferRepository;
  public void setAccountRepository(AccountRepository
  accountRepository) {
    this.accountRepository = accountRepository;
  }
  public void setTransferRepository(TransferRepository
  transferRepository) {
    this.transferRepository = transferRepository;
  }
  // ...
}
```

Similarly, let's define a setter for the repositories' implementations as follows:

Following is the `JdbcAccountRepository.java` file:

```
public class JdbcAccountRepository implements AccountRepository{
  JdbcTemplate jdbcTemplate;
  public setDataSource(DataSource dataSource) {
    this.jdbcTemplate = new JdbcTemplate(dataSource);
  }
  // ...
}
```

Following is the `JdbcTransferRepository.java` file:

```
public class JdbcTransferRepository implements TransferRepository{
    JdbcTemplate jdbcTemplate;
    public setDataSource(DataSource dataSource) {
        this.jdbcTemplate = new JdbcTemplate(dataSource);
}
    // ...
}
```

You can see in the preceding code the JDBC implementation of the repositories as `AccountRepository` and `TransferRepository`. These classes have a setter method with one argument to inject the dependency with the `DataSource` class.

Constructor versus setter injection and best practices

The Spring Framework provides support for both types of dependency injection patterns. Both, the constructor and setter injection pattern, assemble the elements in the system. The choice between the setter and constructor injections depends on your application requirement, and the problem at hand. Let's see the following table, which lists some differences between the constructor and setter injections, and some best practices to select which one is suitable in your application.

Constructors injection	Setter injection
A class with constructor takes arguments; it is very compact sometimes, and clear to understand what it creates.	Here, the object is constructed, but it is not clear whether its attributes are initialized or not.
This is a better choice when the dependency is mandatory.	This is suitable when the dependency is not mandatory.
It allows you to hide the object attributes that are immutable, because it does not have setters for these object attributes. To ensure the immutable nature of the object, use the constructor injection pattern instead of the setter injection.	It doesn't ensure the immutable nature of the object.
It creates circular dependency in your application.	It solves the problem of circular dependency in your application. In this case, the setter injection is a better choice than constructor.

It is not suitable for scalar value dependencies in the application.	If you have simple parameters such as strings and integers as dependencies, the setter injection is better to use, because each setter name indicates what the value is supposed to do.

In the next section, you'll learn how to configure the injector to find the beans and wire them together, and how the injector manages the beans. Here, I will use the Spring configuration for the dependency injection pattern.

Configuring the dependency injection pattern with Spring

In this section, I will explain the process required to configure dependencies in an application. The mainstream injectors are Google Guice, Spring, and Weld. In this chapter, I am using the Spring Framework, so, we will see the Spring configuration here. The following diagram is a high-level view of how Spring works:

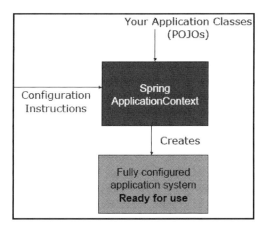

How Spring works using dependency injection pattern

In the preceding diagram, the **Configuration Instruction** is the meta configuration of your application. Here, we define the dependencies in **Your Application Classes (POJOs)**, and initialize the Spring container to resolve the dependency by combining the POJOs and **Configuration Instructions**, and finally, you have a fully configured and executable system or application.

As you have seen in the preceding diagram, the Spring container creates the beans in your application, and assembles them for relationships between those objects via the DI pattern. The Spring container creates the beans based on the configuration that we give to the framework, so, it's your responsibility to tell Spring which beans to create, and how to wire them together.

Spring is very flexible in configuring the dependency of Spring beans. The following are three ways to configure the metadata of your application:

1. **Dependency injection pattern with Java-based configuration**—it is an explicit configuration in Java.
2. **Dependency injection pattern with Annotation-based configuration**—it is an implicit bean discovery, and automatic wiring.
3. **Dependency injection pattern with XML-based configuration**—it is an explicit configuration in XML.

Spring provides three choices to wire beans in Spring. You must select one of the choices, but no single choice is the best match for any application. It depends on your application, and you can also mix and match these choices into a single application. Let's now discuss the dependency injection pattern with Java-based configuration in detail.

Dependency injection pattern with Java-based configuration

As of Spring 3.0, it provides a Java-based Spring configuration to wire the Spring beans. Take a look at the following Java configuration class (`AppConfig.java`) to define the Spring bean and their dependencies. The Java-based configuration for dependency injection is a better choice, because it is more powerful and type-safe.

Creating a Java configuration class - AppConfig.java

Let's create an `AppConfig.java` configuration class for our example:

```
package com.packt.patterninspring.chapter4.bankapp.config;
import org.springframework.context.annotation.Configuration;
@Configuration
public class AppConfig {
    //..
}
```

The preceding `AppConfig` class is annotated with the `@Configuration` annotation, which indicates that it is a configuration class of the application that contains the details on bean definitions. This file will be loaded by the Spring application context to create beans for your application.

Let's now see how you can declare the `TransferService, AccountRepository` and `TransferRepository` beans in `AppConfig`.

Declaring Spring beans into configuration class

To declare a bean in a Java-based configuration, you have to write a method for the desired type object creation in the configuration class, and annotate that method with `@Bean`. Let's see the following changes made in the `AppConfig` class to declare the beans:

```
package com.packt.patterninspring.chapter4.bankapp.config;
import org.springframework.context.annotation.Bean;
import org.springframework.context.annotation.Configuration;
@Configuration
public class AppConfig {
  @Bean
  public TransferService transferService(){
    return new TransferServiceImpl();
  }
  @Bean
  public AccountRepository accountRepository() {
    return new JdbcAccountRepository();
  }
  @Bean
  public TransferRepository transferRepository() {
    return new JdbcTransferRepository();
  }
}
```

In the preceding configuration file, I declared three methods to create instances for `TransferService`, `AccountRepository`, and `TransferRepository`. These methods are annotated with the `@Bean` annotation to indicate that they are responsible for instantiating, configuring, and initializing a new object to be managed by the Spring IoC container. Each bean in the container has a unique bean ID; by default, a bean has an ID same as the `@Bean` annotated method name. In the preceding case, the beans will be named as `transferService`, `accountRepository`, and `transferRepository`. You can also override that default behavior by using the name attribute of the `@Bean` annotation as follows:

```
@Bean(name="service")
public TransferService transferService(){
  return new TransferServiceImpl();
}
```

Now `"service"` is the bean name of that bean `TransferService`.

Let's see how you can inject dependencies for the `TransferService`, `AccountRepository`, and `TransferRepository` beans in `AppConfig`.

Injecting Spring beans

In the preceding code, I declared the beans `TransferService`, `AccountRepository`, and `TransferRepository`; these beans had no dependencies. But, actually, the `TransferService` bean depends on `AccountRepository` and `TransferRepository`. Let's see the following changes made in the `AppConfig` class to declare the beans:

```
package com.packt.patterninspring.chapter4.bankapp.config;
import org.springframework.context.annotation.Bean;
import org.springframework.context.annotation.Configuration;
@Configuration
public class AppConfig {
  @Bean
  public TransferService transferService(){
    return new TransferServiceImpl(accountRepository(),
    transferRepository());
  }
  @Bean
  public AccountRepository accountRepository() {
    return new JdbcAccountRepository();
  }
  @Bean
  public TransferRepository transferRepository() {
    return new JdbcTransferRepository();
```

```
    }
  }
```

In the preceding example, the simplest way to wire up beans in a Java-based configuration is to refer to the referenced bean's method. The `transferService()` method constructs the instance of the `TransferServiceImpl` class by calling the arguments constructor that takes `AccountRepository` and `TransferRepository`. Here, it seems that the constructor of the `TransferServiceImpl` class is calling the `accountRepository()` and `transferRepository()` methods to create instances of `AccountRepository` and `TransferRepository` respectively, but it is not an actual call to create instances. The Spring container creates instances of `AccountRepository` and `TransferRepository`, because the `accountRepository()` and `transferRepository()` methods are annotated with the `@Bean` annotation. Any call to the bean method by another bean method will be intercepted by Spring to ensure the default singleton scope (this will be discussed further in `Chapter 5`, *Understanding the Bean Life cycle and Used Patterns*) of the Spring beans by that method is returned rather than allowing it to be invoked again.

Best approach to configure the dependency injection pattern with Java

In the previous configuration example, I declared the `transferService()` bean method to construct an instance of the `TransferServiceImpl` class by using its arguments constructor. The bean methods, `accountRepository()` and `transferRepository()`, are passed as arguments of the constructor. But in an enterprise application, a lot of configuration files depend on the layers of the application architecture. Suppose the service layer and the infrastructure layer have their own configuration files. That means that the `accountRepository()` and `transferRepository()` methods may be in different configuration files, and the `transferService()` bean method may be in another configuration file. Passing bean methods into the constructor is not a good practice for configuration of the dependency injection pattern with Java. Let's see a different and the best approach to configuring the dependency injection:

```
package com.packt.patterninspring.chapter4.bankapp.config;
import org.springframework.context.annotation.Bean;
import org.springframework.context.annotation.Configuration;
@Configuration
public class AppConfig {
  @Bean
  public TransferService transferService(AccountRepository
  accountRepository, TransferRepository transferRepository){
    return new TransferServiceImpl(accountRepository,
    transferRepository);
```

```
  }
  @Bean
  public AccountRepository accountRepository() {
    return new JdbcAccountRepository();
  }
  @Bean
  public TransferRepository transferRepository() {
    return new JdbcTransferRepository();
  }
}
```

In the preceding code, the `transferService()` method asks for `AccountRepository` and `TransferRepository` as parameters. When Spring calls `transferService()` to create the `TransferService` bean, it autowires `AccountRepository` and `TransferRepository` into the configuration method. With this approach, the `transferService()` method can still inject `AccountRepository` and `TransferRepository` into the constructor of `TransferServiceImpl` without explicitly referring to the `accountRepository()` and `transferRepository()` `@Bean` methods.

Let's now take a look at dependency injection pattern with XML-based configuration.

Dependency injection pattern with XML-based configuration

Spring provides dependency injection with XML-based configuration from the very beginning. It is the primary way of configuring a Spring application. According to me, every developer should have an understanding of how to use XML with a Spring application. In this section, I am going to explain the same example as discussed in the previous section of Java-based configuration with reference to XML-based configuration.

Creating an XML configuration file

In the section on Java-based configuration, we had created an `AppConfig` class annotated with the `@Configuration` annotation. Similarly, for XML-based configuration, we will now create an `applicationContext.xml` file rooted with a `<beans>` element. The following simplest possible example shows the basic structure of XML-based configuration metadata:

Following is the `applicationContext.xml` file:

```
<?xml version="1.0" encoding="UTF-8"?>
<beans xmlns="http://www.springframework.org/schema/beans"
 xmlns:xsi="http://www.w3.org/2001/XMLSchema-instance"
 xsi:schemaLocation="http://www.springframework.org/schema/beans
 http://www.springframework.org/schema/beans/spring-beans.xsd">
 <!-- Configuration for bean definitions go here -->
</beans>
```

The preceding XML file is a configuration file of the application which contains the details on bean definitions. This file is also loaded by the XML-flavored implementation of `ApplicationContext` to create beans for your application. Let's see how you can declare the `TransferService`, `AccountRepository` and `TransferRepository` beans in the preceding XML file.

Declaring Spring beans in an XML file

As with Java, we have to declare a class as a Spring bean into Spring's XML-based configuration by using an element of the Spring-beans schema as a `<bean>` element. The `<bean>` element is the XML analogue to JavaConfig's `@Bean` annotation. We add the following configuration to the XML-based configuration file:

```
<bean id="transferService"
 class="com.packt.patterninspring.chapter4.
 bankapp.service.TransferServiceImpl"/>
<bean id="accountRepository"
 class="com.packt.patterninspring.chapter4.
 bankapp.repository.jdbc.JdbcAccountRepository"/>
<bean id="transferService"
 class="com.packt.patterninspring.chapter4.
 bankapp.repository.jdbc.JdbcTransferRepository"/>
```

In the preceding code, I have created a very simple bean definition. In this configuration, the <bean> element has an `id` attribute to identify the individual bean definition. The `class` attribute is expressed as the fully qualified class name to create this bean. The value of the `id` attribute refers to collaborating objects. So let's see how to configure the collaborating beans to resolve the dependencies in the application.

Injecting Spring beans

Spring provides these two ways to define the DI pattern to inject the dependency with the dependent bean in an application:

- Using constructor injection
- Using setter injection

Using constructor injection

For the DI pattern with the construction injection, Spring provides you two basic options as the <constructor-arg> element and c-namespace introduced in Spring 3.0. c-namespace has less verbosity in the application, which is the only difference between them--you can choose any one. Let's inject the collaborating beans with the construction injection as follows:

```
<bean id="transferService"
 class="com.packt.patterninspring.chapter4.
 bankapp.service.TransferServiceImpl">
 <constructor-arg ref="accountRepository"/>
 <constructor-arg ref="transferRepository"/>
</bean>
<bean id="accountRepository"
 class="com.packt.patterninspring.chapter4.
 bankapp.repository.jdbc.JdbcAccountRepository"/>
<bean id="transferRepository"
 class="com.packt.patterninspring.chapter4.
 bankapp.repository.jdbc.JdbcTransferRepository"/>
```

In the preceding configuration, the <bean> element of `TransferService` has two <constructor-arg>. This tells it to pass a reference to the beans whose IDs are `accountRepository` and `transferRepository` to the constructor of `TransferServiceImpl`.

As of Spring 3.0, the c-namespace, similarly, has a more succinct way of expressing constructor args in XML. For using this namespace, we have to add its schema in the XML file, as follows:

```
<?xml version="1.0" encoding="UTF-8"?>
<beans xmlns="http://www.springframework.org/schema/beans"
 xmlns:xsi="http://www.w3.org/2001/XMLSchema-instance"
 xmlns:c="http://www.springframework.org/schema/c"
 xsi:schemaLocation="http://www.springframework.org/schema/beans
 http://www.springframework.org/schema/beans/spring-beans.xsd">
<bean id="transferService"
 class="com.packt.patterninspring.chapter4.
 bankapp.service.TransferServiceImpl"
 c:accountRepository-ref="accountRepository" c:transferRepository-
 ref="transferRepository"/>
<bean id="accountRepository"
 class="com.packt.patterninspring.chapter4.
 bankapp.repository.jdbc.JdbcAccountRepository"/>
<bean id="transferRepository"
 class="com.packt.patterninspring.chapter4.
 bankapp.repository.jdbc.JdbcTransferRepository"/>
 <!-- more bean definitions go here -->
</beans>
```

Let's see how to set up these dependencies with the setter injection.

Using setter injection

Using the injection, Spring also provides you with two basic options as the `<property>` element and p-namespace introduced in Spring 3.0. The p-namespace also reduced verbosity of code in the application, which is the only difference between them, you can choose any one. Let's inject the collaborating beans with the setter injection as follows:

```
<bean id="transferService"
 class="com.packt.patterninspring.chapter4.
 bankapp.service.TransferServiceImpl">
 <property name="accountRepository"  ref="accountRepository"/>
 <property name="transferRepository" ref="transferRepository"/>
</bean>
<bean id="accountRepository"
 class="com.packt.patterninspring.chapter4.
 bankapp.repository.jdbc.JdbcAccountRepository"/>
<bean id="transferRepository"
 class="com.packt.patterninspring.chapter4.
 bankapp.repository.jdbc.JdbcTransferRepository"/>
```

In the preceding configuration, the `<bean>` element of `TransferService` has two `<property>` elements which tell it to pass a reference to the beans whose IDs are `accountRepository` and `transferRepository` to the setter methods of `TransferServiceImpl`, as follows:

```
package com.packt.patterninspring.chapter4.bankapp.service;

import com.packt.patterninspring.chapter4.bankapp.model.Account;
import com.packt.patterninspring.chapter4.bankapp.model.Amount;
import com.packt.patterninspring.chapter4.bankapp.
 repository.AccountRepository;
import com.packt.patterninspring.chapter4.bankapp.
 repository.TransferRepository;

public class TransferServiceImpl implements TransferService {
  AccountRepository accountRepository;
  TransferRepository transferRepository;
  public void setAccountRepository(AccountRepository
  accountRepository) {
    this.accountRepository = accountRepository;
  }
  public void setTransferRepository(TransferRepository
  transferRepository) {
      this.transferRepository = transferRepository;
  }
  @Override
  public void transferAmmount(Long a, Long b, Amount amount) {
    Account accountA = accountRepository.findByAccountId(a);
    Account accountB = accountRepository.findByAccountId(b);
    transferRepository.transfer(accountA, accountB, amount);
  }
}
```

In the preceding file, if you use this Spring bean without setter methods, the properties `accountRepository` and `transferRepository` will be initialized as null without injecting the dependency.

As of Spring 3.0, the p-namespace, similarly, has a more succinct way of expressing property in XML. For using this namespace, we have to add its schema in the XML file as follows:

```
<?xml version="1.0" encoding="UTF-8"?>
<beans xmlns="http://www.springframework.org/schema/beans"
  xmlns:xsi="http://www.w3.org/2001/XMLSchema-instance"
  xmlns:p="http://www.springframework.org/schema/p"
  xsi:schemaLocation="http://www.springframework.org/schema/beans
  http://www.springframework.org/schema/beans/spring-beans.xsd">
<bean id="transferService"
 class="com.packt.patterninspring.chapter4.bankapp.
 service.TransferServiceImpl"
 p:accountRepository-ref="accountRepository" p:transferRepository-
 ref="transferRepository"/>
<bean id="accountRepository"
 class="com.packt.patterninspring.chapter4.
 bankapp.repository.jdbc.JdbcAccountRepository"/>
<bean id="transferRepository"
 class="com.packt.patterninspring.chapter4.
 bankapp.repository.jdbc.JdbcTransferRepository"/>
<!-- more bean definitions go here -->
</beans>
```

Let's now take a look at the dependency injection pattern with Annotation-based configuration.

Dependency injection pattern with Annotation-based configuration

As discussed in the previous two sections, we defined the DI pattern with Java-and XML-based configurations, and these two options define dependencies explicitly. It creates the Spring beans by using either the `@Bean` annotated method in the `AppConfig` Java file, or the `<bean>` element tag in the XML configuration file. By these methods, you can also create the bean for those classes which lie outside the application, that is, classes that exist in third-party libraries. Now let's discuss another way to create Spring beans, and define the dependencies between them by using implicit configuration through the Stereotype annotations.

What are Stereotype annotations?

The Spring Framework provides you with some special annotations. These annotations are used to create Spring beans automatically in the application context. The main stereotype annotation is @Component. By using this annotation, Spring provides more Stereotype meta annotations such as @Service, used to create Spring beans at the Service layer, @Repository, which is used to create Spring beans for the repositories at the DAO layer, and @Controller, which is used to create Spring beans at the controller layer. This is depicted in the following diagram:

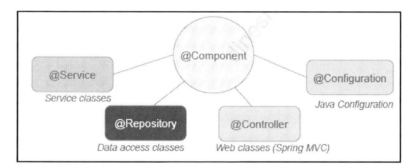

By using these annotations, Spring creates automatic wiring in these two ways:

- **Component scanning:** In this, Spring automatically searches the beans to be created in the Spring IoC container
- **Autowiring:** In this, Spring automatically searches the bean dependencies in the Spring IoC container

Implicitly, the DI pattern configuration reduces the verbosity of an application, and minimizes explicit configuration. Let's demonstrate component scanning and autowiring in the same example as discussed previously. Here, Spring will create the beans for TransferService, TransferRepository, and AccountRepository by discovering them, and automatically inject them to each other as per the defined dependencies.

Creating auto searchable beans using Stereotype annotations

Let's see the following `TransferService` interface. Its implementation is annotated with `@Component`. Please refer to the following code:

```
package com.packt.patterninspring.chapter4.bankapp.service;
public interface TransferService {
  void transferAmmount(Long a, Long b, Amount amount);
}
```

The preceding interface is not important for this approach of configuration--I have taken it just for loose coupling in the application. Let's see its implementation, which is as follows:

```
package com.packt.patterninspring.chapter1.bankapp.service;
import org.springframework.stereotype.Component;
@Component
public class TransferServiceImpl implements TransferService {
  @Override
  public void transferAmmount(Long a, Long b, Amount amount) {
    //business code here
  }
}
```

You can see in the preceding code that `TransferServiceImpl` is annotated with the `@Component` annotation. This annotation is used to identify this class as a component class, which means, it is eligible to scan and create a bean of this class. Now there is no need to configure this class explicitly as a bean either by using XML or Java configuration--Spring is now responsible for creating the bean of the `TransferServiceImpl` class, because it is annotated with `@Component`.

As mentioned earlier, Spring provides us meta annotations for the `@Component` annotation as `@Service`, `@Repository`, and `@Controller`. These annotations are based on a specific responsibility at different layers of the application. Here, `TransferService` is the service layer class; *as a best practice of Spring configuration,* we have to annotate this class with the specific annotation, `@Service`, rather than with the generic annotation, `@Component`, to create the bean of this class. The following is the code for the same class annotated with the `@Service` annotation:

```
package com.packt.patterninspring.chapter1.bankapp.service;
import org.springframework.stereotype.Service;
@Service
public class TransferServiceImpl implements TransferService {
  @Override
  public void transferAmmount(Long a, Long b, Amount amount) {
```

```
            //business code here
    }
}
```

Let's see other classes in the application--these are the `implementation` classes of
`AccountRepository`--and the `TransferRepository` interfaces are the repositories
working at the DAO layer of the application. *As a best practice,* these classes should be
annotated with the `@Repository` annotation rather than using the `@Component` annotation
as shown next.

`JdbcAccountRepository.java` implements the `AccountRepository` interface:

```
package com.packt.patterninspring.chapter4.bankapp.repository.jdbc;
import org.springframework.stereotype.Repository;
import com.packt.patterninspring.chapter4.bankapp.model.Account;
import com.packt.patterninspring.chapter4.bankapp.model.Amount;
import com.packt.patterninspring.chapter4.bankapp.repository.
    AccountRepository;
@Repository
public class JdbcAccountRepository implements AccountRepository {
    @Override
    public Account findByAccountId(Long accountId) {
        return new Account(accountId, "Arnav Rajput", new
        Amount(3000.0));
    }
}
```

And `JdbcTransferRepository.java` implements the `TransferRepository` interface:

```
package com.packt.patterninspring.chapter4.bankapp.repository.jdbc;
import org.springframework.stereotype.Repository;
import com.packt.patterninspring.chapter4.bankapp.model.Account;
import com.packt.patterninspring.chapter4.bankapp.model.Amount;
import com.packt.patterninspring.chapter4.bankapp.
    repository.TransferRepository;
@Repository
public class JdbcTransferRepository implements TransferRepository {
    @Override
    public void transfer(Account accountA, Account accountB, Amount
    amount) {
        System.out.println("Transfering amount from account A to B via
        JDBC implementation");
    }
}
```

In Spring, you have to enable component scanning in your application, because it is not enabled by default. You have to create a configuration Java file, and annotate it with `@Configuration` and `@ComponentScan`. This class is used to search out classes annotated with `@Component`, and to create beans from them.

Let's see how Spring scans the classes which are annotated with any stereotype annotations.

Searching beans using component scanning

The following minimum configuration is required to search beans using component scanning in a Spring application:

```
package com.packt.patterninspring.chapter4.bankapp.config;

import org.springframework.context.annotation.ComponentScan;
import org.springframework.context.annotation.Configuration;

@Configuration
@ComponentScan
public class AppConfig {
}
```

The `AppConfig` class defines a Spring wiring configuration class same as the Java-based Spring configuration in the previous section. There is one thing to be observed here--the `AppConfig` file has one more `@ComponentScan`, as earlier it had only the `@Configuration` annotation. The configuration file `AppConfig` is annotated with `@ComponentScan` to enable component scanning in Spring. The `@ComponentScan` annotation scans those classes that are annotated with `@Component` by default in the same package as the configuration class. Since the `AppConfig` class is in the `com.packt.patterninspring.chapter4.bankapp.config` package, Spring will scan only this package and its sub packages. But our component application classes are in the `com.packt.patterninspring.chapter1.bankapp.service` and `com.packt.patterninspring.chapter4.bankapp.repository.jdbc` packages, and these are not subpackages of `com.packt.patterninspring.chapter4.bankapp.config`. In this case, Spring allows to override the default package scanning of the `@ComponentScan` annotation by setting a base package for component scanning. Let's specify a different base package. You only need to specify the package in the `value` attribute of `@ComponentScan`, as shown here:

```
@Configuration
@ComponentScan("com.packt.patterninspring.chapter4.bankapp")
public class AppConfig {
}
```

Or you can define the base packages with the `basePackages` attribute, as follows:

```
@Configuration
@ComponentScan(basePackages="com.packt.patterninspring.
chapter4.bankapp")
public class AppConfig {
}
```

In the `@ComponentScan` annotation, the `basePackages` attribute can accept an array of Strings, which means that we can define multiple base packages to scan component classes in the application. In the previous configuration file, Spring will scan all classes of `com.packt.patterninspring.chapter4.bankapp` package, and all the subpackages underneath this package. *As a best practice,* always define the specific base packages where the components classes exist. For example, in the following code, I define the base packages for the service and repository components:

```
package com.packt.patterninspring.chapter4.bankapp.config;
import org.springframework.context.annotation.ComponentScan;
import org.springframework.context.annotation.Configuration;
@Configuration
@ComponentScan(basePackages=
{"com.packt.patterninspring.chapter4.
bankapp.repository.jdbc","com.packt.patterninspring.
chapter4.bankapp.service"})
public class AppConfig {
}
```

Now Spring scans only
`com.packt.patterninspring.chapter4.bankapp.repository.jdbc` and
`com.packt.patterninspring.chapter4.bankapp.service packages`, and its
subpackages if they exist. instead of doing a wide range scanning like in the earlier examples.

Rather than specify the packages as simple String values of the `basePackages` attribute of `@ComponentScan`, Spring allows you to specify them via classes or interfaces as follows:

```
package com.packt.patterninspring.chapter4.bankapp.config;
import org.springframework.context.annotation.ComponentScan;
import org.springframework.context.annotation.Configuration;
import com.packt.patterninspring.chapter4.bankapp.
 repository.AccountRepository;
import com.packt.patterninspring.chapter4.
 bankapp.service.TransferService;
@Configuration
@ComponentScan(basePackageClasses=
{TransferService.class,AccountRepository.class})
```

```
public class AppConfig {

}
```

As you can see in the preceding code, the `basePackages` attribute has been replaced with `basePackageClasses`. Now Spring will identify the component classes in those packages where `basePackageClasses` will be used as the base package for component scanning.

It should find the `TransferServiceImpl`, `JdbcAccountRepository`, and `JdbcTransferRepository` classes, and automatically create the beans for these classes in the Spring container. Explicitly, there is no need to define the bean methods for these classes to create Spring beans. Let's turn on component scanning via XML configuration, then you can use the `<context:component-scan>` element from Spring's context namespace. Here is a minimal XML configuration to enable component scanning:

```
<?xml version="1.0" encoding="UTF-8"?>
<beans xmlns="http://www.springframework.org/schema/beans"
xmlns:xsi="http://www.w3.org/2001/XMLSchema-instance"
xmlns:context="http://www.springframework.org/schema/context"
xsi:schemaLocation="http://www.springframework.org/schema/beans
http://www.springframework.org/schema/beans/spring-beans.xsd
http://www.springframework.org/schema/context
http://www.springframework.org/schema/context/spring-context.xsd">
<context:component-scan base-
package="com.packt.patterninspring.chapter4.bankapp" />
</beans>
```

In the preceding XML file, the `<context:component-scan>` element is same the `@ComponentScan` annotation in the Java-based configuration for component scanning.

Annotating beans for autowiring

Spring provides support for automatic bean wiring. This means that Spring automatically resolves the dependencies that are required by the dependent bean by finding other collaborating beans in the application context. Bean Autowiring is another way of DI pattern configuration. It reduces verbosity in the application, but the configuration is spread throughout the application. Spring's `@Autowired` annotation is used for auto bean wiring. This `@Autowired` annotation indicates that autowiring should be performed for this bean.

In our example, we have `TransferService` which has dependencies of `AccountRepository` and `TransferRepository`. Its constructor is annotated with `@Autowired` indicating that when Spring creates the `TransferService` bean, it should instantiate that bean by using its annotated constructor, and pass in two other beans, `AccountRepository` and `TransferRepository`, which are dependencies of the `TransferService` bean. Let's see the following code:

```
package com.packt.patterninspring.chapter4.bankapp.service;
import org.springframework.beans.factory.annotation.Autowired;
import org.springframework.stereotype.Service;
import com.packt.patterninspring.chapter4.bankapp.model.Account;
import com.packt.patterninspring.chapter4.bankapp.model.Amount;
import com.packt.patterninspring.chapter4.bankapp.
 repository.AccountRepository;
importcom.packt.patterninspring.chapter4.
 bankapp.repository.TransferRepository;
@Service
public class TransferServiceImpl implements TransferService {
  AccountRepository accountRepository;
  TransferRepository transferRepository;
@Autowired
public TransferServiceImpl(AccountRepository accountRepository,
TransferRepository transferRepository) {
  super();
  this.accountRepository = accountRepository;
  this.transferRepository = transferRepository;
}
@Override
public void transferAmmount(Long a, Long b, Amount amount) {
  Account accountA = accountRepository.findByAccountId(a);
  Account accountB = accountRepository.findByAccountId(b);
  transferRepository.transfer(accountA, accountB, amount);
}
}
```

 Note--As of Spring 4.3, the `@Autowired` annotation is no more required if you define only one construct with arguments in that class. If class has multiple argument constructors, then you have to use the `@Autowired` annotation on any one of them.

The `@Autowired` annotation is not limited to the construction; it can be used with the setter method, and can also be used directly in the field, that is, an `autowired` class property directly. Let's see the following line of code for setter and field injection.

Using @Autowired with setter method

Here you can annotate the setter method's `setAccountRepository` and `setTransferRepository` with the `@Autowired` annotation. This annotation can be used with any method. There is no specific reason to use it with the setter method only. Please refer to the following code:

```
public class TransferServiceImpl implements TransferService {
  //...
  @Autowired
  public void setAccountRepository(AccountRepository
  accountRepository) {
    this.accountRepository = accountRepository;
  }
  @Autowired
  public void setTransferRepository(TransferRepository
  transferRepository) {
    this.transferRepository = transferRepository;
  }
  //...
}
```

Using @Autowired with the fields

Here you can annotate those class properties which are required for this class to achieve a business goal. Let's see the following code:

```
public class TransferServiceImpl implements TransferService {
  @Autowired
  AccountRepository accountRepository;
  @Autowired
  TransferRepository transferRepository;
  //...
}
```

In the preceding code, the `@Autowired` annotation resolves the dependency by `type` and then by `name` if the property name is the same as the bean name in the Spring container. By default, the `@Autowired` dependency is a required dependency--it raises an exception if the dependency is not resolved, it doesn't matter whether we have used it with a constructor or with the setter method. You can override the required behavior of the `@Autowired` annotation by using the `required` attribute of this annotation. You can set this attribute with the Boolean value `false` as follows:

```
@Autowired(required = false)
public void setAccountRepository(AccountRepository
accountRepository) {
   this.accountRepository = accountRepository;
}
```

In the preceding code, we have set the required attribute with the Boolean value `false`. In this case, Spring will attempt to perform autowiring, but if there are no matching beans, it will leave the bean unwired. But as a best practice of code, you should avoid setting its value as false until it is absolutely necessary.

The Autowiring DI pattern and disambiguation

The `@Autowiring` annotation reduces verbosity in the code, but it may create some problems when two of the same type of beans exist in the container. Let's see what happens in that situation, with the following example:

```
@Service
public class TransferServiceImpl implements TransferService {
@Autowired
public TransferServiceImpl(AccountRepository accountRepository) {
... }
}
```

The preceding snippet of code shows that the `TransferServiceImpl` class has a dependency with a bean of type `AccountRepository`, but the Spring container contains two beans of the same type, that is, the following:

```
@Repository
public class JdbcAccountRepository implements AccountRepository
{..}
@Repository
public class JpaAccountRepository implements AccountRepository {..}
```

As seen from the preceding code, there are two implementations of the
AccountRepository interface--one is JdbcAccountRepository and another is
JpaAccountRepository. In this case, the Spring container will throw the following
exception at startup time of the application:

```
At startup: NoSuchBeanDefinitionException, no unique bean of type
[AccountRepository] is defined: expected single bean but found 2...
```

Resolving disambiguation in Autowiring DI pattern

Spring provides one more annotation, @Qualifier, to overcome the problem of
disambiguation in autowiring DI. Let's see the following snippet of code with the
@Qualifier annotation:

```
@Service
public class TransferServiceImpl implements TransferService {
@Autowired
public TransferServiceImpl( @Qualifier("jdbcAccountRepository")
AccountRepository accountRepository) { ... }
```

Now I have wired the dependency by name rather than by type by using the @Qualifier
annotation. So, Spring will search the bean dependency with the name
"jdbcAccountRepository" for the TransferServiceImpl class. I have given the names
of the beans as follows:

```
@Repository("jdbcAccountRepository")
public class JdbcAccountRepository implements AccountRepository
{..}
@Repository("jpaAccountRepository")
public class JpaAccountRepository implements AccountRepository {..}
```

@Qualifier, also available with the method injection and field injection component names,
should not show implementation details unless there are two implementations of the same
interface.

Let's now discuss some best practices to choose the DI pattern configuration for your Spring
application.

Resolving dependency with Abstract Factory pattern

If you want to add the `if...else` conditional configuration for a bean, you can do so, and also add some custom logic if you are using Java configuration. But in the case of an XML configuration, it is not possible to add the `if...then...else` conditions. Spring provides the solution for conditions in an XML configuration by using the Abstract Factory Pattern. Use a factory to create the bean(s) you want, and use any complex Java code that you need in the factory's internal logic.

Implementing the Abstract Factory Pattern in Spring (FactoryBean interface)

The Spring Framework provides the `FactoryBean` interface as an implementation of the Abstract Factory Pattern. A `FactoryBean` is a pattern to encapsulate interesting object construction logic in a class. The `FactoryBean` interface provides a way to customize the Spring IoC container's instantiation logic. You can implement this interface for objects that are themselves factories. Beans implementing `FactoryBean` are auto-detected.

The definition of this interface is as follows:

```
public interface FactoryBean<T> {
  T getObject() throws Exception;
  Class<T> getObjectType();
  boolean isSingleton();
}
```

As per the preceding definition of this interface, the dependency injection using the FactoryBean and it causes `getObject()` to be invoked transparently. The `isSingleton()` method returns `true` for singleton, else it returns `false`. The `getObjectType()` method returns the object type of the object returned by the `getObject()` method.

Implementation of FactoryBean interface in Spring

FactoryBean is widely used within Spring as the following:

- EmbeddedDatabaseFactoryBean
- JndiObjectFactoryBean
- LocalContainerEntityManagerFactoryBean
- DateTimeFormatterFactoryBean
- ProxyFactoryBean
- TransactionProxyFactoryBean
- MethodInvokingFactoryBean

Sample implementation of FactoryBean interface

Suppose you have a TransferService class whose definition is thus:

```
package com.packt.patterninspring.chapter4.bankapp.service;
import com.packt.patterninspring.chapter4.
 bankapp.repository.IAccountRepository;
public class TransferService {
  IAccountRepository accountRepository;
  public TransferService(IAccountRepository accountRepository){
    this.accountRepository = accountRepository;
  }
  public void transfer(String accountA, String accountB, Double
  amount){
    System.out.println("Amount has been tranferred");
  }
}
```

And you have a FactoryBean whose definition is thus:

```
package com.packt.patterninspring.chapter4.bankapp.repository;
import org.springframework.beans.factory.FactoryBean;
public class AccountRepositoryFactoryBean implements
FactoryBean<IAccountRepository> {
  @Override
  public IAccountRepository getObject() throws Exception {
    return new AccountRepository();
  }
  @Override
  public Class<?> getObjectType() {
    return IAccountRepository.class;
  }
  @Override
```

```
    public boolean isSingleton() {
      return false;
    }
  }
```

You could wire up an `AccountRepository` instance using a hypothetical
`AccountRepositoryFactoryBean` like this:

```xml
<?xml version="1.0" encoding="UTF-8"?>
<beans xmlns="http://www.springframework.org/schema/beans"
xmlns:xsi="http://www.w3.org/2001/XMLSchema-instance"
xmlns:c="http://www.springframework.org/schema/c"
xsi:schemaLocation="http://www.springframework.org/schema/beans
http://www.springframework.org/schema/beans/spring-beans.xsd">
<bean id="transferService" class="com.packt.patterninspring.
 chapter4.bankapp.service.TransferService">
 <constructor-arg ref="accountRepository"/>
</bean>
<bean id="accountRepository"
 class="com.packt.patterninspring.chapter4.
  bankapp.repository.AccountRepositoryFactoryBean"/>
</beans>
```

In the preceding example, the `TransferService` class depends on the
`AccountRepository` bean, but in the XML file, we have defined
`AccountRepositoryFactoryBean` as an `accountRepository` bean. The
`AccountRepositoryFactoryBean` class implements the `FactoryBean` interface of Spring.
The result of the `getObject` method of `FactoryBean` will be passed, and not the actual
`FactoryBean` itself. Spring injects that object returned by `FactoryBean`'s
`getObjectType()` method, and the object type returned by `FactoryBean`'s
`getObjectType()`; the scope of this bean is decided by the `FactoryBean`'s
`isSingleton()` method.

The following is the same configuration for the `FactoryBean` interface in a Java
Configuration:

```java
package com.packt.patterninspring.chapter4.bankapp.config;
import org.springframework.context.annotation.Bean;
import org.springframework.context.annotation.Configuration;
import com.packt.patterninspring.chapter4.bankapp.
 repository.AccountRepositoryFactoryBean;
import com.packt.patterninspring.chapter4.
 bankapp.service.TransferService;
@Configuration
public class AppConfig {
  public TransferService transferService() throws Exception{
```

```
        return new TransferService(accountRepository().getObject());
    }
@Bean
public AccountRepositoryFactoryBean accountRepository(){
    return new AccountRepositoryFactoryBean();
}
}
```

As other normal beans in the Spring container, the Spring `FactoryBean` also has all the other characteristics of any other Spring bean, including the life cycle hooks and services that all beans in the Spring container enjoy.

Best practices for configuring the DI pattern

The following are the best practices for configuring the DI pattern:

- Configuration files should be separated categorically. Application beans should be separate from infrastructure beans. Currently, it's a bit difficult to follow.

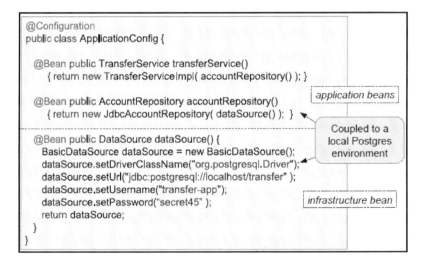

- Always specify the component name; never rely on generated names by the container.
- It is a best practice to give a name along with a description of what the pattern does, where to apply it, and the problems it addresses.

- The best practices for component scanning are as follows:
  - The components are scanned at startup, and it scans the JAR dependencies as well.
  - **Bad practice:** It scans all the packages of com and org. It increases the startup time of the application. Avoid such type of component scanning:

```
@ComponenttScan (( {{ "org", "com" }} ))
```

  - **Optimized:** It scans only the specific packages as defined by us.

```
@ComponentScan ( {
 "com.packt.patterninspring.chapter4.
 bankapp.repository",
 "com.packt.patterninspring.chapter4.bankapp.service"}
 )
```

- Best practices in choosing implicit configuration:
  - Choose annotation-based configurations for frequently changing beans
  - It allows for very rapid development
  - It is a single place to edit the configuration
- Best practices in choosing explicit via Java configuration:
  - It is centralized in one place
  - Strong type checking enforced by the compiler
  - Can be used for all classes
- Spring XML Best Practices: XML has been around for a long time, there are many shortcuts and useful techniques available in XML configuration as well, they are listed follow:
  - factory-method and factory-bean attributes
  - Bean Definition Inheritance
  - Inner Beans
  - p and c namespaces
  - Using collections as Spring beans

Summary

After reading this chapter, you should now have a good idea about DI design patterns, and the best practices for applying those patterns. Spring deals with the plumbing part, so, you can focus on solving the domain problem by using the dependency injection pattern. The DI pattern frees the object of the burden of resolving its dependencies. Your object is handed everything that it needs to work. The DI pattern simplifies your code, improves code reusability, and testability. It promotes programming to interfaces, and conceals the implementation details of dependencies. The DI pattern allows for centralized control over the object's life cycle. You can configure DI via two ways--explicit configuration and implicit configuration. Explicit configuration can be configured through XML-or Java-based configuration; it provides centralized configuration. But implicit configuration is based on annotations. Spring provides stereotype annotations for Annotation-based configuration. This configuration reduces the verbosity of code in the application, but it spreads out across the application files.

In the upcoming `Chapter 5`, *Understanding the Bean Life Cycle and Used Patterns*, we will explore the life cycle of the Spring bean in the container.

5
Understanding the Bean Life Cycle and Used Patterns

In the previous chapter, you saw how Spring creates beans in the container. You also learned how to configure the dependency injection pattern using XML, Java, and Annotation. In this chapter, we will go into more detail, beyond injecting beans and the configuration of dependencies in a Spring application. Here, you will explore the life and scope of beans in the container, and learn how the Spring container works on the defined Spring bean configuration with XML, Annotation, and Java. Spring allows us to control not only the various configurations for the DI pattern and dependency values that are to be injected into the object created from a particular bean definition, but also the life and scope of the beans created from a particular bean definition.

When I was writing this chapter, my two and a half year old son, Arnav, came to me and started playing a video game on my mobile. He was wearing a T-Shirt, which had an interesting quote on it, and these lines described his whole day. The lines went like this-- *My Perfect Day: Wake up, Play Video Games, Eat, Play Video Games, Eat, Play Video Games, and Sleep*.

Actually, these lines perfectly reflected his life cycle for each day, as he woke up, played, ate, and played again before, finally, going to sleep. With this example, I just wanted to demonstrate that everything has a life cycle. We could discuss the life cycle of a butterfly, a star, a frog, or a plant. But let's talk about something more interesting--the life cycle of a bean!

Every bean in the Spring container has a life cycle and its own scope. The Spring container manages the life of the beans in a Spring application. We can customize it in some phases by using Spring-aware interfaces. This chapter will talk about the life of a bean in the container, and how it is managed using design patterns in the various phases of its life. By the end of this chapter, you would have a fair idea of the bean life cycle and its various phases in the container. You will also learn about the many types of bean scope in Spring. This chapter will cover the following points:

- The Spring bean life cycle, and its phases, which are listed as follows:
    - The initialization phase
    - The Use phase
    - The destruction phase
- Spring callbacks
- Understanding bean scopes
    - Singleton pattern
    - Prototype pattern
    - Custom scopes
    - Other bean scopes

Now let's take a moment to see how Spring manages the life cycle of a bean from creation to destruction in the Spring application

The Spring bean life cycle and its phases

In a Spring application, the term life cycle applies to any class of application--Standalone Java, Spring Boot application, or Integration/System Test. Also, life cycle applies to all three dependency injection styles--XML, Annotations, and Java configuration. You define the configuration for beans as per business goals. But Spring creates these beans and manages the life cycle of the Spring beans. Spring loads the bean configurations either in Java or XML through `ApplicationContext`. After loading these beans, the Spring container handles the creation and instantiation of these beans as per your configuration. Let's divide the Spring application life cycle into three phases as follows:

- The initialization phase
- The Use phase
- The destruction phase

Please refer to the following diagram:

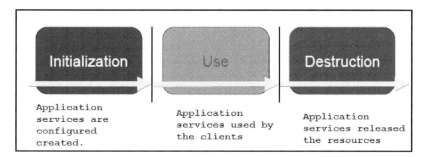

As you can see in the preceding diagram, each Spring bean goes through these three phases in the complete life cycle. Each phase has some set of operations to be performed for each Spring bean (depending on the configuration). Spring fits in to manage your application life cycle. It plays an important role in all three phases.

Now let's take a moment to see how Spring works in the first, initialization phase.

The initialization phase

In this phase, first of all Spring loads all the configuration files of any style-XML, Annotations, and Java configuration. This phase prepares the beans for use. The application is not usable until this phase is complete. This phase, actually, creates the application services for use, and it allocates the system resources to the bean. Spring provides `ApplicationContext` to load the bean configurations; once the application context is created, the initialization phase completes. Let's see how Spring loads the configuration files in Java or XML.

Creating the application context from configuration

Spring provides multiple implementations of `ApplicationContext` to load the various styles of configuration file. These are listed next:

- For Java configuration, the following is used:

```
ApplicationContext context = new
AnnotationConfigApplicationContext(AppConfig.class);
```

- For XML configuration, the implementation is as follows:

```
ApplicationContext context = new
ClassPathXmlApplicationContext("applicationContext.xml");
```

In the preceding codes, Spring loads the Java configuration files by using the `AnnotationConfigApplicationContext` class, and the XML configuration files by using the `ClassPathXmlApplicationContext` class for the Spring container. Spring behaves the same for all types of configuration. It does not matter what configuration styles you use in your application. The following diagram shows what exactly happens in this phase:

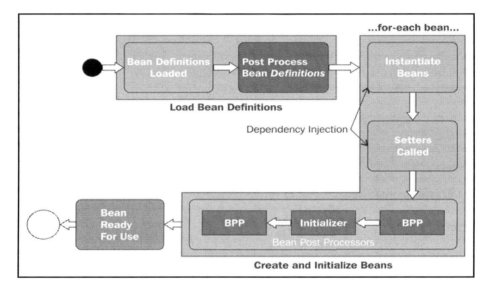

As you can see in the preceding diagram, the initialization phase is divided into these two steps:

- Load bean definitions
- Initialize bean instances

Load bean definitions

In this step, all the configuration files--`@Configuration` classes or XML files-are processed. For Annotation-based configuration, all the classes annotated with `@Components` are scanned to load the bean definitions. All XML files are parsed, and the bean definitions are added to a `BeanFactory`. Each bean is indexed under its `id`. Spring provides multiple `BeanFactoryPostProcessor` beans, so, it is invoked to resolve runtime dependencies such as reading values from external property files. In a Spring application, `BeanFactoryPostProcessor` can modify the definition of any bean. The following diagram describes this step:

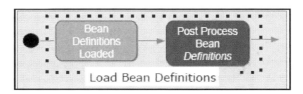

As shown in the preceding diagram, Spring first loads the bean definitions, and then calls `BeanFactoryProcessor` for some beans to modify its definitions accordingly. Let's see this with an example. We have two configuration files--`AppConfig.java` and `InfraConfig.java`, which are defined as follows:

- Following is the `AppConfig.java` file:

```
@Configuration
public class AppConfig {
  @Bean
  public TransferService transferService(){ ... }
  @Bean
  public AccountRepository accountRepository(DataSource
  dataSource){ ... }
}
```

- Following is the `InfraConfig.java` file:

```
@Configuration
public class InfraConfig {
  @Bean
  public DataSource dataSource () { ... }
}
```

These Java configuration files are loaded by the **ApplicationContext** to the container, and indexed with its `id`, as shown in the following diagram:

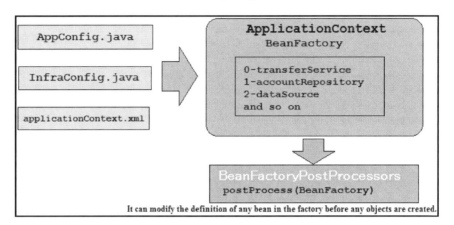

In the last diagram, Spring beans are indexed under its IDs into Spring's `BeanFactory`, and then, that `BeanFactory` object is passed as an argument to the `postProcess()` method of `BeanFactoryPostProcessor`. The `BeanFactoryPostProcessor` can modify the bean definition for some beans; this depends on the bean configurations provided by the developer. Let's see how `BeanFactoryPostProcessor` works, and how to override it in our application:

1. `BeanFactoryPostProcessor` works on the bean definitions or the configuration metadata of the bean before the beans are actually created.
2. Spring provides several useful implementations of `BeanFactoryPostProcessor`, such as reading properties and registering a custom scope.
3. You can write your own implementation of the `BeanFactoryPostProcessor` interface.
4. If you define a `BeanFactoryPostProcessor` in one container, it will only be applied to the bean definitions in that container.

The following is the code snippet for `BeanFactoryPostProcessor`:

```
public interface BeanFactoryPostProcessor {
  public void postProcessBeanFactory
    (ConfigurableListableBeanFactory
    beanFactory);
}
```

Let's now see the following examples of the BeanFactoryPostProcessor extension point:

Reading external property files (database.properties**)**

Here, we'll use the DataSource bean to be configured with the database values such as username, password, db url, and driver, as follows:

```
jdbc.driver=org.hsqldb.jdbcDriver
jdbc.url=jdbc:hsqldb:hsql://production:9002
jdbc.username=doj
jdbc.password=doj@123
```

The following is the DataSource bean definition in the configuration file:

```
@Configuration
@PropertySource ( "classpath:/config/database.properties" )
public class InfraConfig {
 @Bean
 public DataSource dataSource(
 @Value("${jdbc.driver}") String driver,
 @Value("${jdbc.url}") String url,
 @Value("${jdbc.user}") String user,
 @Value("${jdbc.password}") String pwd) {
    DataSource ds = new BasicDataSource();
    ds.setDriverClassName( driver);
    ds.setUrl( url);
    ds.setUser( user);
    ds.setPassword( pwd ));
    return ds;
 }
}
```

So, in the preceding code, how do we resolve the @Value and ${..} variables? We need a PropertySourcesPlaceholderConfigurer to evaluate them. This is a BeanFactoryPostProcessor. If you are using the XML configuration, the <context:property-placeholder/> namespace creates a PropertySourcesPlaceholderConfigurer for you.

Loading the bean definition is a one-time process at the time of loading the configuration file, but the initializing phase for bean instances is executed for each bean in the container. Let's have a look at the initialization of bean instances in the application.

Initializing bean instances

After loading the bean definitions into the `BeanFactory`, the Spring IoC container instantiates the beans for the application; the following diagram shows the process flow:

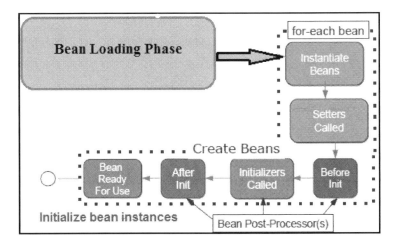

As you can see in the preceding diagram, the bean initialization step is executed for each bean in the container. We can summarize the bean creation process as follows:

- Each bean is eagerly instantiated by default. It is created in the right order with its dependencies injected unless marked as lazy.
- Spring provides multiple `BeanPostProcessor`, so, each bean goes through a post-processing phase such as `BeanFactoryPostProcessor`, which can modify the bean definition. However, the `BeanPostProcessor` can change the instance of the bean.
- After execution of this phase, the bean is fully initialized and ready for use. It is tracked by its `id` till the context is destroyed, except for the prototype beans.

In the next section, we'll discuss how to customize the Spring container by using a `BeanPostProcessor`.

Customizing beans using a BeanPostProcessor

The `BeanPostProcessor` is an important extension point in Spring. It can modify bean instances in any way. It is used to enable a powerful feature such as the AOP proxy. You can write your own `BeanPostProcessor` in your application to create a custom `post-processor`--the class must implement the `BeanPostProcessor` interface. Spring provides several implementations of `BeanPostProcessor`. In Spring, the `BeanPostProcessor` interface has two callback methods, as follows:

```
public interface BeanPostProcessor {
    Object postProcessBeforeInitialization(Object bean, String
    beanName) throws BeansException;
    Object postProcessAfterInitialization(Object bean, String
    beanName) throws BeansException;
}
```

You can implement these two methods of the `BeanPostProcessor` interface to provide your own custom logic for bean instantiation, dependency-resolution, and so on. You can configure multiple `BeanPostProcessor` implementations to add custom logic to the Spring container. You can also manage the order of execution of these `BeanPostProcessor` by setting the order property. `BeanPostProcessor` work on Spring bean instances after instantiation of the bean by the Spring container. The scope of the `BeanPostProcessor` is within the Spring container, which means that beans that are defined in one container are not post-processed by a `BeanPostProcessor` defined in another container.

Any class in a Spring application is registered as a `post-processor` with the container; it is created for each bean instance by the Spring container. And the Spring container calls the `postProcessBeforeInitialization()` method before the container initialization methods (Initializing Bean's `afterPropertiesSet()` and the bean's `init` method). It also calls the `postProcessAfterInitialization()` method after any bean initialization callbacks. The Spring AOP uses the `post-processor` to provide proxy-wrapping logic (Proxy design pattern) although we can take any action by using the `post-processor`.

Spring's `ApplicationContext` automatically detects those beans which implement the `BeanPostProcessor` interface, and registers these beans as `post-processors`. These beans are called at the time of any other bean creation. Let's explore the following example of `BeanPostProcessor`.

Let's create a custom bean `post-processor` as follows:

```
package com.packt.patterninspring.chapter5.bankapp.bpp;
import org.springframework.beans.BeansException;
import org.springframework.beans.factory.config.BeanPostProcessor;
import org.springframework.stereotype.Component;
@Component
public class MyBeanPostProcessor implements
BeanPostProcessor {
  @Override
  public Object postProcessBeforeInitialization
  (Object bean, String beanName) throws BeansException {
    System.out.println("In After bean Initialization
    method. Bean name is "+beanName);
    return bean;
  }
  public Object postProcessAfterInitialization(Object bean, String
  beanName) throws BeansException {
    System.out.println("In Before bean Initialization method. Bean
    name is "+beanName);
    return bean;
    }
}
```

This example illustrates basic usage, here this example shows a `post-processor` prints the
string to the system console for each bean registered with the container. This
`MyBeanPostProcessor` class annotated with `@Component` that means this class same as
other bean class in the application context, now run the following demo class. Please refer to
the following code:

```
public class BeanLifeCycleDemo {
  public static void main(String[] args) {
    ConfigurableApplicationContext applicationContext = new
    AnnotationConfigApplicationContext(AppConfig.class);
    applicationContext.close();
  }
}
```

This is the output that we'll get on the console:

```
<terminated> BeanLifeCycleDemo [Java Application] C:\Program Files\Java\jre1.8.0_131\bin\javaw.exe (04-Jul-2017, 11:27:21 PM)
Jul 04, 2017 11:27:23 PM org.springframework.context.annotation.AnnotationConfigApplicationContext prepareRefresh
INFO: Refreshing org.springframework.context.annotation.AnnotationConfigApplicationContext@6e2c634b: startup date [
In After bean Initialization method. Bean name is org.springframework.context.event.internalEventListenerProcessor
In Before bean Initialization method. Bean name is org.springframework.context.event.internalEventListenerProcessor
In After bean Initialization method. Bean name is org.springframework.context.event.internalEventListenerFactory
In Before bean Initialization method. Bean name is org.springframework.context.event.internalEventListenerFactory
In After bean Initialization method. Bean name is appConfig
In Before bean Initialization method. Bean name is appConfig
In After bean Initialization method. Bean name is transferService
In Before bean Initialization method. Bean name is transferService
Jul 04, 2017 11:27:23 PM org.springframework.context.annotation.AnnotationConfigApplicationContext doClose
INFO: Closing org.springframework.context.annotation.AnnotationConfigApplicationContext@6e2c634b: startup date [Tue
```

As you can see in the preceding output, a string of both the callback methods is printed for each bean method in the Spring container. Spring provides many pre-implemented `BeanPostProcessor` for some specific features, as follows:

- `RequiredAnnotationBeanPostProcessor`
- `AutowiredAnnotationBeanPostProcessor`
- `CommonAnnotationBeanPostProcessor`
- `PersistenceAnnotationBeanPostProcessor`

The namespace `<context:annotation-config/>` in the XML configuration enables several `post-processor` in the same application context in which it is defined.

Let us now move on to our next section, and see how we can enable the Initializer extension point by using `BeanPostProcessor`.

The Initializer extension point

This special case of a bean `post-processor` causes `init` (`@PostConstruct`) methods to be called. Internally, Spring uses several **BeanPostProcessors (BPPs)** `CommonAnnotationBeanPostProcessor` to enable initialization. The following diagram illustrates the relationship between initializer and BPPs.

Now let's see the following example for the Initializer extension point in XML:

Namespace `<context:annotation-config/>` explicitly enables many `post-processor`, let see the following configuration file in XML:

```xml
<?xml version="1.0" encoding="UTF-8"?>
<beans xmlns="http://www.springframework.org/schema/beans"
 xmlns:xsi="http://www.w3.org/2001/XMLSchema-instance"
 xmlns:c="http://www.springframework.org/schema/c"
 xmlns:context="http://www.springframework.org/schema/context"
 xsi:schemaLocation="http://www.springframework.org/schema/beans
 http://www.springframework.org/schema/beans/spring-beans.xsd
 http://www.springframework.org/schema/context
 http://www.springframework.org/schema/context/
 spring-context-4.3.xsd">
<context:annotation-config/>
<bean id="transferService"
class="com.packt.patterninspring.chapter5.
bankapp.service.TransferService"/>
<bean id="accountRepository"
class="com.packt.patterninspring.chapter5.
bankapp.repository.JdbcAccountRepository"
init-method="populateCache"/>
</beans>
```

In the preceding configuration code, you can see that I have defined some beans out of which one of the bean `accountRepository` repository has the `init` method attribute of the bean tag; this attribute has a value, `populateCache`. This is nothing but an `initializer` method of the `accountRepository` bean. It is called by the container at the time of bean initialization if the `post-processor` is explicitly enabled by the `<context:annotation-config/>` namespace. Let's see the `JdbcAccountRepository` class, shown as follows:

```java
package com.packt.patterninspring.chapter5.bankapp.repository;
import com.packt.patterninspring.chapter5.bankapp.model.Account;
import com.packt.patterninspring.chapter5.bankapp.model.Amount;
import com.packt.patterninspring.chapter5.
bankapp.repository.AccountRepository;
public class JdbcAccountRepository implements AccountRepository {
  @Override
  public Account findByAccountId(Long accountId) {
    return new Account(accountId, "Arnav Rajput", new
    Amount(3000.0));
}
void populateCache(){
  System.out.println("Called populateCache() method");
}
}
```

In the Java configuration, we can use `initMethod` attribute of the `@Bean` annotation as follows:

```
@Bean(initMethod = "populateCache")
public AccountRepository accountRepository(){
    return new JdbcAccountRepository();
}
```

In the Annotation-based configuration, we can use the *JSR-250* annotation, `@PostConstruct` as follows:

```
@PostConstruct
void populateCache(){
    System.out.println("Called populateCache() method");
}
```

We have seen the first phase of a bean life cycle, where Spring loads the bean definitions by using XML-, Java-, and Annotation-based configuration, and after that, the Spring container initializes each bean in the correct order in the Spring application. The next diagram gives an overview of the first phase of the configuration life cycle:

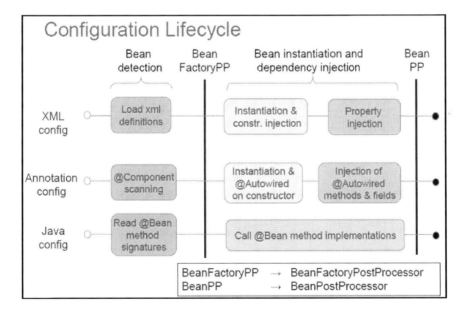

The last diagram shows Spring bean metadata in any style-XML, Annotation, or Java-loaded by the respective implementation of `ApplicationContext`. All XML files are parsed, and loaded with the bean definitions. In Annotation configuration, Spring scans all the components, and loads the bean definitions. In the Java configuration, Spring reads all the `@Bean` methods to load the bean definitions. After loading the bean definitions from all styles of configurations, `BeanFactoryPostProcessor` comes into the picture to modify the definition of some beans, and then the container instantiates the beans. Finally, `BeanPostProcessor` works on the beans, and it can modify and change the bean object. This is the initialization phase. Now let's see the next Use phase of a bean in its life cycle.

The Use phase of beans

In a Spring application, all Spring beans spend 99.99% of their time in this phase. If the initialization phase is completed successfully, then the Spring beans come into this phase. Here, beans are used by clients as application services. These beans process client requests, and carry out application behaviors. In the Use phase, let's see how to invoke a bean obtained from the context **in the application where it is used**. Please refer to the following code:

```
//Get or create application context from somewhere
ApplicationContext applicationContext = new
AnnotationConfigApplicationContext(AppConfig.class);

// Lookup the entry point into the application
TransferService transferService =
context.getBean(TransferService.class);
// and use it
transferService.transfer("A", "B", 3000.1);
```

Suppose the `return` service returns a raw object, then it is simply invoked directly; nothing special here. But if your bean has been wrapped in a proxy, then things become more interesting. Let's explore the following diagram to understand this more clearly:

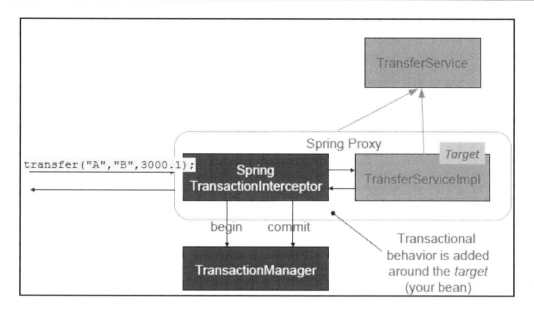

In the preceding diagram, you can see the `service` method call through the `Proxy` class; it is created in the `init` phase by dedicated `BeanPostProcessor`. It wraps your beans in a dynamic proxy, which adds behavior to your bean transparently. It is an implementation of the Decorator Design pattern and Proxy Design pattern.

Let's see how Spring creates a proxy for your bean in the Spring application.

Implementing the Decorator and Proxy patterns in Spring using Proxies

Spring uses two types of proxy in a Spring application. The following are the kind of proxies used by Spring:

- **JDK Proxy**: This is also known as a dynamic proxy. Its API is built into the JDK. For this proxy, the `Java` interface is required.
- **CGLib Proxy**: This is *NOT* built into JDK. However, it is included in Spring JARS, and is used when the interface is not available. It cannot be applied to final classes or methods.

Let's see the features of both the proxies in the following diagram:

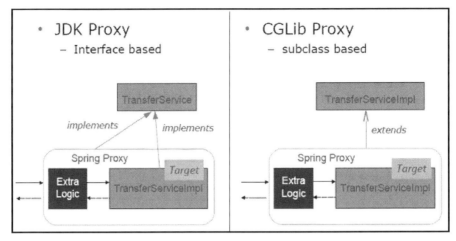

This is all about the Use Phase of the Spring Bean life cycle. Now let's move to the next phase of life cycle, that is, the destruction phase.

The destruction phase of the beans

In this phase, Spring releases any system resource acquired by the application services. These are eligible for garbage collection. When you close an application context, the destruction phase completes. Let's see the following lines of code in this phase:

```
//Any implementation of application context

ConfigurableApplicationContext applicationContext = new
AnnotationConfigApplicationContext(AppConfig.class);

// Destroy the application by closing application context.
applicationContext.close();
```

In the preceding code, what do you think happens when we call the `applicationContext.close()` method in this phase? The process that takes place is given as follows :

- Any bean implementing the `org.springframework.beans.factory.DisposableBean` interface gets a callback from the container when it is destroyed. The `DisposableBean` interface specifies a single method:

```
void destroy() throws Exception;
```

- The `bean` instances are destroyed if instructed to call their `destroy` methods. Beans must have a `destroy` method defined, that is, a `no-arg` method returning `void`.
- The context then destroys itself, and this context is not usable again.
- Only GC actually destroys objects and remember, it is called only when the `ApplicationContext`/JVM exit normally. It is not called for prototype beans.

Let's see how to implement it with the XML Configuration:

```xml
<?xml version="1.0" encoding="UTF-8"?>
<beans xmlns="http://www.springframework.org/schema/beans"
  xmlns:xsi="http://www.w3.org/2001/XMLSchema-instance"
  xmlns:c="http://www.springframework.org/schema/c"
  xmlns:context="http://www.springframework.org/schema/context"
  xsi:schemaLocation="http://www.springframework.org/schema/beans
  http://www.springframework.org/schema/beans/spring-beans.xsd
  http://www.springframework.org/schema/context
  http://www.springframework.org/schema/context/spring-context-
  4.3.xsd">
  <context:annotation-config/>
  <bean id="transferService"
  class="com.packt.patterninspring.chapter5.
  bankapp.service.TransferService"/>
  <bean id="accountRepository"
  class="com.packt.patterninspring.chapter5.
  bankapp.repository.JdbcAccountRepository"
  destroy-method="clearCache"/>
</beans>
```

In the configuration, the `accountRepository` bean has a `destroy` method named `clearCache`:

```
package com.packt.patterninspring.chapter5.bankapp.repository;
import com.packt.patterninspring.chapter5.bankapp.model.Account;
import com.packt.patterninspring.chapter5.bankapp.model.Amount;
import com.packt.patterninspring.chapter5.bankapp.
  repository.AccountRepository;
public class JdbcAccountRepository implements AccountRepository {
 @Override
public Account findByAccountId(Long accountId) {
   return new Account(accountId, "Arnav Rajput", new
   Amount(3000.0));
 }
void clearCache(){
   System.out.println("Called clearCache() method");
 }
}
```

Let's see the same configuration with Java. In the Java configuration, we can use the `destroyMethod` attribute of the `@Bean` annotation as follows:

```
@Bean (destroyMethod="clearCache")
public AccountRepository accountRepository() {
   return new JdbcAccountRepository();
}
```

We can do the same using Annotations. Annotations require `annotation-config` or the component scanner to be activated by using `<context:component-scan ... />`, as seen in the following:

```
public class JdbcAccountRepository {
  @PreDestroy
  void clearCache() {
    // close files, connections...
    // remove external resources...
  }
}
```

You have now seen the Spring bean life cycle in all its phases. In the initialization phase, Bean Post Processors for initialization and proxies. In the Use phase, Spring beans use the magic of proxy. Finally, in the destruction phase, it allows the application to terminate cleanly.

Now that you have seen the bean life cycle, let's learn about bean scopes, and how to create custom bean scopes in the Spring container.

Understanding bean scopes

In Spring, each bean has one scope in the container. You can control not only the bean metadata and its life, but also the scope of that bean. You can create a custom scope of the bean, and register it with the container. You can decide the scope of the bean by configuring it with the bean definition with the XML-, Annotations-, or Java-based configuration.

The Spring application context *creates* all beans *by using* a singleton scope. That means, it is always the same bean each time; it doesn't matter how many times it is injected into another bean or called by other services. Because of this singleton behavior, the scope reduces the cost of instantiating. It is suitable for stateless objects in the application.

In a Spring application, sometimes it is required to save the state of some objects that aren't safe for reuse. For such a requirement, declaring the bean scope as a singleton is not safe, because it may cause unexpected problems when reused later. Spring provides another scope for such a requirement, which is known as the prototype scope of the Spring bean.

Spring defines several scopes under which a bean can be created, and these are as follows:

The singleton bean scope

In Spring, any bean that has a singleton scope has only one instance of the bean created for an application context, where it is defined for the entire application. This is the default behavior of the Spring container. But it is different from the singleton pattern as defined in the **Gang of Four (GoF)** patterns book. In Java, singleton means per object of a particular class per Classloader in the JVM. But in Spring, it implies per instance of a bean per bean definition per Spring IoC container. This is explained in the following diagram:

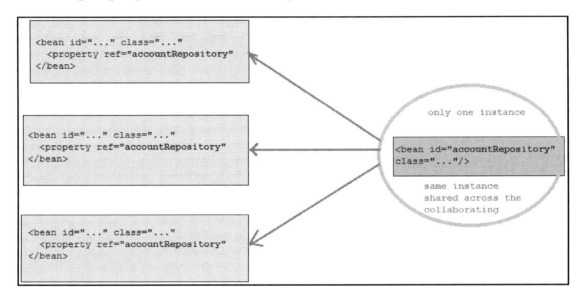

As you can see in the preceding diagram, the same instance of the object is defined by the bean definition, `accountRepository`, injected to other collaborating beans in the same IoC container. Spring stores all singleton bean instances in a cache, and all collaborating beans fetch the dependency of that object returned by the cache.

The prototype bean scope

In Spring, any bean defined with the prototype scope has one instance of the bean created for every time the bean is injected into other collaborating beans. The following figure illustrates the Spring prototype scope:

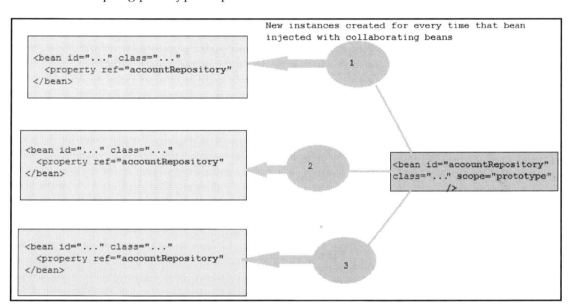

As you can see in the preceding diagram, an `accountRepository` class is configured as a prototype bean, and the container creates a brand new instance for each time that bean is injected into other beans.

The session bean scope

A new instance is created once for every user session in the web environment only.

Consider the following XML configuration for a bean definition:

```
<bean id="..." class="..." scope="session"/>
```

The request bean scope

A new instance is created once for every request in the web environment only.

Consider the following XML configuration for a bean definition:

```
<bean id="..." class="..." scope="request"/>
```

Other scopes in Spring

Spring has other more specialized scopes, which are as follows:

- WebSocket scope
- Refresh scope
- Thread scope (defined, but not registered by default)

Spring also supports the creation of your own custom scope for a bean. We'll discuss this in the following section.

Custom scopes

We can create a custom scope of any bean, and register this scope with the application context. Let's see how to create a custom bean scope with the following example.

Creating custom scopes

For creating your customer scope in the Spring IoC container, Spring provides the `org.springframework.beans.factory.config.Scope` interface. You have to implement this interface to create your own custom scopes. Take a look at the following `MyThreadScope` class as a custom scope in the Spring IoC container:

```
package com.packt.patterninspring.chapter5.bankapp.scope;
import java.util.HashMap;
import java.util.Map;
import org.springframework.beans.factory.ObjectFactory;
import org.springframework.beans.factory.config.Scope;

public class MyThreadScope implements Scope {
  private final ThreadLocal<Object> myThreadScope = new
  ThreadLocal<Object>() {
    protected Map<String, Object> initialValue() {
      System.out.println("initialize ThreadLocal");
```

```
      return new HashMap<String, Object>();
    }
  };
@Override
public Object get(String name, ObjectFactory<?> objectFactory) {
  Map<String, Object> scope = (Map<String, Object>)
  myThreadScope.get();
  System.out.println("getting object from scope.");
  Object object = scope.get(name);
  if(object == null) {
    object = objectFactory.getObject();
    scope.put(name, object);
  }
  return object;
}
@Override
public String getConversationId() {
  return null;
}
@Override
public void registerDestructionCallback(String name, Runnable
callback) {
}
@Override
public Object remove(String name) {
  System.out.println("removing object from scope.");
  @SuppressWarnings("unchecked")
  Map<String, Object> scope = (Map<String, Object>)
  myThreadScope.get();
  return scope.remove(name);
 }
 @Override
 public Object resolveContextualObject(String name) {
   return null;
 }
}
```

In the preceding code, we have overridden multiple methods of the Scope interface as follows:

- **Object get(String name, ObjectFactory objectFactory)**: This method returns the object from the underlying scope
- **Object remove(String name)**: This method removes the object from the underlying scope
- **void registerDestructionCallback(String name, Runnable destructionCallback)**: This method registers the destruction callbacks, and is executed when the specified object with this custom scope is destroyed

Now let's see how to register this custom scope with the Spring IoC container, and how to use it in the Spring application.

You can register this custom bean scope with the Spring IoC container declaratively by using the CustomScopeConfigurer class as follows :

```xml
<?xml version="1.0" encoding="UTF-8"?>
<beans xmlns="http://www.springframework.org/schema/beans"
  xmlns:xsi="http://www.w3.org/2001/XMLSchema-instance"
  xsi:schemaLocation="http://www.springframework.org/schema/beans
  http://www.springframework.org/schema/beans/spring-beans.xsd">
  <bean   class="org.springframework.beans.factory.
  config.CustomScopeConfigurer">
  <property name="scopes">
    <map>
      <entry key="myThreadScope">
        <bean class="com.packt.patterninspring.chapter5.
        bankapp.scope.MyThreadScope"/>
      </entry>
    </map>
  </property>
 </bean>
 <bean id="myBean" class="com.packt.patterninspring.chapter5.
  bankapp.bean.MyBean" scope="myThreadScope">
  <property name="name" value="Dinesh"></property>
 </bean>
</beans>
```

As you can see in the preceding configuration file, I have registered my custom bean scope named `myThreadScope` with the application context by using the `CustomScopeConfigurer` class. This custom scope that I am using is similar to the singleton or prototype scope through the scope attribute of the bean tag in the XML configuration.

Summary

After reading this chapter, you should now have a good idea about the Spring bean life cycle in the container, and the several types of bean scope in a container. You now know that there are three phases of the Spring bean life cycle in the container. The first is the initialization phase. In this phase, Spring loads the bean definitions from XML, Java, or Annotation configurations. After loading these beans, the container constructs each bean, and applies the post-process logic on that bean.

The next is the Use phase, in which the Spring beans are ready to be used, and Spring shows the magic of the proxy pattern.

Finally, the last phase is the destruction phase. In this phase, when the application calls the `close()` method of Spring's `ApplicationContext`, the container calls the clean-up method of each bean to release resources.

In Spring, you can control not only the bean life cycle but also the scope of the bean in the container. The default scope of a bean in the Spring IoC container is the Singleton, but you can override the default scope by defining other scope prototypes with the bean using the scope attribute of the bean tag in XML or the `@Scope` annotation in Java. You can also create your own custom scope, and register it with the container.

Now we'll turn to the magic chapter of this book, that is, Spring **Aspect-Oriented Programming (AOP)**. Much as dependency injection helps decouple components from the other components they collaborate with, AOP helps decouple your application components from tasks that span multiple components in an application. Let's move on to the next chapter, covering Spring Aspect Oriented Programming with Proxy and Decorator Design Pattern.

6
Spring Aspect Oriented Programming with Proxy and Decorator pattern

Before you start reading this chapter, I want to share something with you; as I was writing this chapter, my wife Anamika, was taking a selfie and uploading it to several social media sites such as Facebook and WhatsApp. She keeps a track of the *likes*, However, uploading more photos uses more mobile data, and mobile data costs money. I rarely use social media as I prefer to avoid paying more to the internet company. Every month, the internet company knows how much to bill us. Now consider what would happen if the internet usage, total call duration and bill calculation was meticulously planned and managed by us? It's possible that some obsessive internet users would manage it and I'm really clueless as to how.

Calculating billing for internet usage and calls is an important function, but it is still not predominant for most internet users. For those like my wife, taking selfies, uploading photos to social media, and watching videos on YouTube are the kinds of things that most internet users are actively involved in. Managing and calculating their internet bill is a passive action for internet users.

Similarly some modules of the enterprise applications are like the internet billing calculator for our internet usage. There are some modules in the application that have important functionalities that need to be placed at multiple points in the application. But it is unexpected to explicitly call these functionalities at every points. Functionalities such as logging, security, and transaction management are important for your application but your business objects are not actively participating in it because your business objects need to focus on the business domain problems they're designed for, and leave certain aspects to be handled by someone else.

In software development, there are specific tasks to be performed at certain points in an application. These tasks or functions are known as **cross-cutting concerns**. In an application, all cross-cutting concerns are separate from the business logic of this application. Spring provides a module **Aspect-Oriented Programming (AOP)** to separate these cross-cutting concerns from the business logic.

As in Chapter 4, *Wiring Beans using Dependency Injection Pattern,* you learned about the dependency injection to configure and resolve dependencies of collaborating objects in the application. Whereas DI promotes programming to interface and decoupling application objects from each other, Spring AOP promotes decoupling between the application's business logic and the cross-cutting concerns in the application.

In our bankapp example, transferring money from one account to another account is a business logic but logging this activity and securing the transaction are cross-cutting concerns in our bankapp application. That means logging, security, and transaction are common examples of the application of aspects.

In this chapter, you will explore Spring's support for aspects. It will cover the following points:

- Proxy pattern in Spring
- Adapter design pattern to handle load time weaving
- Decorator design pattern
- Aspect-oriented programming
- Problems resolved by AOP
- Core AOP concepts
- Defining point cuts
- Implementing Advices
- Creating aspects
- Understanding AOP proxies

Before we go further into our Spring AOP discussion, let's first understand the implemented patterns under the Spring AOP Framework, and see how these patterns are applied.

Proxy pattern in Spring

Proxy design pattern provides an object of class that has the functionality of another class. This pattern comes under the structural design pattern of GOF design patterns. According to GOF pattern, *Provide a surrogate or placeholder for another object to control access to it.* The intent of this design pattern is to provide a different class for another class with its functionality to the outer world.

Proxying classes using Decorator pattern in Spring

As you have seen in `Chapter 3`, *Consideration of Structural and Behavioral Patterns*, according to GOF book, *Attach additional responsibilities to an object dynamically. Decorators provide a flexible alternative to subclassing for extending functionality.* This pattern allows you to add and remove behaviors to an individual object at the runtime dynamically or statically without changing the existing behavior of other associated objects from the same class.

In Spring AOP, CGLIB is used to create the proxy in the application. CGLIB proxying works by generating a subclass of the target class at runtime. Spring configures this generated subclass to delegate method calls to the original target--the subclass is used to implement the Decorator pattern, weaving in the advice.

Spring provides two ways to create the proxy in the application.

- CGLIB proxy
- JDK proxy or dynamic proxy

Let's see the following table:

JDK proxy	CGLIB proxy
Also called **dynamic proxies**	NOT built into JDK
API is built into the JDK	Included in Spring JARs
Requirements: Java interface(s)	Used when interface not available
All interfaces proxied	Cannot be applied to final classes or methods

Let's see the following figure:

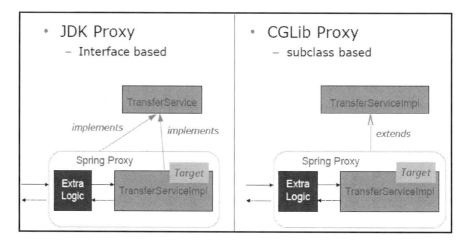

Note--CGLIB proxying has one issue to be considered, that is, final methods can't be advised, as they can't be overridden.

In the following section let's learn more about the cross-cutting concerns.

What are cross-cutting concerns?

In any application, there is some generic functionality that is needed in many places. But this functionality is not related to the application's business logic. Suppose you perform a role-based security check before every business method in your application. Here security is a cross-cutting concern. It is required for any application but it is not necessary from the business point of view, it is a simple generic functionality we have to implement in many places in the application. The following are examples of the cross-cutting concerns for the enterprise application.

- Logging and tracing
- Transaction management
- Security
- Caching

- Error handling
- Performance monitoring
- Custom business rules

Let's see how we will implement these cross-cutting concerns in our application by using aspects of Spring AOP.

What is Aspect-Oriented Programming?

As mentioned earlier, **Aspect-Oriented Programming** (AOP) enables modularization of cross-cutting concerns. It complements **Object-oriented programming (OOP)** which is another programing paradigm. OOP has class and object as key elements but AOP has aspect as key element. Aspects allow you to modularize some functionality across the application at multiple points. This type of functionality is known as **cross-cutting concerns**. For example, security is one of the cross-cutting concerns in the application, because we have to apply it at multiple methods where we want security. Similarly, transaction and logging are also cross-cutting concerns for the application and many more. Let's see in the following figure how these concerns are applied to the business modules:

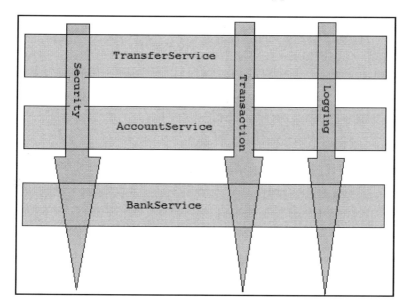

As you can see in the preceding figure, there are three main business modules as **TransferService**, **AccountService**, and **BankService**. All business modules require some common functionality such as **Security**, **Transaction** management and **Logging**.

Let's check out what problems we have to face in the application if we do not use the Spring AOP.

Problems resolved by AOP

As stated earlier, aspects enable modularization of cross-cutting concerns. So if you are not using aspects, then modularization of some cross-cutting functionality is not possible. It tends to mix the cross-cutting functionality with the business modules. If you use a common object-oriented principle to reuse the common functionalities such as security, logging and transaction management, *you need to use* inheritance or composition. But here using inheritance can violate the single responsibility of SOLID principles and also increase object hierarchy. Also, the composition can be complicated to handle across the application. That means, failing to modularize cross-cutting concerns leads to two main problems as follows:

- Code tangling
- Code scattering

Code tangling

It is a coupling of concerns in the application. Code tangling occurs when there is a mixing of cross-cutting concerns with the application's business logic. It promotes tight coupling between the cross-cutting and business modules. Let's see the following code to understand more about code tangling:

```
public class TransferServiceImpl implements TransferService {
  public void transfer(Account a, Account b, Double amount) {
    //Security concern start here
    if (!hasPermission(SecurityContext.getPrincipal()) {
      throw new AccessDeniedException();
    }
    //Security concern end here
    //Business logic start here
    Account aAct = accountRepository.findByAccountId(a);
    Account bAct = accountRepository.findByAccountId(b);
    accountRepository.transferAmount(aAct, bAct, amount);
    ...
  }
}
```

As you can see in the preceding code, security concern code (highlighted) is mixing with application's business logic code. This situation is an example of code tangling. Here we have only included security concern, but in the enterprise application you have to implement multiple cross-cutting concerns such as logging, transaction management and so on. In such cases, it will be even more complicated to manage the code and make any change to the code, which may cause critical bugs in the code as follows in the figure:

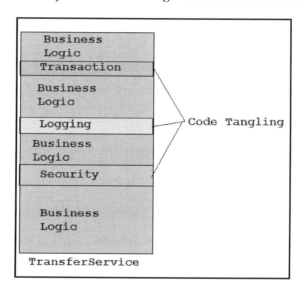

In the preceding figure, you can see there are three cross-cutting concerns which are distributed across the TransferService business class and cross-cutting concerns logic mixing with AccountService's business logic. This coupling between the concerns and application's logic is called **code tangling**. Let's see another main problem if we are using aspects for cross-cutting concern.

Code scattering

This means that the same concern is spread across modules in the application. Code scattering promotes the duplicity of the concern's code across the application modules. Let's see the following code to understand more about code scattering:

```
public class TransferServiceImpl implements TransferService {
    public void transfer(Account a, Account b, Double amount) {
        //Security concern start here
        if (!hasPermission(SecurityContext.getPrincipal())) {
            throw new AccessDeniedException();
        }
```

```
        //Security concern end here
        //Business logic start here
        ...
    }
}

public class AccountServiceImpl implements AccountService {
    public void withdrawl(Account a, Double amount) {
        //Security concern start here
        if (!hasPermission(SecurityContext.getPrincipal()) {
            throw new AccessDeniedException();
        }
        //Security concern end here
        //Business logic start here
        ...
    }
}
```

As you can see in the preceding code, there are two modules for the application, `TransferService` and `AccountService`. Both modules have the same cross-cutting concern code for the security. The bold highlighted code in both business modules are the same, it means there is code duplication here. The following figure illustrates code scattering:

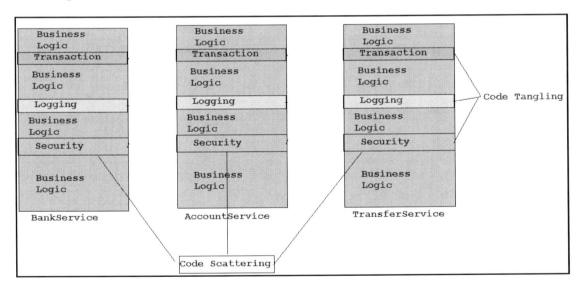

In the preceding figure, there are three business modules **TransferService**, **AccountService**, and **BankService**. Each business module contains cross-cutting concerns such as **Security**, **Logging** and **Transaction** management. All modules have the same code of concerns in the application. It is actually duplication of concerns code across the application.

Spring AOP provides solution for these two problems that is, code tangling and code scattering in the Spring application. Aspects enable modularization of cross-cutting concerns to avoid tangling and to eliminate scattering. Let's see in further section how AOP solves these problems.

How AOP Works to solve problems

Spring AOP allows you to keep cross-cutting concern logic separate from the mainline application logic. That means, you can implement your mainline application logic and only focus on the core problem of the application. And you can write aspects to implement your cross-cutting concerns. Spring provides many aspects out-of-the-box. After creating the aspects, you can add these aspects that is, cross-cutting behaviors to the right places into your application. Let's see the following figure that illustrates the functionality of AOP:

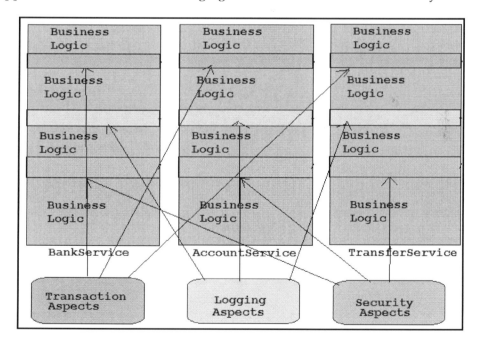

As you can see in the preceding figure, all aspects such as Security, Logging, and Transaction aspect are implemented separately in the application. We have added these aspects at the right places in the applications. Now our application logic is separate from the concerns. Let's see the following section defining the core AOP concepts and use AOP's terminology in your application.

Core AOP terminology and concepts

As with other technologies, AOP has its own vocabularies. Let's start to learn some core AOP concepts and terminology. Spring used the AOP paradigm for the Spring AOP module. But unfortunately, terms used in the Spring AOP Framework are Spring-specific. These terms are used to describe AOP modules and features, but these aren't intuitive. In spite of this, these terms are used in order to understand AOP. Without an understanding of the AOP idiom you will not be able to understand AOP functionality. Basically, AOP is defined in terms of advice, pointcuts, and join points. Let's see the following figure that illustrates about the core AOP concepts and how they are tied together in the framework:

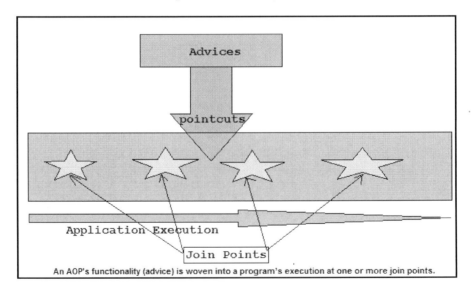

An AOP's functionality (advice) is woven into a program's execution at one or more join points.

In the preceding figure, you can see an AOP functionality, it is known as **Advices** and it is implemented into multiple points. These points are known as **Joint Points**, these are defined by using an expression. These expression are known as **pointcuts**. Let's understand these terms in detail using an example (remember my wife's internet bill story?).

Advice

An internet plan is used for calculating the bill according to data usage in MB or GB by the internet company. The internet company has a list of customers, also and they also company calculates the internet bill for them. So calculating bills and sending it to the customers is a core job for the internet company but not for customers. Likewise, each aspect has its own main job and also has a purpose for doing this job. The job of an aspect is known as advice in the AOP.

As you know now, advice is a job, aspect will perform this job, so there are some questions that come to in mind, when to perform this job and what will be in this job. Will this job be performed before a business method is invoked? Or will it be performed after the business method is invoked? Or will it be performed both before and after method invocation? Or it will be performed when business method throws an exception. Sometime this business method is also called the **advised method**. Let's see the following five kinds of advises used by Spring aspects:

- **Before:** Advice's job executes before the `advised` method is invoked.

 If the advice throws an exception, target will not be called - this is a valid use of a Before Advice.

- **After:** Advice's job executes after the advised method completes regardless of whether an exception has been thrown by the target or not.
- **After-returning:** Advice's job executes after the advised method successfully completes. For example, if a business method returns without throwing an exception.
- **After-throwing:** Advice's job executes if the advised method exits by throwing an exception.
- **Around:** This is one of the most powerful advice of Spring AOP, this advice surrounds the advised method, providing some advice's job before and after the advised method is invoked.

In short, advice's job code to be executed at each selected point that is, Join Point, let's look into another term of AOP.

Join Point

The internet company provides internet to many customers. Each customer has an internet plan and that plan needs to be used for their bill calculation. With the help of each internet plan, the company could potentially calculates the internet bill for all customers. Similarly, your application may have multiple number of places to apply advice. These places in the application are called **join points**. A join point is a point in the execution of a program such as a method call or exception thrown. In these points, Spring aspect inserts concern functionality in your application. Let's see how AOP knows about the join points and discuss another term of AOP concepts.

Pointcut

Internet company makes a number of internet plans according to usage of internet data (customers like my wife need more data) because it is not possible for any internet company to provide same plan for all customers or a unique plan for each customer. Instead, each plan is assigned to the subset of the customers. In the same way, an advice is not necessary to apply to all join points in an application. You can define an expression that selects one or more Join Points in the application. This expression is known as **pointcut**. It helps to narrow down the join points advised by an aspect. Let's see another term of AOP that is Aspect.

Aspect

An internet company knows which customer has what internet plan. On the basis of this information the internet company calculates an internet bill and sends it to the customer. In this example internet company is an aspect, internet plans are pointcuts and customers are join points, and calculating internet bills by the company is an advice. Likewise, in your application, an aspect is a module that encapsulates pointcuts and advice. Aspects know what it does; where and when it does it in the application. Let's see how AOP applies the aspect to the business methods.

Weaving

Weaving is a technique by which aspects are combined with the business code. This is a process of applying aspects to a target object by creating a new proxy object. Weaving can be done at the compile time or at class load time, or at runtime. Spring AOP uses the runtime weaving by using proxy pattern.

You have seen lot of terms used in the AOP. You must know about this terminology whenever your learn about any AOP Framework either AspectJ or Spring AOP. Spring has used AspectJ Framework to implement Spring AOP Framework. Spring AOP supports limited features of AspectJ. Spring AOP provides proxy-based AOP solution. Spring only supports the method joint points. Now you have some basic idea about Spring AOP and how it works, let's move on the next topics how to define pointcuts in the Spring's declarative AOP model.

Defining pointcuts

As mentioned before, pointcuts are used to define a point where advice would be applied. So pointcut is one of the most important elements of an aspect in the application. Let's understand how to define pointcuts. In Spring AOP, we can use expression language to define the pointcuts. Spring AOP uses AspectJ's pointcut expression language for selecting where to apply advice. Spring AOP supports a subset of the pointcut designators available in AspectJ because as you know, Spring AOP is proxy-based and some designators do not support proxy-based AOP. Let's see following table has Spring AOP supported designators.

Spring supported AspectJ designators	Description
execution	It matches the join points by method executions, it is primary pointcut designator supported by Spring AOP.
within	It matches the join points by limit within certain types.
this	It limits matching to join points where the bean reference is an instance of the given type.
target	It limits matching to join points where the target object is of a given type.
args	It limits matching to join points where the arguments are instances of the given types.
@target	It limits matching to join points where the target object has an annotation of the given type.
@args	It limits matching to join points where the runtime, type of the actual arguments passed have annotations of the given type.
@within	It limits matching to join points where the declared type of the target object has the given type annotation.

`@annotation`	It limits matching to join points where the subject of the join point has the given annotation.

As listed earlier, Spring supported pointcut designators, execution is primary pointcut designator. So here I will only show you how to define pointcuts using execution designators. Let's see how to write the pointcut expression in the application.

Writing pointcuts

We can write pointcuts by using execution designator as follows:

- **execution(<method pattern>)**: The method must match the pattern as defined follows
- **Can chain together to create composite pointcuts by using following operators**: `&& (and), || (or), ! (not)`
- **Method pattern**: Following is method pattern:
  - `[Modifiers] ReturnType [ClassType]`
  - `MethodName ([Arguments]) [throws ExceptionType]`

In the preceding method pattern, values within bracket `[ ]` that is, modifiers, `ClassType`, arguments and exceptions are all optional values. There is no need to define it for every pointcut using execution designator. Value without brackets such as `ReturnType`, and `MethodName` are mandatory to define.

Let's define a `TransferService` interface:

```
package com.packt.patterninspring.chapter6.bankapp.service;
public interface TransferService {
    void transfer(String accountA, String accountB, Long amount);
}
```

`TransferService` is a service for transferring amounts from one to another account. Let's say that you want to write a logging aspect that triggers off `TransferService`'s `transfer()` method. The following figure illustrates a pointcut expression that can be used to apply advice whenever the `transfer()` method is executed:

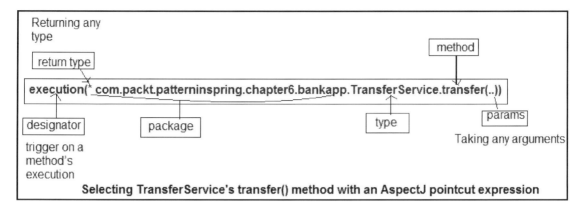

Selecting TransferService's transfer() method with an AspectJ pointcut expression

As in the preceding figure, you can see, I used the `execution()` designator to select join point `TransferService`'s `transfer()` method. In preceding expression in figure, I have used an asterisk at the beginning of the expression. This means that method can return any type. And after asterisk, I have specified a fully qualified class name and name of method as `transfer()`. As method arguments, I have used double dot (..), it means that the pointcut can select a method whose name is `transfer()` with no parameter or any number of parameters.

Let's see following some more pointcut expressions to select join points:

- Any class or package:
    - **execution(void transfer*(String))**: Any method starting with transfer that takes a single String parameter and has a void return type
    - **execution(* transfer(*))**: Any method named `transfer()` that takes a single parameter
    - **execution(* transfer(int, ..))**: Any method named transfer whose first parameter is an int (the " . . " signifies zero or more parameters may follow)
- Restrict by class:
    - `execution(void com.packt.patterninspring.chapter6.bankapp.service.TransferServiceImpl.*(..))`: Any void method in the `TransferServiceImpl` class, it is including any sub-class, but will be ignored if a different implementation is used.

- Restrict by interface:
  - `execution(void com.packt.patterninspring.chapter6.bankapp.service.TransferService.transfer(*))`: Any void `transfer()` method taking one argument, in any object implementing `TransferService`, it is more flexible choice--works if implementation changes.
- Using Annotations
  - `execution(@javax.annotation.security.RolesAllowed void transfer*(..))`: Any void method whose name starts with `transfer` that is annotated with the `@RolesAllowed` annotation.
- Working with packages
  - `execution(* com..bankapp.*.*(..))`: There is one directory between `com` and `bankapp`
  - `execution(* com.*.bankapp.*.*(..))`: There may be several directories between `bankapp` and `com`
  - `execution(* *..bankapp.*.*(..))`: Any sub-package called `bankapp`

Now that you have seen that the basics of writing pointcuts, let's see how to write the advice and declare the aspects that use those pointcuts

Creating aspects

As I said earlier, *aspects* is one of the most important terms in the AOP. Aspect merges the pointcuts and advices in the application. Let's see how to define aspect in the application.

You've already defined the `TransferService` interface as the subject of your aspect's pointcuts. Now let's use AspectJ annotations to create an aspect.

Define aspects using Annotation

Suppose in your bank application, you want to generate log for a money transfer service for auditing and tracking to understand customers' behaviors. A business never succeeds without understanding its customers. Whenever you will think about it from the perspective of a business, an auditing is required but isn't central to the function of the business itself; it's a separate concern. Therefore, it makes sense to define the auditing as an aspect that's applied to a transfer service. Let's see the following code which shows the Auditing class that defines the aspects for this concern:

```java
package com.packt.patterninspring.chapter6.bankapp.aspect;

import org.aspectj.lang.annotation.AfterReturning;
import org.aspectj.lang.annotation.AfterThrowing;
import org.aspectj.lang.annotation.Aspect;
import org.aspectj.lang.annotation.Before;

@Aspect
public class Auditing {

  //Before transfer service
  @Before("execution(* com.packt.patterninspring.chapter6.bankapp.
  service.TransferService.transfer(..))")
  public void validate(){
    System.out.println("bank validate your credentials before
    amount transferring");
  }

  //Before transfer service
  @Before("execution(* com.packt.patterninspring.chapter6.bankapp.
  service.TransferService.transfer(..))")
  public void transferInstantiate(){
    System.out.println("bank instantiate your amount
    transferring");
  }

  //After transfer service
  @AfterReturning("execution(* com.packt.patterninspring.chapter6.
  bankapp.service.TransferService.transfer(..))")
  public void success(){
    System.out.println("bank successfully transferred amount");
  }

  //After failed transfer service
  @AfterThrowing("execution(* com.packt.patterninspring.chapter6.
  bankapp.service.TransferService.transfer(..))")
  public void rollback() {
```

```
        System.out.println("bank rolled back your transferred amount");
    }
}
```

As you can see how the `Auditing` class is annotated with `@Aspect` annotation. It means this class is not just Spring bean, it is an aspect of the application. And `Auditing` class has some methods, these are advices and define some logic within these methods. As we know that before beginning to transfer amount from an account to another, bank will validate (`validate ()`) the use credentials and after that instantiate (`transferInstantiate()`) this service. After successful validation (`success ()`) amount is transferred and the bank audits it. But if the amount transferring fails in any case, then the bank should roll back (`rollback ()`) that amount.

As you can see, all methods of `Auditing` aspects are annotated with advice annotations to indicate when those methods should be called. Spring AOP provides five type advice annotations for defining advice. Let's see in the following table:

Annotation	Advice
`@Before`	It is used for before advice, `advice`'s method executes before the advised method is invoked.
`@After`	It is used for after advice, advice's method execute after the advised method executes normally or abnormally doesn't matter.
`@AfterReturning`	It used for after returning advice, advice's method execute after the advised method complete successfully.
`@AfterThrowing`	It used for after throwing advice, advice's method execute after the method terminate abnormally by throwing an exception.
`@Around`	It is used for around advice, advice's method executes before and after the advised method invoked.

Let's see the implementation of advices and how these work in the application.

Implementing Advice

As you know that, Spring provides five types of advices, let's see work flow of one by one.

Advice type - Before

Let's see the following figure for before advice. This advice executes the before the target method:

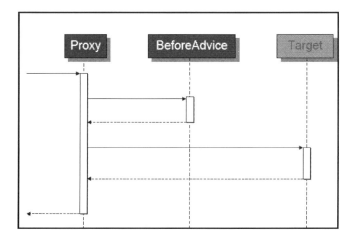

As you can see in figure, before advice is executed first and then it calls the **Target** method. As we know that Spring AOP is proxy-based. So a **Proxy** object is created of target class. It is based on Proxy design pattern and Decorator Design Pattern.

Before Advice example

Let's see the use of @Before annotation:

```
//Before transfer service
@Before("execution(* com.packt.patterninspring.chapter6.
bankapp.service.TransferService.transfer(..))")
public void validate(){
  System.out.println("bank validate your credentials before amount
  transferring");
}

//Before transfer service
@Before("execution(* com.packt.patterninspring.chapter6.
```

```
bankapp.service.TransferService.transfer(..))")
public void transferInstantiate(){
    System.out.println("bank instantiate your amount transferring");
}
```

 Note--if the advice throws an exception, target will not be called--this is a valid use of a Before Advice.

Now you have seen the before advice, let's have a look into another type advice.

Advice Types: After Returning

Let's see the following figure for after returning advice. This advice executes the after the **Target** method executed successfully:

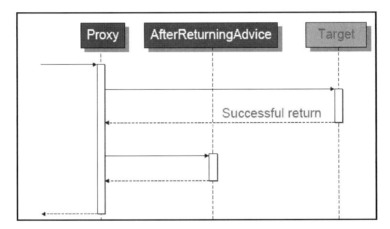

As you can see in figure, the after returning advice is executed after the target returns successfully. This advice will never execute if target throws any exception in the application.

After Returning Advice example

Let's see the use of the `@AfterReturning` annotation:

```
//After transfer service
@AfterReturning("execution(* com.packt.patterninspring.chapter6.
bankapp.service.TransferService.transfer(..))")
public void success(){
   System.out.println("bank successfully transferred amount");
}
```

Now you have seen the after returning advice, let's move to another type advice in the Spring AOP.

Advice Types: After Throwing

Let's see the following figure for after throwing advice. This advice executes the after the target method terminated abnormally. It mean the `target` method throws any exception, then this advice will be executed. Please refer to the following diagram:

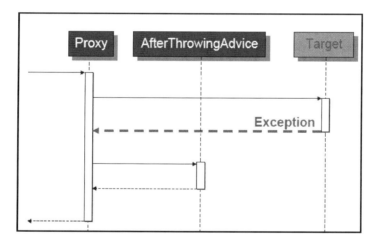

As you can see in figure, the after throwing advice is executed after the target throws an exception. This advice will never execute if the target doesn't throw any exception in the application.

After Throwing Advice example

Let's see the use of the `@AfterThrowing` annotation:

```
//After failed transfer service
@AfterThrowing("execution(* com.packt.patterninspring.chapter6.
bankapp.service.TransferService.transfer(..))")
public void rollback() {
   System.out.println("bank rolled back your transferred amount");
}
```

You can also use the `@AfterThrowing` annotation with the throwing attribute, it only invokes advice if the right exception type is thrown:

```
//After failed transfer service
@AfterThrowing(value = "execution(*
com.packt.patterninspring.chapter6.
bankapp.service.TransferService.transfer(..))", throwing="e"))
public void rollback(DataAccessException e) {
   System.out.println("bank rolled back your transferred amount");
}
```

Execute every time a `TransferService` class throws an exception of type `DataAccessException`.

The `@AfterThrowing` advice will not stop the exception from propagating. However, it can throw a different type of exception.

Advice Types: After

Let's see the following figure for **AfterAdvice**. This advice executes after the **Target** method is terminated normally or abnormally. It doesn't matter that **Target** method throws any exception or executes without any exception:

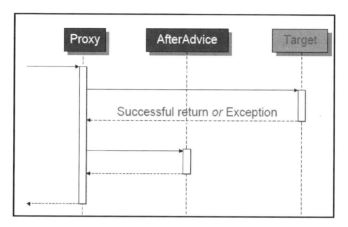

As you can see in figure, the after advice is executed after the `target` method terminates by throwing any exception or normally.

After Advice example

Let's see the use of `@After` annotation:

```
//After transfer service
@After ("execution(* com.packt.patterninspring.chapter6.
bankapp.service.TransferService.transfer(..))")
public void trackTransactionAttempt(){
   System.out.println("bank has attempted a transaction");
}
```

Use `@After` annotation called regardless of whether an exception has been thrown by the target or not.

Advice Types - Around

Let's see the following figure for **AroundAdvice**. This advice executes both times before and after the **Target** method is invoked. This advice is very powerful advice of Spring AOP. Many features of the Spring Framework are implemented by using this advice. This is the only advice in Spring which has capability to stop or proceed the target method execution. Please refer to the following diagram:

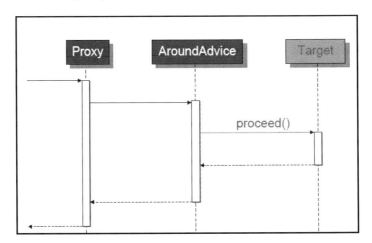

As you can see in the preceding figure, **AroundAdvice** executed two times, first time it is executed before the advised method and second time it is executed after advised method is invoked. And also this advice calls the `proceed()` method to execute the advised method in the application. Let's see the following example:

Around Advice example

Let's see the use of the `@Around` annotation:

```
@Around(execution(*    com.packt.patterninspring.chapter6.
bankapp.service.TransferService.createCache(..)))
public Object cache(ProceedingJoinPoint point){
Object value = cacheStore.get(CacheUtils.toKey(point));
if (value == null) {
  value = point.proceed();
  cacheStore.put(CacheUtils.toKey(point), value);
}
return value;
}
```

Here I used @Around annotation and a ProceedingJoinPoint, it inherits from Join Point and adds the proceed() method. As you can see in this example, this advice proceeds to target only if value is not already in the cache.

You have seen how to implement the advice in the application using annotations and how to create aspect and how to define pointcuts by annotations. In this example, we are using Auditing as an aspect class and it is annotated with @Aspect annotation, but this annotation will not work if you don't enable AOP proxy behavior of the Spring.

Let's see the following Java configuration file, AppConfig.java, you can turn on auto-proxying by applying the @EnableAspectJAutoProxy annotation at the class level:

```
package com.packt.patterninspring.chapter6.bankapp.config;

import org.springframework.context.annotation.Bean;
import org.springframework.context.annotation.ComponentScan;
import org.springframework.context.annotation.Configuration;
import org.springframework.context.annotation.
  EnableAspectJAutoProxy;

import com.packt.patterninspring.chapter6.bankapp.aspect.Auditing;

@Configuration
@EnableAspectJAutoProxy
@ComponentScan
public class AppConfig {
  @Bean
  public Auditing auditing() {
    return new Auditing();
  }
}
```

If you're using XML configuration, let's see how to wire your beans in Spring and how to enable Spring AOP feature by using the <aop:aspectj-autoproxy> element from Spring's AOP namespace:

```
<?xml version="1.0" encoding="UTF-8"?>
<beans xmlns="http://www.springframework.org/schema/beans"
  xmlns:xsi="http://www.w3.org/2001/XMLSchema-instance"
  xmlns:context="http://www.springframework.org/schema/context"
  xmlns:aop="http://www.springframework.org/schema/aop"
  xsi:schemaLocation="http://www.springframework.org/schema/aop
  http://www.springframework.org/schema/aop/spring-aop.xsd
  http://www.springframework.org/schema/beans
  http://www.springframework.org/schema/beans/spring-beans.xsd
  http://www.springframework.org/schema/context
  http://www.springframework.org/schema/context/spring-
```

```
        context.xsd">
        <context:component-scan base-
        package="com.packt.patterninspring.chapter6.bankapp" />
        <aop:aspectj-autoproxy />
        <bean class="com.packt.patterninspring.chapter6.
        bankapp.aspect.Auditing" />
    </beans>
```

Let's see how you can declare aspects in a Spring XML configuration file.

Define aspects using XML configuration

As we know that, we can configure beans in the XML based configuration, similarly you can declare aspects in the XML configuration. Spring provides another AOP namespace and it offers many elements that are used to declare aspects in XML, let's see in the following tables:

Annotation	Parallel XML element	Purpose of XML element
@Before	<aop:before>	It defines before advice.
@After	<aop:after>	It defines after advice.
@AfterReturning	<aop:after-returning>	It defines after returning advice.
@AfterThrowing	<aop:after-throwing>	It defines after throwing advice.
@Around	<aop:around>	It defines around advice.
@Aspect	<aop:aspect>	It defines an aspect.
@EnableAspectJAutoProxy	<aop:aspectj-autoproxy>	It enables annotation-driven aspects using @AspectJ.
@Pointcut	<aop:pointcut>	It defines a pointcut.
--	<aop:advisor>	It define AOP adviser
--	<aop:config>	It is top level AOP element

As you can see in the preceding table, a number of AOP namespace elements are parallel to the corresponding annotation available in the Java based configuration. Let's see the following same example in the XML based configuration, first have a look into the aspect class `Auditing`. Let's remove all of those AspectJ annotations as shown in following code:

```
package com.packt.patterninspring.chapter6.bankapp.aspect;

public class Auditing {
  public void validate(){
    System.out.println("bank validate your credentials before
    amount transferring");
  }
  public void transferInstantiate(){
    System.out.println("bank instantiate your amount
    transferring");
  }
  public void success(){
    System.out.println("bank successfully transferred amount");
  }
  public void rollback() {
    System.out.println("bank rolled back your transferred amount");
  }
}
```

As you can see the preceding code, now our aspect class doesn't indicate that it is an aspect class. It is a basic Java POJO class with some methods. Let's see in next section how to declare advices in XML configuration:

```
<aop:config>
  <aop:aspect ref="auditing">
    <aop:before pointcut="execution(*
    com.packt.patterninspring.chapter6.bankapp.
    service.TransferService.transfer(..))"
    method="validate"/>
    <aop:before pointcut="execution(*
    com.packt.patterninspring.chapter6.bankapp.
    service.TransferService.transfer(..))"
    method="transferInstantiate"/>
    <aop:after-returning pointcut="execution(*
    com.packt.patterninspring.chapter6.
    bankapp.service.TransferService.transfer(..))"
    method="success"/>
    <aop:after-throwing pointcut="execution(*
    com.packt.patterninspring.chapter6.bankapp.
    service.TransferService.transfer(..))"
    method="rollback"/>
  </aop:aspect>
```

```
</aop:config>
```

As you can see, `<aop-config>` is using a top level element. In `<aop:config>`, you declare other elements like `<aop:aspect>`, this element has `ref` attribute and it references to the POJO bean Auditing. It indicates that `Auditing` is an aspect class in the application. Now `<aop-aspect>` element has advices and pointcuts elements. All logics are same as we have defined in Java configuration.

Let's see in the next section how spring create AOP proxy.

Understanding AOP proxies

As you know that, Spring AOP is proxy-based. It mean Spring creates the proxy to weave the aspect between the business logic that is, in `target` object. It is based on the Proxy and Decorator design pattern. Let's see `TransferServiceImpl` class as an implementation of `TransferService` interface:

```java
package com.packt.patterninspring.chapter6.bankapp.service;
import org.springframework.stereotype.Service;
public class TransferServiceImpl implements TransferService {
  @Override
  public void transfer(String accountA, String accountB, Long
  amount) {
    System.out.println(amount+" Amount has been tranfered from
    "+accountA+" to "+accountB);
  }
}
```

Caller invokes this service (`transfer()` method) directly by the object reference, let's see the following figure to illustrate more:

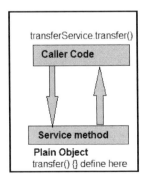

As you can see that caller could directly call the service and do the task assigned to it.

But you declare this `TransferService` as a target for the aspect. Since this is done, things change slightly. Now this class wrapped by proxy and client code actually doesn't call this service directly, it calls routed by this proxy. Let's see the following diagram.

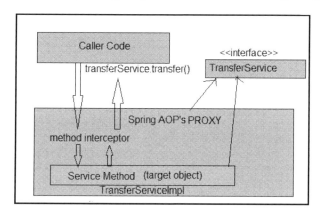

As you can see in the preceding diagram, Spring apply the AOP-proxy to the object in the following sequence:

1. Spring creates a proxy weaving aspect and target.
2. Proxy also implements target interface, that is, `TransferServive` interface.
3. All calls for transfer service method `transfer()` routed through proxy interceptor.
4. Matching advice is executed.
5. Then `target` method is executed.

As preceding list, is the flow when you call the method that has the proxy created by Spring.

You have seen in this chapter the Spring AOP Framework, it has actually implemented some part of the AspectJ Framework using proxy-based aspect weaving. I think, this gave good knowledge about Spring AOP.

Summary

In this chapter, we have seen the Spring AOP Framework and used design patterns behind this module. AOP is a very powerful paradigm and it complements the Object oriented programming. **Aspect-Oriented Programming (AOP)** modularizes cross-cutting concerns such as Logging, Security and Transaction. An aspect is a Java class annotated with @Aspect annotation. It defines a module containing the crosscutting behavior. This module separates from the application's business logic. We can reuse it in our application with other business modules without making any changes.

In Spring AOP, behavior is implemented as an advice method. You have learned in Spring, there are five types as Before, AfterThrowing, AfterReturning, After and Around. Around advice is a very powerful advice, there are interesting features implemented by using Around advice. You've learned how to weave these advices using load time weaving.

You have seen how to declare Pointcuts in the Spring application and pointcuts select joinpoints where advice applies.

Now we'll move to the essential part and look at how spring works in the backend to connect with database and read data for the application. Starting in the next chapter, you'll see how to build applications using JDBC template in Spring.

7
Accessing a Database with Spring and JDBC Template Patterns

In earlier chapters, you learned about Spring core modules like the Spring IoC container, the DI pattern, container life cycle, and the used design patterns. Also you have seen how Spring makes magic using AOP. Now is the right time to move into the battlefield of real Spring applications with persisting data. Do you remember your first application during college days where you dealt with database access? That time, you probably, had to write boring boilerplate code to load database drivers, initialize your data-access framework, open connections, handle various exceptions, and to close connections. You also had to be very careful about that code. If anything went wrong, you would not have been able to make a database connection in your application, even though you would've invested a lot of time in such boring code, apart from writing the actual SQL and business code.

Because we always try to make things better and simpler, we have to focus on the solution to that tedious work for data-access. Spring comes with a solution for the tedious and boring work for data-access--it removes the code of data access. Spring provides data-access frameworks to integrate with a variety of data-access technologies. It allows you to use either JDBC directly or any **object-relational mapping (ORM)** framework, like Hibernate, to persist your data. Spring handles all the low-level code for data access work in your application; you can just write your SQL, application logic, and manage your application's data rather than investing time in writing code for making and closing database connections, and so on.

Now, you can choose any technology, such as JDBC, Hibernate, the **Java Persistence API (JPA)**, or others. to persist your application's data. Irrespective of what you choose, Spring provides support for all these technologies for your application. In this chapter, we will explore Spring's support for JDBC. It will cover the following points:

- The best approach to designing your data access
- Implementing the template design pattern
- Problems with the traditional JDBC
- Solving problems with the Spring `JdbcTemplate`
- Configuring the data source
- Using the object pool design pattern to maintain database connections
- Abstracting database access by the DAO pattern
- Working with `JdbcTemplate`
- The Jdbc callback interfaces
- Best practices for configuring `JdbcTemplate` in the application

Before we go on to discuss more about JDBC and the template design pattern, let's first see the best approach to define the data-access tier in the layered architecture.

The best approach to designing your data-access

In previous chapters, you have seen that one of Spring's goals is to allow you to develop applications by following one of the OOPs principles of coding to interfaces. Any enterprise application needs to read data and write data to any kind of database, and to meet this requirement, we have to write the persistence logic. Spring allows you to avoid the scattering of persistence logic across all the modules in your application. For this, we can create a different component for data access and persistence logic, and this component is known as a **data access object** (**DAO**). Let's see, in the following diagram, the best approach to create modules in layered applications:

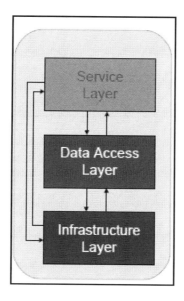

As you can see in the preceding diagram, for a better approach, many enterprise applications consist of the following three logical layers:

- **The service layer** (or application layer): This layer of the application exposes high-level application functions like use-cases and business logic. All application services are defined here.
- **The data access layer**: This layer of the application defines an interface to the application's data repository (such as a Relational or NoSQL database). This layer has the classes and interfaces which have the data-access logic's data persisting in the application.
- **The infrastructure layer**: This layer of the application exposes low-level services to the other layers, such as configuring DataSource by using the database URL, user credentials, and so on. Such configuration comes under this layer.

In the previous figure, you can see that the **Service Layer** collaborates with the **Data Access Layer**. To avoid coupling between the application logic and data-access logic, we should expose their functionality through interfaces, as interfaces promote decoupling between the collaborating components. If we use the data-access logic by implementing interfaces, we can configure any particular data-access strategy to the application without making any changes in the application logic in the **Service Layer**. The following diagram shows the proper approach to designing our data-access layer:

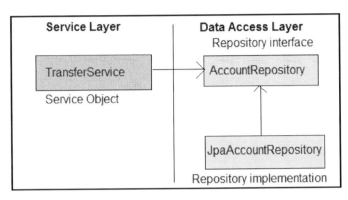

As shown in the preceding figure, your application service objects, that is, **TransferService**, don't handle their own data access. Instead, they delegate data access to the repositories. The repository's interface, that is, **AccountRepository** in your application, keeps it loosely coupled to the service object. You could configure any variant of the implementations-either the Jpa implementation of **AccountRepository** (**JpaAccountRepository**), or the Jdbc implementation of **AccountRepository** (**JdbcAccountRepository**).

Spring not only provides loose coupling between the application components working at the different layers in the layered architecture, but also helps to manage the resources in the enterprise layered architecture application. Let's see how Spring manages the resources, and what design pattern is using by Spring to solve the resource management problem.

The resource management problem

Let's understand the resource management problem with the help of a real example. You must've ordered pizza online sometime. If so, what are the steps involved in the process, from the time of ordering the pizza till its delivery? There are many steps to this process-- We first go to the online portal of the pizza company, select the size of the pizza and the toppings. After that, we place our order and check out. The order is accepted by the nearest pizza shop; they prepare our pizza accordingly, put the toppings on accordingly, wrap this pizza in the bag, the delivery boy comes to your place and hands over the pizza to you, and, finally, you enjoy your pizza with your friend. Even though there are many steps to this process, you're actively involved in only a couple of them. The pizza company is responsible for cooking the pizza and delivering it smoothly. You are involved only when you need to be, and other steps are taken care of by the pizza company. As you saw in this example, there are many steps involved in managing this process, and we also have to assign the resources to each step accordingly such that it is treated as a complete task without any break in the flow. This is a perfect scenario for a powerful design pattern, the template method pattern. The Spring framework implements this template design pattern to handle such type scenarios in the DAO layer of an application. Let's see what problems we face if we don't use Spring, and work with the traditional application instead.

In a traditional application, we work with the JDBC API to access the data from the database. It is a simple application where we access and persist the data using the JDBC API, and for this application, the following steps are required:

1. Define the connection parameters.
2. Access a data source, and establish a connection.
3. Begin a transaction.
4. Specify the SQL statement.
5. Declare the parameters, and provide parameter values.
6. Prepare and execute the statement.
7. Set up the loop to iterate through the results.
8. Do the work for each iteration--execute the business logic.
9. Process any exception.
10. Commit or roll back the transaction.
11. Close the connection, statement, and resultset.

If you use the Spring Framework for the same application, then you have to write the code for some steps of the preceding list of steps, while spring takes care of all the steps involving the low-level processes such as establishing a connection, beginning a transaction, processing any exception in the data layer, and closing the connection. Spring manages these steps by using the Template method design pattern, which we'll study in the next section.

Implementing the template design pattern

Define the skeleton of an algorithm in an operation, deferring some steps to subclasses. Template Method lets subclasses redefine certain steps of an algorithm without changing the algorithm's structure.

-GOF Design Pattern

We discussed the Template method design pattern in `Chapter 3`, *Consideration of Structural and Behavioral Patterns*. It is widely used, and comes under the structural design pattern of the GOF design pattern family. This pattern defines the outline or skeleton of an algorithm, and leaves the details to specific implementations later. This pattern hides away large amounts of boilerplate code. Spring provides many template classes, such as `JdbcTemplate`, `JmsTemplate`, `RestTemplate`, and `WebServiceTemplate`. Mostly, this pattern hides the low-level resource management as discussed earlier in the pizza example.

In the example, the process is ordering a pizza for home delivery from an online portal. The process followed by the pizza company has some fixed steps for each customer, like taking the order, preparing the pizza, adding the toppings according to the customer's specifications, and delivering it to the customer's address. We can add these steps, or define these steps to a specific algorithm. The system can then implement this algorithm accordingly.

Spring implements this pattern to access data from a database. In a database, or any other technology, there are some steps that are always common, such as establishing a connection to the database, handling transactions, handling exceptions, and some clean up actions which are required for each data access process. But there are also some steps which are not fixed, but depend on the application's requirement. It is the responsibility of the developer to define these steps. But spring allows us to separate the fixed and dynamic parts of the data-access process into different parts as templates and callbacks. All fixed steps come under the template, and dynamic custom steps come under callbacks. The following figure describes the two in detail:

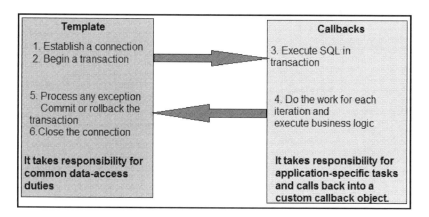

As you can see in the preceding figure, all the fixed parts of the process for data access wraps to the template classes of the Spring Framework as open and close connection, open and close statements, handling exceptions, and managing resources. But the other steps like writing SQLs, declaring connection parameters, and so on are parts of the callbacks, and callbacks are handled by the developer.

Spring provides several implementations of the Template method design pattern such as `JdbcTemplate`, `JmsTemplate`, `RestTemplate`, and `WebServiceTemplate`, but in this chapter, I will explain only its implementation for the JDBC API as `JdbcTemplate`. There is another variant of `JdbcTemplate-NamedParameterJdbcTemplate`, which wraps a `JdbcTemplate` to provide named parameters instead of the traditional JDBC "?" placeholders.

Problems with the traditional JDBC

The following are the problems we have to face whenever we work with the traditional JDBC API:

- **Redundant results due to error-prone code**: The traditional JDBC API required a lot of tedious code to work with the data access layer. Let's see the following code to connect the Database and execute the desired query:

```
public List<Account> findByAccountNumber(Long accountNumber) {
  List<Account> accountList = new ArrayList<Account>();
  Connection conn = null;
  String sql = "select account_name,
  account_balance from ACCOUNT where account_number=?";
  try {
    DataSource dataSource = DataSourceUtils.getDataSource();
    conn = dataSource.getConnection();
```

```
        PreparedStatement ps = conn.prepareStatement(sql);
        ps.setLong(1, accountNumber);
        ResultSet rs = ps.executeQuery();
        while (rs.next()) {
          accountList.add(new Account(rs.getString(
            "account_name"), ...));
        }
    } catch (SQLException e) { /* what to be handle here? */ }
    finally {
      try {
        conn.close();
      } catch (SQLException e) { /* what to be handle here ?*/ }
    }
    return accountList;
  }
```

As you can see in the preceding code, there are some lines which are highlighted; only this bold code matters-the rest is boilerplate. Also, this code handles the SQLException in the application inefficiently, because the developer doesn't know what should be handled there. Let's now look at another problem in the traditional JDBC code.

- **Leads to poor exception handling**: In the preceding code, the exceptions in the application are handled very poorly. The developers are not aware of what exceptions are to be handled here. SQLException is a checked Exception, which means it forces the developers to handle errors, but if you can't handle it, you must declare it. It is a very bad way of handling exceptions, and the intermediate methods must declare exception(s) from all methods in the code. It is a form of tight coupling.

Solving problems with Spring's JdbcTemplate

Spring's JdbcTemplate solves both the problems listed in the last section. JdbcTemplate greatly simplifies the use of the JDBC API, and it eliminates repetitive boilerplate code. It alleviates the common causes of bugs, and handles SQLExceptions properly without sacrificing power. It provides full access to the standard JDBC constructs. Let's see the same code using Spring's JdbcTemplate class to solve these two problems:

- **Removing redundant code from the application using JdbcTemplate**: Suppose you want a count of the accounts in a bank. The following code is required if you use the JdbcTemplate class:

```
int count = jdbcTemplate.queryForObject("SELECT COUNT(*)
  FROM ACCOUNT", Integer.class);
```

If you want to access the list of accounts for a particular user ID:

```
List<Account> results = jdbcTemplate.query(someSql,
  new RowMapper<Account>() {
    public Account mapRow(ResultSet rs, int row) throws
      SQLException {
        // map the current row to an Account object
    }
});
```

As you can see in the preceding code, you don't need to write the code for Open and Close database connection, for preparing a statement to execute query, and so on.

- **Data Access Exceptions**: Spring provides a consistent exception hierarchy to handle technology-specific exceptions like SQLException to its own exception class hierarchy with DataAccessException as the root exception. Spring wraps these original exceptions into different unchecked exceptions. Now Spring does not force the developers to handle these exceptions at development time. Spring provides the DataAccessException hierarchy to hide whether you are using JPA, Hibernate, JDBC, or similar. Actually, it is a hierarchy of sub-exceptions, and not just one exception for everything. It is consistent across all the supported data access technologies. The following diagram depicts the Spring Data Access Exception hierarchy:

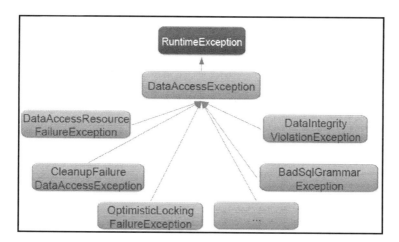

- As you can see in the preceding figure, Spring's `DataAccessException` extends the `RuntimeException`, that is, it is an unchecked exception. In an enterprise application, unchecked exceptions can be thrown up the call hierarchy to the best place to handle it. The good thing is that the methods in between don't know about it in the application.

Let's first discuss how to configure Spring with a data source to be able to connect the database, before declaring the templates and repositories in a Spring application.

Configuring the data source and object pool pattern

In the Spring Framework, DataSource is part of the JDBC API, and it provides a connection to the database. It hides many boilerplate codes for connection pooling, exception handling, and transaction management issues from the application code. As a developer, you let it focus on your business logic only. Don't worry about connection pooling, exception handling, and managing transactions; it is the responsibility of the application administrators how they set up the container managed data source in production. You just write the code, and test that code.

In an enterprise application, we can retrieve DataSource in several ways. We can use the JDBC driver to retrieve DataSource, but it is not the best approach to create DataSource in the production environment. As performance is one of the key issues during application development, Spring implements the object pool pattern to provide DataSource to the application in a very efficient way. The object pool pattern says that *creation of objects is expensive rather than reuse.*

Spring allows us to implement the object pool pattern for reusing the DataSource object in the application. You can use either the application server and container-managed pool (JNDI), or you can create a container by using third-party libraries such as DBCP, c3p0, and so on. These pools help to manage the available data sources in a better way.

In your Spring application, there are several options to configure the data-source beans, and they are as follows:

- Configuring data source using a JDBC driver
- Implementing the object pool design pattern to provide data source objects
    - Configuring the data source using JNDI
    - Configuring the data source using pool connections
        - Implementing the Builder pattern to create an embedded data source
- Let's see how to configure a data-source bean in a Spring application.

Configuring a data source using a JDBC driver

Using a JDBC driver to configure a data-source bean is the simplest data source in Spring. The three data source classes provided by Spring are as follows:

- `DriverManagerDataSource`: It always creates a new connection for every connection request
- `SimpleDriverDataSource`: It is similar to the `DriverManagerDataSource` except that it works with the JDBC driver directly
- `SingleConnectionDataSource`: It returns the same connection for every connection request, but it is not a pooled data source

Let's see the following code for configuring a data source bean using the `DriverManagerDataSource` class of Spring in your application:

In Java-based configuration, the code is as follows:

```
DriverManagerDataSource dataSource = new DriverManagerDataSource();
dataSource.setDriverClassName("org.h2.Driver");
dataSource.setUrl("jdbc:h2:tcp://localhost/bankDB");
dataSource.setUsername("root");
dataSource.setPassword("root");
```

In XML-based configuration, the code will be like this:

```
<bean id="dataSource"
 class="org.springframework.jdbc.datasource
 .DriverManagerDataSource">
 <property name="driverClassName" value="org.h2.Driver"/>
 <property name="url" value="jdbc:h2:tcp://localhost/bankDB"/>
 <property name="username" value="root"/>
 <property name="password" value="root"/>
</bean>
```

The data source defined in the preceding code is a very simple data source, and we can use it in the development environment. It is not a suitable data source for production. I, personally, prefer to use JNDI to configure the data source for the production environment. Let's see how.

Let's implement the object pool design pattern to provide data source objects *by* configuring the data source *using* JNDI.

In a Spring application, you can configure a data source by using the JNDI lookup. Spring provides the `<jee:jndi-lookup>` element from Spring's JEE namespace. Let's see the code for this configuration.

In XML configuration, the code is given as follows:

```
<jee:jndi-lookup id="dataSource"
 jndi-name="java:comp/env/jdbc/datasource" />
```

In Java configuration, the code is as follows:

```
@Bean
public JndiObjectFactoryBean dataSource() {
    JndiObjectFactoryBean jndiObject = new JndiObjectFactoryBean();
    jndiObject.setJndiName("jdbc/datasource");
    jndiObject.setResourceRef(true);
    jndiObject.setProxyInterface(javax.sql.DataSource.class);
    return jndiObject;
}
```

Application servers like WebSphere or JBoss allow you to configure data sources to be prepared via JNDI. Even a web container like Tomcat allows you to configure data sources to be prepared via JNDI. These servers manage the data sources in your application. It is beneficial, because the performance of the data source will be greater, as the application servers are often pooled. And they can be managed completely external to the application. This is one of the best ways to configure a data source to be retrieved via JNDI. If you are not able to retrieve through the JNDI lookup in production, you can choose another, better option, which we'll discuss next.

Configuring the data source using pool connections

The following open-sources technologies provide pooled data sources:

- Apache commons DBCP
- c3p0
- BoneCP

The following code configures DBCP's `BasicDataSource`.

The XML-based DBCP configuration is given as follows:

```
<bean id="dataSource"
  class="org.apache.commons.dbcp.BasicDataSource"
  destroy-method="close">
  <property name="driverClassName" value="org.h2.Driver"/>
  <property name="url" value="jdbc:h2:tcp://localhost/bankDB"/>
  <property name="username" value="root"/>
  <property name="password" value="root"/>
  <property name="initialSize" value="5"/>
  <property name="maxActive" value="10"/>
</bean>
```

The Java-based DBCP configuration is as follows:

```
@Bean
public BasicDataSource dataSource() {
    BasicDataSource dataSource = new BasicDataSource();
    dataSource.setDriverClassName("org.h2.Driver");
    dataSource.setUrl("jdbc:h2:tcp://localhost/bankDB");
    dataSource.setUsername("root");
    dataSource.setPassword("root");
    dataSource.setInitialSize(5);
    dataSource.setMaxActive(10);
    return dataSource;
}
```

As you can see in the preceding code, there are many other properties which are introduced for a pooled data sources provider. The properties of the `BasicDataSource` class in Spring are listed next:

- `initialSize`: This is the number of connections created at the time of initialization of the pool.
- `maxActive`: This is the maximum number of connections that can be allocated from the pool at the time of initialization of the pool. If you set this value to 0, that means there's no limit.
- `maxIdle`: This is the maximum number of connections that can be idle in the pool without extras being released. If you set this value to 0, that means there's no limit.
- `maxOpenPreparedStatements`: This is the maximum number of prepared statements that can be allocated from the statement pool at the time of initialization of the pool. If you set this value to 0, that means there's no limit.
- `maxWait`: This is the maximum waiting time for a connection to be returned to the pool before an exception is thrown. If you set it to 1, it means wait indefinitely.
- `minEvictableIdleTimeMillis`: This is the maximum time duration a connection can remain idle in the pool before it's eligible for eviction.
- `minIdle`: This is the minimum number of connections that can remain idle in the pool without new connections being created.

Implementing the Builder pattern to create an embedded data source

In application development, the embedded database is very useful, because it doesn't require a separate database server that your application connects. Spring provides one more data source for embedded databases. It is not powerful enough for the production environment. We can use the embedded data source for the development and testing environment. In Spring, the jdbc namespace configures an embedded database, H2, as follows:

In XML configuration, H2 is configured as follows:

```
<jdbc:embedded-database id="dataSource" type="H2">
 <jdbc:script location="schema.sql"/>
 <jdbc:script location="data.sql"/>
</jdbc:embedded-database>
```

In Java configuration, H2 is configured as follows:

```
@Bean
public DataSource dataSource(){
  EmbeddedDatabaseBuilder builder =
    new EmbeddedDatabaseBuilder().setType(EmbeddedDatabaseType.H2);
  builder.addScript("schema.sql");
  builder.addScript("data.sql");
  return builder.build();
}
```

As you can see in the preceding code, Spring provides the EmbeddedDatabaseBuilder class. It actually implements the Builder design pattern to create the object of the EmbeddedDatabaseBuilder class.

Let's see one more design pattern in the next section.

Abstracting database access using the DAO pattern

The data access layer works as an aspect between the business layer and the database. Data accessing depends on the business call, and it varies depending on the source of the data for example database, flat files, XML, and so on. So, we can abstract all access by providing an interface. This is known as the data access object pattern. From the application's point of view, it makes no difference when it accesses a relational database or parses XML files using a DAO.

In an earlier version, EJB provided entity beans managed by the container; they were distributed, secure, and transactional components. These beans were very transparent to the client, that is, for the service layer in the application, they had automatic persistence without the care of underlying database. But mostly, the features offered by these entity beans were not required for your application, as you needed to persist data to the database. Due to *this*, some non-required features of the entity beans, like network traffic, increased, and your application's performance was impacted. And that time, the entity beans needed to run inside the EJB containers, which is why it was very difficult to test.

In a nutshell, if you are working with the traditional JDBC API or earlier EJB versions, you will face the following problems in your application:

- In a traditional JDBC application, you merge the business tier logic with persistence logic.
- The Persistence tier or DAO layer is not consistent for the service layer or business tier. But DAO should be consistent for the service layer in an enterprise application.
- In a traditional JDBC application, you have to handle a lot of boilerplate code like making and closing connection, preparing statement, handling exceptions, and so on. It degrades reusability and increases development time.
- With EJB, the entity bean was created *as* an overhead to the application, and was difficult to test.

Let's see how spring solves these problems.

The DAO pattern with the Spring Framework

Spring provides a comprehensive JDBC module to design and develop JDBC-based DAOs. These DAOs in the application take care of all the boilerplate code of the JDBC API, and help to provide a consistent API for data access. In the Spring JDBC, DAO is a generic object to access data for the business tier, and it provides a consistent interface to the services at the business tier. The main goal behind the DAO's classes is to abstract the underlying data access logic from the services at the business tier.

In our previous example, we saw how the pizza company helped us to understand the resource management problem, and now, we will continue with our bank application. Let's see the following example on how to implement DAOs in an application. Suppose, in our bank application, we want the total number accounts in a branch in the city. For this, we will first create an interface for the DAO. It promotes programming to interface, as discussed earlier. It is one of the best practices of the design principles. This DAO interface will be injected with the services at the business tier, and we can create a number of concrete classes of the DAO interface according to the underlying databases in the application. That means our DAO layer will be consistent for the business layer. Let's create a DAO interface as following:

```
package com.packt.patterninspring.chapter7.bankapp.dao;
public interface AccountDao {
  Integer totalAccountsByBranch(String branchName);
}
```

Let's see a concrete implementation of the DAO interface using Spring's JdbcDaoSupport class:

```
package com.packt.patterninspring.chapter7.bankapp.dao;

import org.springframework.jdbc.core.support.JdbcDaoSupport;
public class AccountDaoImpl extends JdbcDaoSupport implements
 AccountDao {
    @Override
    public Integer totalAccountsByBranch(String branchName) {
      String sql = "SELECT count(*) FROM Account WHERE branchName =
       "+branchName;
      return this.getJdbcTemplate().queryForObject(sql,
       Integer.class);
    }
}
```

In the preceding code, you can see that the `AccountDaoImpl` class implements the `AccountDao` DAO interface, and it extends Spring's `JdbcDaoSupport` class to ease development with JDBC-based. This class provides a `JdbcTemplate` to its subclasses by using `getJdbcTemplate()`. The `JdbcDaoSupport` class is associated with a data source, and supplies the `JdbcTemplate` object for use in the DAO.

Working with JdbcTemplate

As you learned earlier, Spring's `JdbcTemplate` solves two main problems in the application. It solves the redundant code problem as well as poor exception handling of the data access code in the application. Without `JdbcTemplate` in your application, only 20% of the code is required for querying a row, but 80% is boilerplate which handles exceptions and manages resources. If you use `JdbcTemplate`, then there is no need to worry about the 80% boilerplate code. Spring's `JdbcTemplate`, in a nutshell, is responsible for the following:

- Acquisition of the connection
- Participation in the transaction
- Execution of the statement
- Processing of the result set
- Handling any exceptions
- Release of the connection

Let's see when to use `JdbcTemplate` in the application, and how to create it.

When to use JdbcTemplate

`JdbcTemplate` is useful in standalone applications, and anytime when JDBC is needed. It is suitable in utility or test code to clean up messy legacy code. Also, in any layered application, you can implement a repository or data access object. Let's see how to create it in an application.

Creating a JdbcTemplate in an application

If you want to create an object of the `JdbcTemplate` class to access data in your Spring application, you need to remember that it requires a `DataSource` to create the database connection. Let's create a template once, and reuse it. Do not create one for each thread, it is thread-safe after construction:

```
JdbcTemplate template = new JdbcTemplate(dataSource);
```

Let's configure a `JdbcTemplate` bean in Spring with the following `@Bean` method:

```
@Bean
public JdbcTemplate jdbcTemplate(DataSource dataSource) {
   return new JdbcTemplate(dataSource);
}
```

In the preceding code, we use the constructor injection to inject the `DataSource` with the `JdbcTemplate` bean in the Spring application. The `dataSource` bean being referenced can be any implementation of `javax.sql.DataSource`. Let's see how to use the `JdbcTemplate` bean in your JDBC-based repository to access the database in your application.

Implementing a JDBC-based repository

We can use the Spring's `JdbcTemplate` class to implement the repositories in a Spring application. Let's see how to implement the repository class based on the JDBC template:

```
package com.packt.patterninspring.chapter7.bankapp.repository;

import java.sql.ResultSet;
import java.sql.SQLException;

import javax.sql.DataSource;

import org.springframework.jdbc.core.JdbcTemplate;
import org.springframework.jdbc.core.RowMapper;
import org.springframework.stereotype.Repository;
import com.packt.patterninspring.chapter7.bankapp.model.Account;
@Repository
public class JdbcAccountRepository implements AccountRepository{
   JdbcTemplate jdbcTemplate;
   public JdbcAccountRepository(DataSource dataSource) {
      super();
      this.jdbcTemplate = new JdbcTemplate(dataSource);
   }
```

```
@Override
public Account findAccountById(Long id){
   String sql = "SELECT * FROM Account WHERE id = "+id;
   return jdbcTemplate.queryForObject(sql,
    new RowMapper<Account>(){
      @Override
      public Account mapRow(ResultSet rs, int arg1) throws
      SQLException {
         Account account = new Account(id);
         account.setName(rs.getString("name"));
         account.setBalance(new Long(rs.getInt("balance")));
         return account;
      }
   });
  }
}
```

In the preceding code, the DataSource bean is injected with the JdbcAccountRepository class by using the constructor injection. By using this DataSource, we created a JdbcTemplate object for accessing the data. The following methods are provided by JdbcTemplate to access data from the database:

- queryForObject(..): This is a query for simple java types (int, long, String, Date ...) and for custom domain objects.
- queryForMap(..): This is used when expecting a single row. JdbcTemplate returns each row of a ResultSet as a Map.
- queryForList(..): This is used when expecting multiple rows.

 Note that queryForInt and queryForLong have been deprecated since Spring 3.2; you can just use queryForObject instead (API improved in Spring 3).

Often, it is useful to map relational data into domain objects, for example, a ResultSet to an Account in the last code. Spring's JdbcTemplate supports this by using a callback approach. Let's discuss Jdbc callback interfaces in the next section.

Jdbc callback interfaces

Spring provides three callback interfaces for JDBC as follows:

- **Implementing RowMapper**: Spring provides a `RowMapper` interface for mapping a single row of a `ResultSet` to an object. It can be used for both single and multiple row queries. It is parameterized as of Spring 3.0:

```
public interface RowMapper<T> {
  T mapRow(ResultSet rs, int rowNum)
  throws SQLException;
}
```

- Let's understand this with the help of an example.

Creating a RowMapper class

In the following example, a class, `AccountRowMapper`, implements the `RowMapper` interface of the Spring Jdbc module:

```
package com.packt.patterninspring.chapter7.bankapp.rowmapper;

import java.sql.ResultSet;
import java.sql.SQLException;
import org.springframework.jdbc.core.RowMapper;
import com.packt.patterninspring.chapter7.bankapp.model.Account;
public class AccountRowMapper implements RowMapper<Account>{
  @Override
  public Account mapRow(ResultSet rs, int id) throws SQLException {
    Account account = new Account();
    account.setId(new Long(rs.getInt("id")));
    account.setName(rs.getString("name"));
    account.setBalance(new Long(rs.getInt("balance")));
    return account;
  }
}
```

In the preceding code, a class, `AccountRowMapper`, maps a row of the result set to the domain object. This row-mapper class implements the `RowMapper` callback interface of the Spring Jdbc module.

Query for single row with JdbcTemplate

Let's now see how the row-mapper maps a single row to the domain object in the application in the following code:

```
public Account findAccountById(Long id){
   String sql = "SELECT * FROM Account WHERE id = "+id;
   return jdbcTemplate.queryForObject(sql, new AccountRowMapper());
}
```

Here, there is no need to add typecasting for the Account object. The `AccountRowMapper` class maps the rows to the Account objects.

Query for multiple rows

The following code shows how the row mapper maps multiple rows to the list of domain objects:

```
public List<Account> findAccountById(Long id){
   String sql = "SELECT * FROM Account ";
   return jdbcTemplate.queryForList(sql, new AccountRowMapper());
}
```

RowMapper is the best choice when each row of a `ResultSet` maps to a domain object.

Implementing RowCallbackHandler

Spring provides a simpler `RowCallbackHandler` interface when there is no return object. It is used to stream rows to a file, converting the rows to XML, and filtering them before adding to a collection. But filtering in SQL is much more efficient, and is faster than the JPA equivalent for big queries. Let's look at the following example:

```
public interface RowCallbackHandler {
   void processRow(ResultSet rs) throws SQLException;
}
```

Example for using a RowCallbackHandler

The following code is an example of a `RowCallbackHandler` in the application:

```
package com.packt.patterninspring.chapter7.bankapp.callbacks;
import java.sql.ResultSet;
import java.sql.SQLException;
import org.springframework.jdbc.core.RowCallbackHandler;
public class AccountReportWriter implements RowCallbackHandler {
   public void processRow(ResultSet resultSet) throws SQLException {
```

```
    // parse current row from ResultSet and stream to output
    //write flat file, XML
  }
}
```

In preceding code, we have created a RowCallbackHandler implementation; the AccountReportWriter class implements this interface to process the result set returned from the database. Let's see the following code how to use AccountReportWriter call back class:

```
@Override
public void generateReport(Writer out, String branchName) {
  String sql = "SELECT * FROM Account WHERE branchName = "+
  branchName;
  jdbcTemplate.query(sql, new AccountReportWriter());
}
```

RowCallbackHandler is the best choice when no value should be returned from the callback method for each row, especially for large queries.

Implementing ResultSetExtractor

Spring provides a ResultSetExtractor interface for processing an entire ResultSet at once. Here, you are responsible for iterating the ResultSet, for example, for mapping the entire ResultSet to a single object. Let's see the following example:

```
public interface ResultSetExtractor<T> {
  T extractData(ResultSet rs) throws SQLException,
  DataAccessException;
}
```

Example for using a ResultSetExtractor

The following line of code implements the ResultSetExtractor interface in the application:

```
package com.packt.patterninspring.chapter7.bankapp.callbacks;

import java.sql.ResultSet;
import java.sql.SQLException;
import java.util.ArrayList;
import java.util.List;

import org.springframework.dao.DataAccessException;
import org.springframework.jdbc.core.ResultSetExtractor;
```

```
import com.packt.patterninspring.chapter7.bankapp.model.Account;

public class AccountExtractor implements
 ResultSetExtractor<List<Account>> {
   @Override
   public List<Account> extractData(ResultSet resultSet) throws
    SQLException, DataAccessException {
      List<Account> extractedAccounts = null;
      Account account = null;
      while (resultSet.next()) {
         if (extractedAccounts == null) {
            extractedAccounts = new ArrayList<>();
            account = new Account(resultSet.getLong("ID"),
             resultSet.getString("NAME"), ...);
         }
         extractedAccounts.add(account);
      }
      return extractedAccounts;
   }
}
```

This preceding class, `AccountExtractor`, implements `ResultSetExtractor`, and it is used to create an object for the entire data of the result set returned from the database. Let's see how to use this class in your application:

```
public List<Account> extractAccounts() {
   String sql = "SELECT * FROM Account";
   return jdbcTemplate.query(sql, new AccountExtractor());
}
```

The previous code is responsible for accessing all the accounts of a bank, and for preparing a list of accounts by using the `AccountExtractor` class. This class implements the `ResultSetExtractor` callback interface of the Spring Jdbc module.

`ResultSetExtractor` is the best choice when multiple rows of a `ResultSet` map to a single object.

Best practices for Jdbc and configuring JdbcTemplate

Instances of the `JdbcTemplate` class are thread-safe once configured. As a best practice of configuring the `JdbcTemplate` in a Spring application, it should be constructed in the constructor injection or setter injection of the data source bean in your DAO classes by passing that data source bean as a constructor argument of the `JdbcTemplate` class. This leads to DAOs that look, in part, like the following:

```
@Repository
public class JdbcAccountRepository implements AccountRepository{
  JdbcTemplate jdbcTemplate;
  public JdbcAccountRepository(DataSource dataSource) {
    super();
    this.jdbcTemplate = new JdbcTemplate(dataSource);
  }
  //...
}
Let's see some best practices to configure a database and write
the code for the DAO layer:
```

- If you want to configure the embedded database at the time of development of the application, as the best practice, the embedded database will always be assigned a uniquely generated name. This is because in the Spring container, the embedded database is made available by configuring a bean of type `javax.sql.DataSource`, and that data source bean is injected to the data access objects.

- Always use object pooling; this can be achieved in two ways:
  - **Connection pooling**: It allows the pool manager to keep the connections in a *pool* after they are closed
  - **Statement pooling**: It allows the driver to reuse the prepared Statement objects.
    - Choose the commit mode carefully
    - Consider removing the auto-commit mode for your application, and use manual commit instead to better control the commit logic, as follows:

```
Connection.setAutoCommit(false);
```

Summary

An application without data is like a car without fuel. Data is the heart of an application. Some applications may exist in the world without data, but these applications are simply showcase applications such as static blogs. Data is an important part of an application, and you need to develop data-access code for your application. This code should very simple, robust, and customizable.

In a traditional Java application, you could use JDBC to access the data. It is a very basic way, but sometimes, it is very messy to define specifications, handle JDBC exceptions, make database connections, load drivers, and so on. Spring simplifies these things by removing the boilerplate code and simplifying JDBC exception handling. You just write your SQL that should be executed in the application, and the rest is managed by the Spring framework.

In this chapter, you have seen how Spring provides support at the backend for data access and data persistence. JDBC is useful, but using the JDBC API directly is a tedious and error-prone task. `JdbcTemplate` simplifies data access, and enforces consistency. Data access with Spring uses the layered architecture principles-the higher layers should not know about data management. It isolates SQLException via Data Access Exceptions, and creates a hierarchy to make them easier to handle.

In the next chapter, we'll continue to discuss data access and persistence with the ORM framework, like Hibernate and JPA.

8
Accessing Database with Spring ORM and Transactions Implementing Patterns

In `Chapter 7`, *Accessing Database with Spring and JDBC Template Patterns*, we have learned how to access database using JBDC and how Spring can remove boilerplate code from the developer end to the framework by using template pattern and callbacks. In this chapter, we will learn one advanced step of accessing database using the **Object Relational Mapping (ORM)** Framework and managing transactions across the application.

When my son, Arnav, was one and a half years old, he used to play with a dummy mobile phone. But as he grew up, his needs too outgrew dummy mobiles to smartphones.

Similarly, when your application has a small set of data for a business tier, then JDBC works fine, but as your application grows and becomes more complex, it becomes difficult to map tables to the objects in the application. JDBC is the dummy small phone of the data access world. But with complex applications, we need Object Relational Mapping solutions that are able to map object properties to database columns. We also need more sophisticated platforms for our application at the data access layer, which create the queries and statements independently from the database technologies for us, and which we can define declaratively or programmatically.

Many ORM Frameworks are available to provide services at the data access layer of an application. Examples of such services include object relational mapping, lazy loading of data, eager loading of data, cascading, and so on. These ORM services save you from writing a lot of code for error handling, and managing resources in the application. The ORM Frameworks decrease the development time, and help to write error-free code, so that you just focus on the business requirements only. Spring doesn't implement its own ORM solution, but it provides support for many persistence frameworks such as Hibernate, the **Java Persistence API (JPA)**, iBATIS, and **Java Data Objects (JDO)**. Spring also provides integration points to the ORM Frameworks so that we can easily integrate the ORM Framework in our Spring application.

Spring provides support for all these technologies in your application. In this chapter, we will explore Spring's support for ORM solutions, and cover the following topics:

- ORM Framework and used patterns
    - The data access object pattern
    - Creating DAOs using the Factory design pattern in Spring
    - The Data Mapper pattern
    - The domain model pattern
    - Proxy for the lazy loading pattern
    - The Hibernate template pattern
- Integrating Hibernate with Spring
    - Configuring Hibernate's `SessionFactory` in a Spring container
    - Implementing DAOs based on plain Hibernate API
    - Transaction management strategies in Spring
    - Declarative transaction implementation and demarcation
    - Programmatic transaction implementation and demarcation
    - Best practices for Spring ORM and transaction modules in the application

Before we go on to discuss more about the ORM Frameworks, let's first look at some design patterns used in the **data access layer** (**DAL**) of the application.

ORM Framework and the patterns used

Spring provides support for several ORM Frameworks, such as Hibernate, the **Java Persistence API (JPA)**, iBATIS, and **Java Data Objects (JDO)**. By using any ORM solution in your application, you can easily persist and access data in the form of POJO objects from relational databases. The Spring ORM module is an extension of the previously discussed Spring JDBC DAO module. Spring provides ORM templates, such as JDBC-based templates, to work in the integration tier or data access layer. The following are the ORM Frameworks and integration supported by the Spring Framework:

- Hibernate
- Java Persistence API
- Java Data Objects
- iBATIS
- Data access object implementations
- Transaction strategies

You can use Spring's dependency injection feature to configure ORM solutions in your application. Spring also adds important enhancements to the ORM layer in your data access applications. The following are the benefits of using the Spring Framework to create your ORM DAOs:

- **Easier development and testing**: Spring's IoC container manages the beans for ORM DAOs. You can easily swap the implementation of the DAO interface by using Spring's dependency injection feature. It also makes it easy to test persistence-related code in isolation.
- **Common data access exceptions**: Spring provides a consistent data exception hierarchy to handle exceptions at the persistence layer. It wraps all the checked exceptions from the ORM tool, and converts these exceptions to unchecked general exceptions which are not related to any specific ORM solution and are DB-specific.
- **General resource management**: Resources such as `DataSource`, DB connections, Hibernates `SessionFactory`, JPA `EntityManagerFactory`, and others are managed by the Spring IoC container. Spring also manages transactions--local or global--using JTA.
- **Integrated transaction management**: Spring provides declarative and programmatic transaction management in your application. For declarative transaction management, you can use the `@Transactional` annotation.

The main approach to Spring's integration with the ORM solution is loose coupling between the application's layers; that is, the business layer and the data access layer. It is clear application layering, and is independent of any specific database and transaction technology. Business services in the application are no longer dependent on data access and a specific transaction strategy. Because Spring manages the resources used in the integration layer, you don't need to look up resources for specific data access technologies. Spring provides templates for the ORM solution to remove the boilerplate codes, and it provides a consistent approach across all ORM solutions.

In `Chapter 7`, *Accessing Database with Spring and JDBC Template Patterns*, you saw how Spring solves two major problems of the integration layer in the application. The first problem was *redundant code for managing resources from the application*, and the second problem was *handling checked exceptions* in the application at development time. Similarly, the Spring ORM module also provides solutions to these two problems, as we'll discuss in the following sections.

Resource and transaction management

In the Spring JDBC module, resources such as connection handling, statements handling, and exceptions handling are managed by the Spring's JdbcTemplate. It also translates SQL error codes of the database specific to meaningful unchecked exception classes. The same is true for the Spring ORM module--Spring manages both local and global transactions in the enterprise application by using the respective Spring transaction managers. Spring provides transaction managers for all supported ORM technologies. For example, Spring offers the Hibernate transaction manager for Hibernate, the JPA transaction manager for JPA, and JTA support for global or distributed transactions.

Consistent exception handling and translation

In the Spring JDBC module, Spring provides `DataAccessException` to handle all types of database-specific SQL error code, and generates meaningful exception classes. In the Spring ORM module, as we already know, Spring supports integration for several ORM solutions, such as Hibernate, JPA, or JDO in a DAO, and these persistence technologies provide their own native exception classes as `HibernateException`, `PersistenceException`, or `JDOException` depending on the technology. These native exceptions of the ORM Frameworks are unchecked exceptions, so we don't have to handle them in the application. The caller of the DAO services cannot do specific handling unless the application is strongly ORM based, or does not need any special exception treatment. Spring provides a consistent approach throughout the ORM Frameworks; you don't need to implement specific code for any ORM in a Spring application. It enables exception translation by using the `@Repository` annotation. If any class in the Spring application is annotated with `@Repository` annotation, then that class is eligible for Spring `DataAccessException` translation. Take for example the following code for the `AccountDaoImpl` class:

```
@Repository
public class AccountDaoImpl implements AccountDao {
  // class body here...
}

<beans>
  <!-- Exception translation bean post processor -->
  <bean class="org.springframework.dao.annotation.
  PersistenceExceptionTranslationPostProcessor"/>
  <bean id="accountDao" class="com.packt.patterninspring.chapter8.
  bankapp.dao.AccountDaoImpl"/>
</beans>
```

As you can see in the preceding code, the `PersistenceExceptionTranslationPostProcessor` class is a bean `post processor`, which automatically searches for all exception translators and also advises all the registered beans annotated with the `@Repository` annotation in the container. It applies the discovered exception translators to those annotated beans, and these translators can intercept and apply the appropriate translation on the thrown exceptions.

Let's see some more design patterns that are implemented in the Spring ORM module to provide the best enterprise solution for the integration tier of an enterprise application.

The data access object pattern

The **data access object (DAO)** pattern is a very popular design pattern for the persistent layer in a J2EE application. It separates the business logic layer and persistence layer. The DAO pattern is based on the encapsulation and abstraction object-oriented principles. The context for using the DAO pattern is to access and persist data depending on the underlying vendor implementation and type of storage, such as object-oriented database, flat files, relational databases, and so on. Using the DAO pattern, you can create a DAO interface, and implement this DAO interface to abstract and encapsulate all access to the data source. This DAO implementation manages the database's resources like connections with the data source.

The DAO interfaces are very generic to all the underlying data source mechanisms, and don't need to change for any changes in the low-level persistence technologies. This pattern allows you to adopt any different data access technologies without affecting the business logic in the enterprise application. Let's see the following figure to understand more about the DAO pattern:

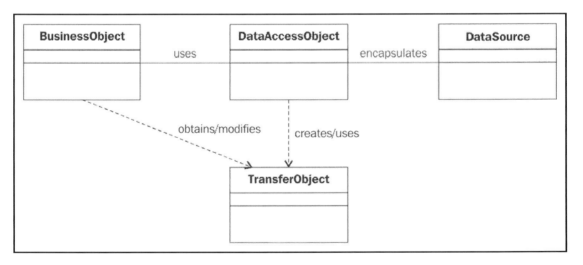

As you can see in the preceding diagram, the following participants work on this pattern:

- **BusinessObject**: This object works on the business layer, and is a client for the data access layer. It requires data for business modeling, and for preparing Java objects for the helper or controllers in the application.

- **DataAccessObject**: This is a primary object of the DAO pattern. This object hides all the low-level implementation of the underlying database implementation for the **BusinessObject**.
- **DataSource**: This is also an object to contain all the low-level information about the underlying database implementation, such as an RDBMS, flat files, or XML.
- **TransferObject**: This is also an object, and it is used as a data carrier. This object is used by **DataAccessObject** to return data to the business object.

Let's see the following example of the DAO pattern, where `AccountDao` is a `DataAccessObject` interface, and `AccountDaoImpl` is the implementation class of the `AccountDao` interface:

```
public interface AccountDao {
   Integer totalAccountsByBranch(String branchName);
}

public class AccountDaoImpl extends JdbcDaoSupport implements
AccountDao {
   @Override
   public Integer totalAccountsByBranch(String branchName) {
      String sql = "SELECT count(*) FROM Account WHERE branchName =
      "+branchName;
      return this.getJdbcTemplate().queryForObject(sql,
      Integer.class);
   }

}
```

Creating DAOs using the Factory design pattern in Spring

As we know, there are a lot of design patterns that play a role in the Spring Framework. As discussed in Chapter 2, *Overview of GOF Design Patterns*--Core Design patterns, the Factory pattern is a creational design pattern, and it is used to create an object without exposing the underlying logic to the client, and to assign a new object to the caller using a common interface or abstract class. You can make the DAO pattern highly flexible by using the `Factory` method and Abstract Factory design patterns.

Let's see in our example where do we are implementing this strategy in which a factory produces the DAOs for a single database implementation. Please refer to the following diagram:

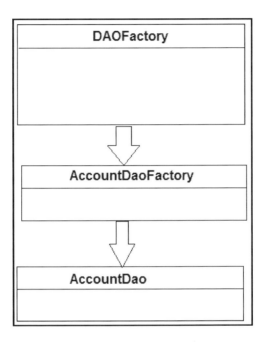

You can see in the preceding diagram that the **AccountDao** object is produced by **AccountDaoFactory**, and **AccountDaoFactory** is a factory for **AccountDao**. We can change the underlying database at any time such that we do not need to change the business code-- the factory takes care of these things, Spring provides support to maintain all the DAOs in the bean factory and in the factory for DAOs as well.

The Data Mapper pattern

> *A layer of Mappers that moves data between objects and a database while keeping them independent of each other and the mapper itself.*
> *- By* **Martin Fowler**: *Patterns of Enterprise Application Architecture*

The ORM Framework provides mapping between the object and relational databases, because we know that Objects and tables in the relational databases have different ways of storing the data for the application. Also, objects and tables have mechanisms for structuring data. In your Spring application, if you use any ORM solution such as Hibernate, JPA, or JDO, then you don't need worry about the mapping mechanism between the object and relational databases. Let's see the following diagram to understand more about the Data Mapper pattern:

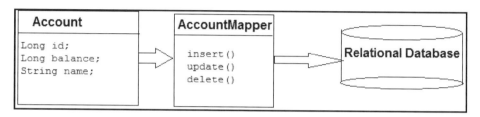

As shown in the preceding diagram, **Account**, an object, is mapped to the relational database through **AccountMapper**. It works like a mediator layer between the Java object and the underlying database in the application. Let's see another pattern used in the data access layer.

The domain model pattern

An object model of the domain that incorporates both behaviour and data.
-by Martin Fowler: Patterns of Enterprise Application Architecture

A domain model is an object that has behavior and data, so, the behavior defines the business logic of the enterprise application, and data is information about the business's output. A domain model combines data and process. In an enterprise application, data model lies under the business layer to insert the business logic, and it returns data from the business behaviors. Let's see the following diagram for more clarity on this:

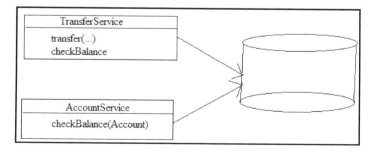

As you can see in the preceding diagram, we have defined two domain models in our application as per as our business requirements. Business behavior for transferring money from one account to another account has been defined in the **TransferService** class. The classes **TransferService** and **AccountService** come under the domain model pattern in the enterprise application.

Proxy for the lazy loading pattern

Lazy loading is a design pattern, and this design pattern is used by some ORM solutions such as Hibernate in the enterprise application to defer initialization of an object until it is called by another object at a point where it is needed. The purpose of this design pattern is memory optimization in the application. The lazy loading design pattern in Hibernate is achieved by using a virtual proxy object. In Lazy loading demonstration, we use a proxy, but this is not part of the proxy pattern.

Spring's Hibernate template pattern

Spring provides a helper class to access data in the DAO layer--this class is based on the GoF template method design pattern. Spring provides the `HibernateTemplate` class for providing database operations such as `save`, `create`, `delete`, and `update`. The `HibernateTemplate` class ensures that only one Hibernate session is used per transaction.

Let's see Spring's support for Hibernate in the next section.

Integrating Hibernate with Spring

Hibernate is a persistence ORM Framework, it is open source, and it provides not only simple object relationship mapping between Java objects and database tables, but also provides a lot of sophisticated features for your application to improve performance, and helps in better resource utilization such as caching, lazy loading, eager fetching, and distributed caching.

Spring Framework provides full support to integrate the Hibernate Framework, and Spring has some inbuilt libraries for full utilization of the Hibernate Framework. We can use Spring's DI pattern and IoC container to configure Hibernate in your application.

Let's see in the following section how to configure Hibernate in the Spring IoC container.

Configuring Hibernate's SessionFactory in a Spring container

As the best approach for configuring Hibernate and other persistence technologies in any enterprise application, business objects should be separate from the hard-coded resource lookups such as a JDBC `DataSource` or Hibernate `SessionFactory`. You can define these resources as beans in the Spring container. But business objects require the references of these resources, such as `SessionFactory` and JDBC `DataSource`, to access them. Let's see the following DAO class which has `SessionFactory` to access data for the application:

```
public class AccountDaoImpl implements AccountDao {
  private SessionFactory sessionFactory;

  public void setSessionFactory(SessionFactory sessionFactory) {
    this.sessionFactory = sessionFactory;
  }
   //.....
}
```

As you can see in the preceding code, the DAO class, `AccountDaoImpl`, follows the dependency injection pattern. It is injected with Hibernate's `SessionFactory` object to access the data, and fits nicely into a Spring IoC container. Here, Hibernate's `SessionFactory` is singleton object; it produces the main object of `org.hibernate.Session` interface of Hibernate. `SessionFactory` manages the `Session` object of Hibernate, and is also responsible for opening and closing the `Session` object. The `Session` interface has actual data-access functionality such as `save`, `update`, `delete`, and `load` objects from the database. In the application, `AccountDaoImp` or any other repository uses this Hibernate `Session` object to perform all of its persistence needs.

Spring provides inbuilt Hibernate modules, and you could use Spring's Hibernate session-factory beans in your application.

The `org.springframework.orm.hibernate5.LocalSessionFactoryBean` bean is the implementation of the `FactoryBean` interface of Spring. `LocalSessionFactoryBean` is based on the Abstract Factory pattern, and it produces Hibernate `SessionFactory` in the application. You can configure the Hibernate `SessionFactory` as a bean in Spring's context in your application as follows:

```
@Bean
public LocalSessionFactoryBean sessionFactory(DataSource
dataSource) {
  LocalSessionFactoryBean sfb = new LocalSessionFactoryBean();
  sfb.setDataSource(dataSource);
```

```
sfb.setPackagesToScan(new String[] {
  "com.packt.patterninspring.chapter8.bankapp.model" });
  Properties props = new Properties();
  props.setProperty("dialect",
  "org.hibernate.dialect.H2Dialect");
  sfb.setHibernateProperties(props);
  return sfb;
}
```

In the preceding code, we have configured `SessionFactory` as a bean by using the Spring's `LocalSessionFactoryBean` class. This bean method takes `DataSource` as an argument; `DataSource` specifies how and where to find a database connection. We also specified a property, `setPackagesToScan`, for `LocalSessionFactoryBean` with a package named "`com.packt.patterninspring.chapter8.bankapp.model`" to be scanned, and set a property of `SessionFactory` is `hibernateProperties` to find what kind of database we will deal with in the application.

Let's see how to implement DAOs for the persistence layer of the application after configuring the Hibernate `SessionFactory` bean in the Spring application context.

Implementing DAOs based on the plain Hibernate API

Let's create the following DAO implanting class:

```
package com.packt.patterninspring.chapter8.bankapp.dao;

import org.hibernate.SessionFactory;
import org.springframework.stereotype.Repository;
import org.springframework.beans.factory.annotation.Autowired;
@Repository
public class AccountDaoImpl implements AccountDao {
  @Autowired
  private SessionFactory sessionFactory;

  public void setSessionFactory(SessionFactory sessionFactory) {
    this.sessionFactory = sessionFactory;
  }
  @Override
  public Integer totalAccountsByBranch(String branchName) {
    String sql = "SELECT count(*) FROM Account WHERE branchName =
    "+branchName;
    return this.sessionFactory.getCurrentSession().createQuery(sql,
    Integer.class).getSingleResult();
```

```
    }
    @Override
    public Account findOne(long accountId) {
      return (Account)
      this.sessionFactory.currentSession().
      get(Account.class, accountId);
    }
    @Override
    public Account findByName(String name) {
      return (Account) this.sessionFactory.currentSession().
      createCriteria(Account.class)
      .add(Restrictions.eq("name", name))
      .list().get(0);
    }
    @Override
    public List<Account> findAllAccountInBranch(String branchName) {
      return (List<Account>) this.sessionFactory.currentSession()
      .createCriteria(Account.class).add(Restrictions.eq("branchName",
      branchName)).list();
    }
  }
}
```

As you can see in the preceding code, `AccountDaoImpl` is a DAO implementation class, which is injected with Hibernate's `SessionFactory` bean by using the `@Autowired` annotation. The DAO implementations described earlier will throw unchecked Hibernate `PersistenceExceptions`--it is not desirable to let these propagate up to the service layer or other users of the DAOs. But the Spring AOP module allows translation to Spring's rich, vendor-neutral `DataAccessException` hierarchy--it hides the access technology used. Spring provides this capability out of the box by annotating the DAO implementation class with `@Repository`, and you just need to define a Spring-provided `BeanPostProcessor`, that is, `PersistenceExceptionTranslationPostProcessor`.

Let's add an exception translation to our Hibernate DAO implementation class; we can do this by just adding a `PersistenceExceptionTranslationPostProcessor` bean to the Spring application context, as follows:

```
@Bean
public BeanPostProcessor persistenceTranslation() {
  return new PersistenceExceptionTranslationPostProcessor();
}
```

The preceding registered bean `PersistenceExceptionTranslationPostProcessor` is responsible for adding an adviser for the beans which are annotated with the `@Repository` annotation, and it is re-thrown as a Spring-specific unchecked data access exception for any platform-specific exceptions caught in the code.

Let's see, in the next section, how Spring manages transactions across the business and persistence layers of the Spring application.

Transaction management strategies in Spring

Spring provides comprehensive support for transaction management in a Spring application. This is one the most compelling features of the Spring Framework. Mostly, this feature forces software industries to develop enterprise applications with the Spring Framework. The Spring Framework provides a consistent way to manage transactions across the application using any persistence technology, such as Java Transaction API , JDBC, Hibernate, Java Persistence API, and Java Data Objects. Spring supports declarative transaction management as well as programmatic transaction management.

There are two types of Java transactions, which are as follows:

- **Local transactions - single resource**: Local transactions managed by the underlying resource; these are resource-specific. Let's explain this with the help of the following diagram:

  As you can see in the preceding diagram, there is a transaction working between the application and the database platforms to ensure that every unit of task follows the ACID property of the databases.

- **Global (distributed) transactions - multiple**: Global transactions, which are managed by separate, dedicated transaction managers, enable you to work with multiple transactional resources. Take a look at the following diagram to understand more about Global or distributed transactions:

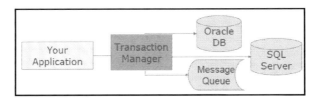

As you can see in the last diagram, a **Transaction Manager** works with multiple database technologies in the application. A global transaction is independent of platform-specific persistence technologies.

Spring provides the same API for both types of transactions in Java applications. The Spring Framework provides a consistent programming model in any environment by either configuring the transactions declaratively, or by configuring the transaction programmatically.

Let's move on to the following sections to see how to configure transactions in Spring applications.

Declarative transaction demarcation and implementation

Spring supports declarative transaction management. Spring separates transaction demarcation from transaction implementation. Demarcation is expressed declaratively via the Spring AOP. We always recommend using Spring's declarative transaction demarcation and implementation in your Spring application, because the declarative programming model enables you to replace the external transaction demarcation API from the code, and you can configure it by using Spring AOP transaction interceptor. Transactions are, basically, cross-cutting concerns; this declarative transaction model allows you to keep your application's business logic separate from the repetitive transaction demarcation code.

As mentioned earlier, Spring provides a consistent model for handling transactions in a Spring application, and provides an interface PlatformTransactionManager to hide the implementation details. There are several implementations available for this interface in the Spring Framework, and some of these are listed next:

- DataSourceTransactionManager
- HibernateTransactionManager
- JpaTransactionManager
- JtaTransactionManager
- WebLogicJtaTransactionManager
- WebSphereUowTransactionManager

The following is a key interface:

```
public interface PlatformTransactionManager {
  TransactionStatus getTransaction(
    TransactionDefinition definition) throws TransactionException;
   void commit(TransactionStatus status) throws
     TransactionException;
   void rollback(TransactionStatus status) throws
     TransactionException;
}
```

In the preceding code, the getTransaction() method returns a TransactionStatus object. This object contains the status of transactions; either it is new or it returns existing in the current call stack. It depends on the TransactionDefinition parameter. As in JDBC or ORM modules, Spring also provides a consistent way to handle exceptions thrown by any transaction manager. The getTransaction() method throws a TransactionException exception, which is an unchecked exception.

Spring uses the same API for global and local transactions in the application. Very minor changes are required to move from local transaction to the global transaction in the application-that is just change the transaction manager.

Deploying the transaction manager

There are two steps for deploying a transaction in your Spring application. The first step is that you have to implement or configure a pre-implemented Spring transaction manager class with your application. The second step is to declare transaction demarcation, that is, where you want to place the Spring transaction.

Step 1 - Implementing the transaction manager

Create the bean for the required implementation just like any other Spring bean. You can configure, as appropriate, the transaction manager for any persistence technologies such as JDBC, JMS, JTA, Hibernate, JPA, and so on. But in the following example, here is the manager for a DataSource using JDBC:

In Java configuration, let's see how to define the `transactionManager` bean in the application:

```
@Bean
public PlatformTransactionManager transactionManager(DataSource
dataSource) {
    return new DataSourceTransactionManager(dataSource);
}
```

In XML configuration, the bean can be created like this:

```
<bean id="transactionManager"
 class="org.springframework.jdbc.datasource.
 DataSourceTransactionManager">
 <property name="dataSource" ref="dataSource"/>
</bean>
```

In the preceding code, we use `dataSource` bean; a `dataSource` bean must be defined elsewhere. The bean ID, `"transactionManager"`, is the default name. We can change it, but then must specify the alternative name everywhere, and that is not so easy to do!

Step 2 - Declaring the transaction demarcation

As the best approach, the service layer of the application is the best place to demarcate the transactions. Let's see this in the following code:

```
@Service
public class TransferServiceImpl implements TransferService{
  //...
  @Transactional
  public void transfer(Long amount, Long a, Long b){
    // atomic unit-of-work
  }
  //...
}
```

As you can see in the preceding code, `TransferServiceImpl` is our service class at the service layer of the application. This service is the best place to demarcate the transactions for units of work. Spring provides the `@Transactional` annotation to demarcate the transactions; this annotation can be used at either the class level or the method level of the service classes in the application. Let's look `@Transactional` at the class level:

```
@Service
@Transactional
public class TransferServiceImpl implements TransferService{
  //...
  public void transfer(Long amount, Account a, Account b){
    // atomic unit-of-work
  }
  public Long withdraw(Long amount,  Account a){
    // atomic unit-of-work
  }
  //...
}
```

If you declare the `@Transactional` annotation at the class level, all business methods in this service will be transactional methods.

 Note--Method visibility should be public if you are using the `@Transactional` annotation. If you use this annotation with a non-public method, such as `protected`, `private`, or `package-visible`, no error or exception is thrown, but this annotated method does not show the transactional behavior.

But only using this annotation in the Spring application is not enough. We have to enable the transaction management feature of the Spring Framework by using the `@EnableTransactionManagement` annotation in the Java configuration file of Spring, or we can use the namespace `<tx:annotation-driven/>` in the XML configuration file. Let's look the following code, for example:

```
@Configuration
@EnableTransactionManagement
public class InfrastructureConfig {
  //other infrastracture beans definitions
  @Bean
  public PlatformTransactionManager transactionManager(){
      return new DataSourceTransactionManager(dataSource());
  }
}
```

As you can see in the preceding code, `InfrastructureConfig` is the Java configuration file of the Spring application--here, we define infrastructure-related beans, and one of the `transactionManager` beans too has been defined here. This configuration class annotated with one more annotation is `@EnableTransactionManagement`--this annotation defines a Bean Post-Processor in the application, and it proxies `@Transactional` beans. Now, take a look at the following diagram:

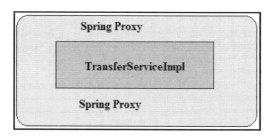

As you see in the preceding diagram, the `TransferServiceImpl` class is wrapped in a Spring proxy.

But to know what happens exactly with the `@Transactional` beans in the application, let's see the following steps:

1. The `target` object is wrapped in a proxy; it uses an Around advice as we have discussed in Chapter 6, Spring Aspect Oriented Programming with Proxy & Decorator Pattern.
2. The Proxy implements the following behavior:

    1. Start transaction before entering the business method.

    2. Commit at the end of the business method.

    3. Roll back if the business method throws a `RuntimeException`--it is the default behavior of a Spring transaction, but you can override it for checked and custom exceptions also.

3. The transaction context is now bound to the current thread in the application.
4. All steps controlled by the configuration either in XML, Java or Annotations.

Now take a look at the following diagram of a local JDBC configuration with the associated transaction manager:

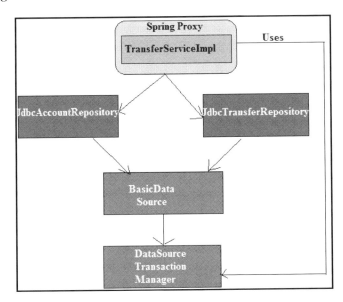

In the previous diagram, we have defined a local data source using JDBC and a **DataSource Transaction Manager**.

In the next section, we'll discuss how to implement and demarcate transactions programmatically in the application.

Programmatic transaction demarcation and implementation

Spring allows you to implement and demarcate transactions programmatically in the application by using the `TransactionTemplate` and a `PlatformTransactionManager` implementation directly. But declarative transaction management is highly recommended, because it provides a clean code and a very flexible configuration.

Let's see how to implement the transactions in the application programmatically:

```
package com.packt.patterninspring.chapter8.bankapp.service;

import org.springframework.beans.factory.annotation.Autowired;
import org.springframework.stereotype.Service;
import org.springframework.transaction.PlatformTransactionManager;
import org.springframework.transaction.TransactionStatus;
import org.springframework.transaction.support.TransactionCallback;
import org.springframework.transaction.support.TransactionTemplate;

import com.packt.patterninspring.chapter8.bankapp.model.Account;
import com.packt.patterninspring.chapter8.bankapp.
  repository.AccountRepository;

@Service
public class AccountServiceImpl implements AccountService {
  //single TransactionTemplate shared amongst all methods in this
  instance
  private final TransactionTemplate transactionTemplate;
  @Autowired
  AccountRepository accountRepository;
  // use constructor-injection to supply the
  PlatformTransactionManager
  public AccountServiceImpl(PlatformTransactionManager
  transactionManager) {
    this.transactionTemplate = new
    TransactionTemplate(transactionManager);
  }
  @Override
  public Double cheeckAccountBalance(Account account) {
    return transactionTemplate.execute(new
    TransactionCallback<Double>() {
      // the code in this method executes in a transactional
      context
      public Double doInTransaction(TransactionStatus status) {
        return accountRepository.checkAccountBalance(account);
      }
    });  }
}
```

In the preceding application code, we have used `TransactionTemplate` explicitly to execute the application logic in a transactional context. The `TransactionTemplate` is also based on the template method design pattern, and it has the same approach as other templates in the Spring Framework, such as the JdbcTemplate. Similar to JdbcTemplate, `TransactionTemplate` also uses a callback approach, and it makes application code free from having the boilerplate code for managing transactional resources. We constructed an object of the `TransactionTemplate` class in the Service class construction, and passed an object of `PlatformTransactionManager` as an argument to the constructor of the `TransactionTemplate` class. We also wrote a `TransactionCallback` implementation that contains the business logic code of your application, which shows tight coupling between the application logic and transactional code.

We have seen in this chapter how efficiently Spring manages transactions in an enterprise application. Let's now study some best practices that we have to keep in mind whenever we work on the any enterprise application.

Best practices for Spring ORM and transaction module in an application

The following are the practices that we have to follow in the design and development of an application:

Avoid using Spring's `HibernateTemplate` helper class in the DAO implementation, and use `SessionFactory` and `EntityManager` in your application. Because of the contextual session capability of Hibernate, use `SessionFactory` directly in your DAOs. Additionally, use `getCurrentSession()` method to access the transactional current session in order to perform persistence operations in the application. Please refer to the following code:

```
@Repository
public class HibernateAccountRepository implements
AccountRepository {
  SessionFactory sessionFactory;
  public HibernateAccountRepository(SessionFactory
  sessionFactory) {
    super();
    this.sessionFactory = sessionFactory;
  }
//...
}
```

In your application, always use the @Repository annotation for data access objects or repositories; it provides exception translation. Please refer to the following code:

```
@Repository
public class HibernateAccountRepository{//...}
```

The service layer must be separate even though business methods in the services only delegate their responsibilities to the corresponding DAO methods.

Always implement transactions at the service layer of the application and not the DAO layer--this is the best place for transactions. Please refer to the following code:

```
@Service
@Transactional
public class AccountServiceImpl implements AccountService {//...}
```

Declarative transaction management is more powerful and convenient to configure in the application, and is a highly recommend approach to use in a Spring application. It separates the cross-cutting concerns from business logic.

Always throw runtime exceptions instead of checked exceptions from the service layer.

Be careful of the readOnly flag for the @Transactional annotation. Mark transactions as readOnly=true when service methods only contain queries.

Summary

In Chapter 7, *Accessing Database with Spring and JDBC Template Patterns*, we saw that Spring provides JdbcTemplate class based on the GOF template method design pattern. This class handles all the required boilerplate codes underlying the tradition JDBC API. But when we work with the Spring JDBC module, mapping tables to the objects becomes very tedious. In this chapter, we saw the solution to map objects to tables in a relational database--we can do much more with a relational database by using ORM in a complex application. Spring supports integration with several ORM solutions like Hibernate, JPA, and others. These ORM Frameworks enable the declarative programming model for the data persistence instead of using the JDBC programming model.

We also looked at the several design patterns that are implemented in the data access layer or integration tier. These patterns are implemented as a feature in the Spring Framework as proxy pattern for lazy loading, Facade pattern for integration with business tier, DAO patterns for data accessing, and so on.

In the next chapter, we'll see how we can improve our application's performance in production by using Spring's support for cache patterns.

9
Improving Application Performance Using Caching Patterns

In previous chapters, we have seen how Spring works in the backend to access data for the application. We also saw how the Spring JDBC Module provides the `JdbcTemplate` helper class for database access. Spring provides support for integration with ORM solutions such as Hibernate, JPA, JDO, and so on, and manages transactions across application. Now, in this chapter, we will see how Spring provides caching support to improve application performance.

Do you ever face a volley of questions from your wife when you return home very late in the night from your office? Yes, I know it is very irritating to answer so many questions when you are tired and exhausted. It is even more irritating when you're asked the same questions over and over again..

Some questions can be answered with a *Yes* or *No*, but for some questions, you have to explain in detail. Consider what will happen if you are asked another lengthy question again after some time! Similarly, there are some stateless components in an application, where the components have been designed in such a way that they ask the same questions over and over again to complete each task individually. Similar to some questions asked by your wife, some questions in the system take a while to fetch the appropriate data--it may have some major complex logic behind it, or maybe, it has to fetch data from the database, or call a remote service.

If we know that the answer of a question is not likely to change frequently, we can remember the answer to that question for later when it is asked again by the same system. It doesn't make sense to go through the same channel to fetch it again, as it will impact your application's performance, and will be a wasteful use of your resources. In an enterprise application, caching is a way to store those frequently needed answers so that we fetch from the cache instead of going through the proper channel to get the answer for the same question over and over again. In this chapter, we will discuss Spring's Cache Abstraction feature, and how Spring declaratively supports caching implementation. It will cover the following points:

- What is a cache?
- Where do we do this caching?
- Understanding the cache abstraction
- Enabling caching via the Proxy pattern
- Declarative Annotation-based caching
- Declarative XML-based caching
- Configuring the cache storage
- Implementing custom cache annotations
- Caching best practices

Let's begin.

What is cache?

In very simple terms, **cache** is a memory block where we store preprocessed information for the application. In this context, a key-value storage, such as a map, may be a cache in the application. In Spring, cache is an interface to abstract and represent caching. A cache interface provides some methods for placing objects into a cache storage, it can retrieve from the cache storage for given key, it can update the object in the cache storage for a given key, it remove the object from the cache storage for a given key. This cache interface provides many functions to operate with cache.

Where do we use caching?

We use caching in cases where a method always returns the same result for the same argument(s). This method could do anything such as calculate data on the fly, execute a database query, and request data via RMI, JMS, and a web-service, and so on. A unique key must be generated from the arguments. That's the cache key.

Understanding cache abstraction

Basically, caching in Java applications is applied to the Java methods to reduce the number of executions for the same information available in the cache. That means, whenever these Java methods are invoked, the cache abstraction applies the cache behavior to these methods based on the given arguments. If the information for the given argument is already available in the cache, then it is returned without having to execute the target method. If the required information is not available in the cache, then the `target` method is executed, and the result is cached and returned to the caller. Cache abstraction also provides other cache-related operations such as updating and/or removing the contents in the cache. These operations are useful when the data changes in the application sometimes.

Spring Framework provides cache abstraction for Spring applications by using the `org.springframework.cache.Cache` and `org.springframework.cache.CacheManager` interfaces. Caching requires the use of an actual storage to store the cache data. But cache abstraction only provides caching logic. It doesn't provide any physical storage to store the cached data. So, developers need to implement the actual storage for caching in the application. If you have a distributed application, then you will need to configure your cache provider accordingly. It depends on the use cases of your application. You can either make a copy of the same data across nodes for a distributed application, or you can make a centralized cache.

There are several cache providers in the market, which you could use as per as your application requirement. Some of them are as follows:

- Redis
- `OrmLiteCacheClient`
- `Memcached`
- In Memory Cache
- Aws DynamoDB Cache Client
- Azure Cache Client

To implement cache abstraction in your application, you have to take care of the following tasks:

- **Caching declaration**: This means that you have to recognize those methods in the application that need to be cached, and annotate these methods either with caching annotations, or you can use XML configuration by using Spring AOP
- **Cache configuration**: This means that you have to configure the actual storage for the cached data--the storage where the data is stored and read from

Let's now see how we can enable Spring's cache abstraction in a Spring application.

Enabling caching via the Proxy pattern

You can enable Spring's cache abstraction in the following two ways:

- Using Annotation
- Using the XML namespace

Spring transparently applies caching to the methods of Spring beans by using AOP. Spring applies proxy around the Spring beans where you declare the methods that need to be cached. This proxy adds the dynamic behavior of caching to the Spring beans. The following diagram illustrates the caching behavior:

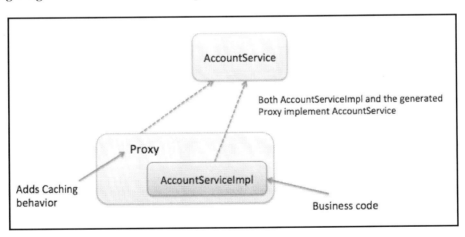

In the preceding diagram, you can see that Spring applies **Proxy** to the **AccountServiceImpl** class to add the caching behavior. Spring uses the GoF proxy pattern to implement caching in the application.

Let's look at how to enable this feature in a Spring application.

Enabling the caching proxy using Annotation

As you already know, Spring provides lots of features, but they are, mostly, disabled. You must enable these feature before using it. If you want to use Spring's cache abstraction in your application, you have to enable this feature. If you are using Java configuration, you can enable cache abstraction of Spring by adding the @EnableCaching annotation to one of your configuration classes. The following configuration class shows the @EnableCaching annotation:

```
package com.packt.patterninspring.chapter9.bankapp.config;

import org.springframework.cache.CacheManager;
import org.springframework.cache.annotation.EnableCaching;
import org.springframework.cache.concurrent.
  ConcurrentMapCacheManager;
import org.springframework.context.annotation.Bean;
import org.springframework.context.annotation.ComponentScan;
import org.springframework.context.annotation.Configuration;

@Configuration
@ComponentScan(basePackages=
{"com.packt.patterninspring.chapter9.bankapp"})
@EnableCaching //Enable caching
public class AppConfig {
 @Bean
 public AccountService accountService() { ... }

 //Declare a cache manager
 @Bean
 public CacheManager cacheManager() {
     CacheManager cacheManager = new ConcurrentMapCacheManager();
     return cacheManager;
 }
}
```

In the preceding Java configuration file, we added the @EnableCaching annotation to the configuration class AppConfig.java; this annotation indicates to the Spring Framework to enable Spring cache behavior for the application.

Let's now look at how to enable Spring's cache abstraction by using XML configuration.

Enabling the Caching Proxy using the XML namespace

If you're configuring your application with XML, you can enable annotation-driven caching with the `<cache:annotation-driven>` element from Spring's cache namespace, as follows:

```xml
<?xml version="1.0" encoding="UTF-8"?>
<beans xmlns="http://www.springframework.org/schema/beans"
 xmlns:xsi="http://www.w3.org/2001/XMLSchema-instance"
 xmlns:context="http://www.springframework.org/schema/context"
 xmlns:jdbc="http://www.springframework.org/schema/jdbc"
 xmlns:tx="http://www.springframework.org/schema/tx"
 xmlns:aop="http://www.springframework.org/schema/aop"
 xmlns:cache="http://www.springframework.org/schema/cache"
 xsi:schemaLocation="http://www.springframework.org/schema/jdbc
 http://www.springframework.org/schema/jdbc/spring-jdbc-4.3.xsd
 http://www.springframework.org/schema/cache
 http://www.springframework.org/schema/cache/spring-cache-4.3.xsd
 http://www.springframework.org/schema/beans
 http://www.springframework.org/schema/beans/spring-beans.xsd
 http://www.springframework.org/schema/context
 http://www.springframework.org/schema/context/spring-context.xsd
 http://www.springframework.org/schema/aop
 http://www.springframework.org/schema/aop/spring-aop-4.3.xsd
 http://www.springframework.org/schema/tx
 http://www.springframework.org/schema/tx/spring-tx-4.3.xsd">
 <!-- Enable caching -->
 <cache:annotation-driven />
 <context:component-scan base-
 package="com.packt.patterninspring.chapter9.bankapp"/>
 <!-- Declare a cache manager -->
 <bean id="cacheManager"
 class="org.springframework.cache.concurrent.
 ConcurrentMapCacheManager" />
</beans>
```

As seen in the preceding configuration files, whether you use Java configuration or XML configuration, the annotation `@EnableCaching` and namespace `<cache:annotation-driven>` enables Spring's cache abstraction by creating an aspect with pointcuts that trigger off of Spring's caching annotations.

Let's see how to use Spring's caching annotations to define cache boundaries.

Declarative Annotation-based caching

In Spring applications, Spring's abstraction provides the following Annotations for caching declaration:

- `@Cacheable`: This indicates that before execution of the actual method, look at the return value of that method in the cache. If the value is available, return this cached value, if the value is not available, then invoke the actual method, and put the returned value into the cache.
- `@CachePut`: This updates the cache without checking if the value is available or not. It always invokes the actual method.
- `@CacheEvict`: This is responsible for triggering cache eviction.
- `@Caching`: This is used for grouping multiple annotations to be applied on a method at once.
- `@CacheConfig`: This indicates to Spring to share some common cache-related settings at the class level.

Let us now take a closer look at each annotation.

The @Cacheable annotation

`@Cacheable` marks a method for caching. Its result is stored in a cache. For all subsequent invocations of that method with the same arguments, it will fetch data from the cache using a key. The method will not be executed. The following are the `@Cacheable` attributes:

- **value**: This is the name of cache to use
- **key**: This is the key for each cached data item
- **condition**: This is a SpEL expression to evaluate true or false; if it is false, then the result of caching is not applied to the method call
- **unless**: This too is a SpEL expression; if it is true, it prevents the return value from being put in the cache

You can use SpEL and argument(s) of method. Let's look at the following code for the simplest declaration of the `@Cacheable` annotation. It requires the name of the cache associated with that method. Please refer to the following code:

```
@Cacheable("accountCache ")
public Account findAccount(Long accountId) {...}
```

In the preceding code, the `findAccount` method is annotated with the `@Cacheable` annotation. This means that this method is associated with a cache. The name of the cache is **accountCache**. Whenever this method is called for a particular `accountId`, the cache is checked for the return value of this method for the given `accountId`. You can also give multiple names to the cache as shown next:

```
@Cacheable({"accountCache ", "saving-accounts"})
public Account findAccount(Long accountId) {...}
```

The @CachePut annotation

As mentioned earlier, the `@Cacheable` and `@CachePut` annotations both have the same goal, that is, to populate a cache. But their working is slightly different from each other. `@CachePut` marks a method for caching, and its result is stored in a cache. For each invocation of that method with the same arguments, it always invokes the actual method without checking whether the return value of that method is available in the cache or not. The following are `@CachePut` attributes:

- **value**: This is the name of the cache to use
- **key**: This is the key for each cached data item
- **condition**: This is a SpEL expression to evaluate true or false; if false, then the result of caching is not applied to the method call
- **unless**: This is also a SpEL expression; if it is true, it prevents the return value from being put in the cache

You can also use SpEL and argument(s) of method for the `@CachePut` annotation. The following code is the simplest declaration of the `@CachePut` annotation:

```
@CachePut("accountCache ")
public Account save(Account account) {...}
```

In the preceding code, when `save()` is invoked, it saves the `Account`. Then the returned Account is placed in the `accountCache` cache.

As mentioned earlier, the cache is populated by the method based on the argument of the method. It is actually a default cache key. In case of the `@Cachable` annotation, the `findAccount(Long accountId)` method has `accountId` as an argument, the `accountId` is used as the cache key for this method. But in case of the `@CachePut` annotation, the only parameter of `save()` is an Account. It is used as the cache key. It doesn't seem fine to use `Account` as a cache key. In this case, you need the cache key to be the ID of the newly saved Account and not the Account itself. So, you need to customize the key generation behavior. Let's see how you can customize the cache key.

Customizing the cache key

You can customize the cache key by using a key attribute of `@Cacheable` and the `@CachePut` annotation. The cache key is derived by a SpEL expression using properties of the object as highlighted key attribute in the following snippet of code. Let's look at the following examples:

```
@Cacheable(cacheNames=" accountCache ", key="#accountId")
public Account findAccount(Long accountId)

@Cacheable(cacheNames=" accountCache ", key="#account.accountId")
public Account findAccount(Account account)

@CachePut(value=" accountCache ", key="#account.accountId")
Account save(Account account);
```

You can see in the preceding code snippets how we have created the cache key by using the key attribute of the `@Cacheable` annotation.

Let's see another attribute of these annotations in a Spring application.

Conditional caching

Spring's caching annotations allow you to turn off caching for some cases by using the condition attribute of @Cacheable and @CachePut annotations. These are given a SpEL expression to evaluate the conditional value. If the value of the conditional expression is true, the method is cached. If the value of the conditional expression is false, the method is not cached, but is executed every time without performing any caching operations no matter what values in the cache or what arguments are used. Let's see an example. The following method will be cached only if the passed argument has a value greater than or equal to 2000:

```
@Cacheable(cacheNames="accountCache", condition="#accountId >=
2000")
public Account findAccount(Long accountId);
```

There is a one more attribute of the @Cacheable and @CachePut annotations-- unless. This is also given a SpEL expression. This attribute may seem the same as the condition attribute but there is some difference between them. Unlike condition, the unless expressions are evaluated after the method has been called. It prevents the value from being placed in the cache. Let's see the following example--We only want to cache when the bank name does not contain HDFC:

```
@Cacheable(cacheNames="accountCache", condition="#accountId >=
2000", unless="#result.bankName.contains('HDFC')")
public Account findAccount(Long accountId);
```

As you can see in the preceding code snippet, we have used both attributes--condition and unless. But the unless attribute has a SpEL expression as #result.bankName.contains('HDFC'). In this expression, the result is a SpEL extension or cache SpEL metadata. The following is a list of the caching metadata that is available in SpEL:

Expression	Description
#root.methodName	The name of the cached method
#root.method	The cached method, that is, the method being invoked
#root.target	It evaluates the target object being invoked
#root.targetClass	It evaluates the class of the target object being invoked
#root.caches	An array of caches against which the current method is executed
#root.args	An array of the arguments passed into the cached method

`#result`	The return value from the cached method; only available in unless expressions for `@CachePut`

 Spring's `@CachePut` and `@Cacheable` annotations should never be used on the same method, because they have different behaviors. The `@CachePut` annotation forces the execution of the cache method in order to update the caches. But the `@Cacheable` annotation executes the cached method only if the return value of the method is not available on the cache.

You have seen how to add information to the cache by using Spring's `@CachePut` and `@Cacheable` annotations in a Spring application. But how can we remove that information from the cache? Spring's cache abstraction provides another annotation for removing cached data from the cache--the `@CacheEvict` annotation. Let's see how to remove the cached data from the cache by using the `@CacheEvict` annotation.

The @CacheEvict annotation

Spring's cache abstraction not only allows populating caches, but also allows removing the cached data from the cache. There is a stage in the application where you have to remove stale or unused data from the cache. In that case, you can use the `@CacheEvict` annotation, because it doesn't add anything to the cache unlike the `@Cacheable` annotation. The `@CacheEvict` annotation is used only to perform cache eviction. Let's see how this annotation makes the `remove()` method of `AccountRepository` as a cache eviction:

```
@CacheEvict("accountCache ")
void remove(Long accountId);
```

As you can see in the preceding code snippet, the value associated with the argument, `accountId`, is removed from the `accountCache` cache when the `remove()` method is invoked. The following are `@Cacheable` attributes:

- **value**: This is an array of names of the cache to use
- **key**: This is a SpEL expression to evaluate the cache key to be used
- **condition**: This is a SpEL expression to evaluate true or false; if it is false, then the result of caching is not being applied to the method call
- **allEntries**: This implies that if the value of this attribute is true, all entries will be removed from the caches

- **beforeInvocation**: This means that if the value of this attribute is true, the entries are removed from the cache before the method is invoked, and if the value of this attribute is false (the default), the entries are removed after a successful method invocation

> We can use the @CacheEvict annotation on any method, even a void one, because it only removes the value from the cache. But in case of the @Cacheable and @CachePut annotations, we have to use a non-void return value method, because these annotations require a result to be cached.

The @Caching annotation

Spring's cache abstraction allows you to use multiple annotations of the same type for caching a method by using the @Caching annotation in a Spring application. The @Caching annotation groups other annotations such as @Cacheable, @CachePut, and @CacheEvict for the same method. For example:

```
@Caching(evict = {
  @CacheEvict("accountCache "),
  @CacheEvict(value="account-list", key="#account.accountId") })
  public List<Account> findAllAccount(){
  return (List<Account>) accountRepository.findAll();
}
```

The @CacheConfig annotation

Spring's cache abstraction allows you to annotate @CacheConfig at the class level to avoid repeated mentioning in each method. In some cases, applying customizations of the caches to all methods can be quite tedious. Here, you can use the @CacheConfig annotation to all operations of the class. For example:

```
@CacheConfig("accountCache ")
public class AccountServiceImpl implements AccountService {

  @Cacheable
  public Account findAccount(Long accountId) {
    return (Account) accountRepository.findOne(accountId);
  }
}
```

You can see in the preceding code snippet that the `@CacheConfig` annotation is used at the class level, and it allows you to share the `accountCache` cache with all the `cacheable` methods.

 Since Spring's cache abstraction module uses proxies, you should use the cache annotations only with public visibility methods. In all non-public methods, these annotations do not raise any error, but non-public methods annotated with these annotations do not show any caching behaviors.

We have already seen that Spring also offers XML namespace to configure and implement cache in a Spring application. Let's see how in the next section.

Declarative XML-based caching

To keep your configuration codes of caching separate from business codes, and to maintain loose coupling between the Spring-specific annotations and your source code, XML-based caching configuration is much more elegant than the annotation-based one. So, to configure Spring cache with XML, let's use the cache namespace along with the AOP namespace, because caching is an AOP activity, and it uses the Proxy pattern behind the declarative caching behavior.

```xml
<?xml version="1.0" encoding="UTF-8"?>
<beans xmlns="http://www.springframework.org/schema/beans"
 xmlns:xsi="http://www.w3.org/2001/XMLSchema-instance"
 xmlns:context="http://www.springframework.org/schema/context"
 xmlns:aop="http://www.springframework.org/schema/aop"
 xmlns:cache="http://www.springframework.org/schema/cache"
 xsi:schemaLocation="http://www.springframework.org/schema/cache
 http://www.springframework.org/schema/cache/spring-cache-4.3.xsd
 http://www.springframework.org/schema/beans
 http://www.springframework.org/schema/beans/spring-beans.xsd
 http://www.springframework.org/schema/context
 http://www.springframework.org/schema/context/spring-context.xsd
 http://www.springframework.org/schema/aop
 http://www.springframework.org/schema/aop/spring-aop-4.3.xsd">
<!-- Enable caching -->
<cache:annotation-driven />
<!-- Declare a cache manager -->
<bean id="cacheManager"class="org.springframework.cache.
concurrent.ConcurrentMapCacheManager" />
</beans>
```

You can see in the preceding XML file that we have included the cache and aop namespaces. The cache namespace defines the caching configurations by using the following elements:

XML element	Caching Description
`<cache:annotation-driven>`	It is equivalent to @EnableCaching in Java configuration, and is used to enable the caching behavior of Spring.
`<cache:advice>`	It defines caching advice
`<cache:caching>`	It is equivalent to the @Caching annotation, and is used to group a set of caching rules within the caching advice
`<cache:cacheable>`	It is equivalent to the @Cacheable annotation; it makes any method cacheable
`<cache:cache-put>`	It is equivalent to the @CachePut annotation, and is used to populate a cache
`<cache:cache-evict>`	It is equivalent to the @CacheEvict annotation, and is used for cache eviction.

Let's see the following example based on XML-based configuration.

Create a configuration file, spring.xml as follows:

```xml
<?xml version="1.0" encoding="UTF-8"?>
<beans xmlns="http://www.springframework.org/schema/beans"
xmlns:xsi="http://www.w3.org/2001/XMLSchema-instance"
xmlns:context="http://www.springframework.org/schema/context"
xmlns:aop="http://www.springframework.org/schema/aop"
xmlns:cache="http://www.springframework.org/schema/cache"
xsi:schemaLocation="http://www.springframework.org/schema/cache
http://www.springframework.org/schema/cache/spring-cache-4.3.xsd
http://www.springframework.org/schema/beans
http://www.springframework.org/schema/beans/spring-beans.xsd
http://www.springframework.org/schema/context
http://www.springframework.org/schema/context/spring-context.xsd
http://www.springframework.org/schema/aop
http://www.springframework.org/schema/aop/spring-aop-4.3.xsd">
<context:component-scan base-
package="com.packt.patterninspring.chapter9.bankapp.service,
com.packt.patterninspring.chapter9.bankapp.repository"/>

<aop:config>
```

```
    <aop:advisor advice-ref="cacheAccount" pointcut="execution(*
    com.packt.patterninspring.chapter9.bankapp.service.*.*(..))"/>
    </aop:config>
    <cache:advice id="cacheAccount">
      <cache:caching>
        <cache:cacheable cache="accountCache" method="findOne" />
          <cache:cache-put cache="accountCache" method="save"
          key="#result.id" />
          <cache:cache-evict cache="accountCache" method="remove" />
          </cache:caching>
        </cache:advice>

    <!-- Declare a cache manager -->
    <bean id="cacheManager" class="org.springframework.cache.concurrent.
    ConcurrentMapCacheManager" />
    </beans>
```

In the preceding XML configuration file, the highlighted code is the Spring cache configuration. In the cache configuration, the first thing that you see is the declared `<aop:config>` then `<aop:advisor>`, which have references to the advice whose ID is `cacheAccount`, and also has a pointcut expression to match the advice. The advice is declared with the `<cache:advice>` element. This element can have many `<cache:caching>` elements. But, in our example, we have only one `<cache:caching>` element, which has a `<cache:cacheable>` element, a `<cache:cache-put>`, and one `<cache:cache-evict>` element; each declare a method from the pointcut as being cacheable.

Let's see the `Service` class of the application with cache annotations:

```
package com.packt.patterninspring.chapter9.bankapp.service;

import org.springframework.beans.factory.annotation.Autowired;
import org.springframework.cache.annotation.CacheEvict;
import org.springframework.cache.annotation.CachePut;
import org.springframework.cache.annotation.Cacheable;
import org.springframework.stereotype.Service;

import com.packt.patterninspring.chapter9.bankapp.model.Account;
import com.packt.patterninspring.chapter9.
bankapp.repository.AccountRepository;

@Service
public class AccountServiceImpl implements AccountService{
@Autowired
AccountRepository accountRepository;
```

```
@Override
@Cacheable("accountCache")
public Account findOne(Long id) {
   System.out.println("findOne called");
   return accountRepository.findAccountById(id);
}

@Override
@CachePut("accountCache")
public Long save(Account account) {
   return accountRepository.save(account);
}

@Override
@CacheEvict("accountCache")
public void remove(Long id) {
   accountRepository.findAccountById(id);
}
}
```

In the preceding file definition, we have used Spring's cache annotations to create the cache in the application. Now let's see how to configure the cache storage in an application.

Configuring the cache storage

Spring's cache abstraction provides a lot of storage integration. Spring provides `CacheManager` for each memory storage. You can just configure `CacheManager` with the application. Then the `CacheManager` is responsible for controlling and managing the Caches. Let's explore how to set up the `CacheManager` in an application.

Setting up the CacheManager

You must specify a cache manager in the application for storage, and some cache provider given to the `CacheManager`, or you can write your own `CacheManager`. Spring provides several cache managers in the `org.springframework.cache` package, for example, `ConcurrentMapCacheManager`, which creates a `ConcurrentHashMap` for each cache storage unit.

```
@Bean
public CacheManager cacheManager() {
   CacheManager cacheManager = new ConcurrentMapCacheManager();
   return cacheManager;
}
```

`SimpleCacheManager`, `ConcurrentMapCacheManager`, and others are cache managers of the Spring Framework's cache abstraction. But Spring provides support for integration with third-party cache managers, as we will see in the following section.

Third-party cache implementations

Spring's `SimpleCacheManager` is ok for testing, but has no cache control options (overflow, eviction). So we have to use third-party alternatives like the following:

- Terracotta's EhCache
- Google's Guava and Caffeine
- Pivotal's Gemfire

Let's see one of the configurations of third-party cache managers.

Ehcache-based cache

Ehcache is one of the most popular cache providers. Spring allows you to integrate with Ehcache by configuring `EhCacheCacheManager` in the application. Take for example, the following Java configuration:

```
@Bean
public CacheManager cacheManager(CacheManager ehCache) {
   EhCacheCacheManager cmgr = new EhCacheCacheManager();
   cmgr.setCacheManager(ehCache);
   return cmgr;
}
@Bean
public EhCacheManagerFactoryBean ehCacheManagerFactoryBean() {
   EhCacheManagerFactoryBean eh = new EhCacheManagerFactoryBean();
   eh.setConfigLocation(new
   ClassPathResource("resources/ehcache.xml"));
   return eh;
}
```

In the preceding code, the bean method, `cacheManager()`, creates an object of `EhCacheCacheManager`, and set it with the `CacheManager` of Ehcache. Here, Ehcache's `CacheManager` is injected into Spring's `EhCacheCacheManager`. The second bean method, `ehCacheManagerFactoryBean()`, creates and returns an instance of `EhCacheManagerFactoryBean`. Because it's a Factory bean, it will return an instance of `CacheManager`. An XML file, `ehcache.xml`, has the Ehcache configuration. Let's refer to the following code for `ehcache.xml`:

```
<ehcache>
    <cache name="accountCache" maxBytesLocalHeap="50m"
     timeToLiveSeconds="100">
    </cache>
</ehcache>
```

The contents of the `ehcache.xml` file vary from application to application, but you need to declare, at least, a minimal cache. For example, the following Ehcache configuration declares a cache named **accountCache** with 50 MB of maximum heap storage and a time-to-live of 100 seconds:

XML-based configuration

Let's create XML based configuration for the Eache, and it is configuring here `EhCacheCacheManager`. Please refer to the following code:

```
<bean id="cacheManager"
 class="org.springframework.cache.ehcache.EhCacheCacheManager"
 p:cache-manager-ref="ehcache"/>

<!-- EhCache library setup -->
<bean id="ehcache"
  class="org.springframework.cache.ehcache.
  EhCacheManagerFactoryBean" p:config-
  location="resources/ehcache.xml"/>
```

Similarly, in case of the XML configuration, you have to configure the cache manager for ehcache, configure the `EhCacheManagerFactoryBean` class, and set the config-location value with `ehcache.xml`, which has the Ehcache configuration as defined in the previous section.

There are many more third-party caching storages which have integration support with the Spring Framework. In this chapter, I have discussed only the ECache manager.

In the following section, we'll discuss how Spring allows you to create your own custom annotation for caching.

Creating custom caching annotations

Spring's cache abstraction allows you to create custom caching annotations for your application to recognize the cache method for the cache population or cache eviction. Spring's @Cacheable and @CacheEvict annotations are used as Meta annotations to create custom cache annotation. Let's see the following code for custom annotations in an application:

```
@Retention(RetentionPolicy.RUNTIME)
@Target({ElementType.METHOD})
@Cacheable(value="accountCache", key="#account.id")
public @interface SlowService {
}
```

In the preceding code snippet, we have defined a custom annotation named as SlowService, which is annotated with Spring's @Cacheable annotation. If we use @Cacheable in the application, then we have to configure it as the following code:

```
@Cacheable(value="accountCache", key="#account.id")
public Account findAccount(Long accountId)
```

Let's replace the preceding configuration with our defined custom annotation, with the following code:

```
@SlowService
public Account findAccount(Long accountId)
```

As you can see, we use only the @SlowService annotation to make a method cacheable in the application.

Now let's move on to the next section, where we'll see which are the best practices we should consider at the time of cache implementation in anapplication.

Top caching best practices to be used in a web application

In your enterprise web application, proper use of caching enables the web page to be rendered very fast, minimizes the database hits, and reduces the consumption of the server's resources such as memory, network, and so on. Caching is a very powerful technique to boost your application's performance by storing stale data in the cache memory. The following are the best practices which should be considered at the time of design and development of a web application:

- In your Spring web application, Spring's cache annotations such as `@Cacheable`, `@CachePut`, and `@CacheEvict` should be used on concrete classes instead of application interfaces. However, you can annotate the interface method as well, using interface-based proxies. Remember that Java annotations are not inherited from interfaces, which means that if you are using class-based proxies by setting the attribute `proxy-target-class="true"`, then Spring cache annotations are not recognized by the proxying.

- If you have annotated any method with the `@Cacheable`, @CachePut, or `@CacheEvict` annotations, then never call it directly by another method of the same class if you want to benefit from the cache in the application. This is because in direct calling of a cached method, the Spring AOP proxy is never applied.

- In an enterprise application, Java Maps or any key/value collections should never be used as a Cache. Any key/value collection cannot be a Cache. Sometimes, developers use java map as a custom caching solution, but it is not a caching solution, because Cache provides more than a key/value storage, like the following:
  - Cache provides eviction policies
  - You can set the max size limit of Cache
  - Cache provides a persistent store
  - Cache provides weak reference keys
  - Cache provides statistics
    - The Spring Framework provides the best declarative approach to implement and configure the Cache solution in an application. So, always use the cache abstraction layer--it provides flexibility in the application. We know that the `@Cacheable` annotation allows you to separate business logic code from the caching cross-cutting concern.

- Be careful whenever you use cache in the application. Always use cache in a place where it is actually required such as a web service or an expensive database call, because every caching API has an overhead.

- At the time of cache implementation in an application, you have to ensure that the data in the cache is in sync with the data storage. You can use distributed cache managers like Memcached for proper cache strategy implementation to provide considerable performance.

- You should use cache only as second option if data fetching is very difficult from the database because of slow database queries. It is because, whenever we use caching behavior in the application, first the value is checked in the cache if not available then it execute actual method, so it would be unnecessary.

- In this chapter, we saw how caching helps to improve the performance of anapplication. Caching mostly works on the service layer of the application. In your application, there is a data returned by a method; we can cache that data if the application code calls it over and over again from the same requirement. Caching is a great way to avoid execution of the application method for the same requirements. The return value of the method for a specific parameter is stored in a cache whenever this method is invoked for the first time. For further calls of the same method for same parameter, the value is retrieved from that cache. Caching improves application performance by avoiding some resource and time consuming operations for same answers like performing a database query.

Summary

Spring provides Cache Manager to manage caching in a Spring application. In this chapter, you have seen how to define the caching manager for a particular caching technology. Spring provides some annotations for caching such as @Cacheable, @CachePut, and @CacheEvict, which we can use in our Spring application. We can also configure caching in the Spring application by using the XML configuration. Spring framework provides cache namespace to achieve this. The <cache:cacheable>, <cache:cache-put>, and <cache:cache-evict> elements are used instead of the corresponding annotations.

Spring makes it possible to manage caching in anapplication by using Aspect-Oriented Programming. Caching is a cross-cutting concern for the Spring Framework. That means, caching is as an aspect in the Spring application. Spring implements caching by using around advice of the Spring AOP module.

In the next Chapter 10, *Implementing MVC Pattern in a Web Application using Spring*, we will explore how Spring we can use in the web layer and with the MVC pattern.

10
Implementing the MVC Pattern in a Web Application using Spring

In the last couple of chapters in the book, we have seen that all examples were based on a standalone application using the Spring Framework. We have seen how Spring works to provide important features, such as the dependency injection pattern, bean life cycle management, AOP, cache management, and Spring, in the backend using the JDBC and ORM modules. In this chapter, we will see how Spring works in the web environment to address some common problems of any web application, such as workflow, validations, and state management.

Like other modules in the Spring Framework, Spring has introduced its own web framework, known as Spring Web MVC. It is based on the **Model-View-Controller** (**MVC**) pattern. Spring Web MVC supports the presentation tier, and helps you to build a flexible and loosely coupled web-based application. The Spring MVC module addresses the problem of testing the web components in the enterprise application. It allows you to write the test case without using request and response objects in the application. Here, we will discuss more about it.

In this chapter, we will not only discuss the internals of Spring MVC, but also about the different layers of a web application. We will see here the implementation of the MVC pattern including what it is, and why we should use it. We will explore the following topics in this chapter about Spring's MVC web framework:

- Implementing MVC patterns on a web application
- Implementing controllers patterns

- Configuring `DispatcherServlet` as the Front Controller pattern
- Enabling Spring MVC and proxying
- Accepting request parameters
- Processing the forms of a web page
- Implementing a view in the MVC pattern
- Creating JSP views in a web application
- The View Helper pattern
- The Composite View pattern with Apache Tiled ViewResolver

Let's look at all the aforementioned topics in detail.

Implementing the MVC pattern in a web application

The **Model View Controller pattern** (**MVC pattern**) is a J2EE design pattern. It was first introduced by Trygve Reenskaug in his own project to separate the different components of the application. That time, he used this pattern on a desktop-based application. The main approach of this pattern is to promote the separation of concerns principle of the software industry. The MVC pattern divides the system into three kinds of components. Each component in the system has specific responsibilities. Let's see these three components of this pattern:

- **Model**: The model in the MVC pattern is responsible for maintaining data for the view so that it can be rendered in any view template. In short, we can say that the model is a data object, such as a `SavingAccount` in the banking system, and list of accounts of a branch of any bank.
- **View**: The view in the MVC pattern is responsible for rendering the model to itself in a web application for representation of a page. It presents the data of the model in a readable format to the user. There are several technologies that provide the view, such as JSP, JSF page, PDF, XML, and so on.
- **Controller**: This is an actual actionable component in the MVC pattern. In Software, the controller code controls the interaction between the view and model. Interactions such as form submission or clicking a link are part of the controller in an enterprise application. The controller is also responsible for creating and updating the model, and forwarding this model to the view for rendering.

Take a look at the following diagram to understand more about the MVC pattern:

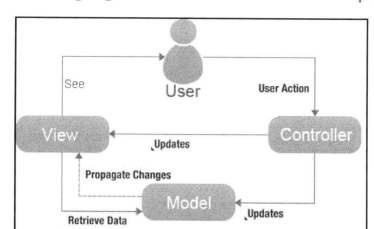

As you can see in the preceding diagram, there are three components in an application, and each component has its own responsibility. As we've already said, the MVC pattern is all about separation of concerns. In a software system, separation of concerns is very important to make the components flexible and easy to test with a clean code structure. In the MVC pattern, the **User** interacts with the **Controller** component through the **View** component, and the **Controller** component triggers the actual action to prepare the **Model** component. That **Model** component propagates the changes to the **View**, and finally, the **View** component renders the model in front of the **User**. This is the whole idea behind the implementation of the MVC pattern. This approach of MVC pattern properly fits most of the applications, especially, desktop applications. This MVC pattern is also known as Model 1 architecture.

But in case you are working with an enterprise web application, things will be slightly different from a desktop application, because keeping a model across the request life cycle can be quite difficult due to the stateless nature of an HTTP protocol. Let's see another modified version of the MVC pattern in the following section, and how the Spring framework adopts it to create the enterprise web application.

Model 2 architecture MVC pattern with Spring

The Model 1 architecture is not very straightforward for a web application. Model 1 also has decentralized navigation control, because in this architecture, each user contains a separate controller and also different logic to determine the next page. That time for web application, Model 1 architecture has Servlet and JSP as the main technologies to develop the web applications.

For a web application, the MVC pattern is implemented as a Model 2 architecture. This pattern provides centralized navigation control logics to easily test and maintain the web application, and it also provides better separation of concerns than Model 1 architecture for web applications. The difference between the MVC pattern based on Model 1 Architecture and the modified MVC pattern based on Model 2 architecture is that the latter incorporates a front controller that dispatches all incoming requests to other controllers. These controllers handle the incoming request, return the model, and select the view. take a look at the following diagram to better understand the Model 2 architecture MVC pattern:

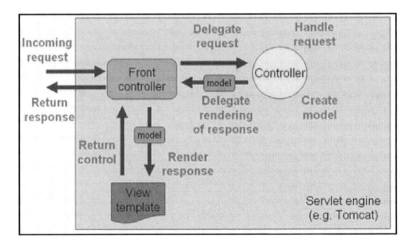

As you can see in the preceding diagram, a new component is introduced for the MVC pattern, that is, the front controller. It is implemented as a `javax.servlet.Servlet` servlet such as `ActionServlet` in struts, `FacesServlet` in JSF, and `DispatcherServlet` in Spring MVC. It handles the incoming requests, and delegates the requests to the specific application controller. That application controller creates and updates the model, and delegates it to the front controller for rendering. Finally, the **Front Controller** determines the specific view, and renders that model data.

The Front Controller design pattern

The Front Controller design pattern is a J2EE pattern; it provides solutions for the following application design problems:

- In a web application based on the Model 1 architecture, too many controllers are required to handle too many requests. It is difficult to maintain and reuse them.
- Each request has its own point of entry in the web application; it should be a single point of entry for each request.
- JSP and Servlet are the main components of the Model 1 MVC pattern, so, these components handle both action and view, violating the *Single Responsibility* principle.

The Front Controller provides the solution to the aforementioned design problems of the web application. In a web application, it works as the main component which routes all requests into framework control. This means that too many requests land on a single controller (Front Controller), and then, these requests are delegated to the specific controllers. Front Controller provides centralized control, and improves the reusability and manageability, because, typically, only the resource is registered with the web container. This controller not only handles too many requests, but also has following responsibilities:

- It initializes the framework to cater to the requests
- It loads the map of all URLs and the components responsible for handling the request
- It prepares the map for the views

Let's see the following diagram for **Front Controller**:

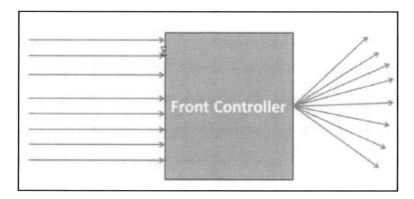

As you can see in the preceding diagram, all application requests land at the **Front Controller**, and it delegates these requests to the configured application controllers.

The Spring Framework provides a module based on the MVC pattern, that is, Model 2 architecture implementation. The Spring MVC module provides out-of-the-box front controller pattern implementation by introducing the `org.springframework.web.servlet.DispatcherServlet` class. This is a simple `servlet` class, and the backbone of the Spring MVC framework. And this Servlet is integrated with the Spring IoC container to benefit the Spring's dependency pattern. Spring's web framework uses Spring for its own configuration, and all controllers are Spring beans; these controllers are testable artifacts.

Let's dive into the internals of Spring MVC in this Chapter, and have a closer look at `org.springframework.web.servlet.DispatcherServlet` in the Spring MVC framework, and how it handles all incoming requests to the web application.

Processing the life of a request

Have you ever played a *wooden labyrinth board game, a maze puzzle with a steel ball bearing*? You might have played it in your childhood. It was a very crazy game. The goal of this game is to send all the steel ball bearings to the center of the wooden labyrinth board through interlinked curvy paths, and these curvy paths have cuts leading to a second curve near the center. All the balls need to navigate to the center of the wooden labyrinth board through these cuts between the curvy paths. If one steel ball reaches the center, then we have to be careful about this ball so that it does not move away from the center when trying to move another ball to the center. You can see this in the following diagram:

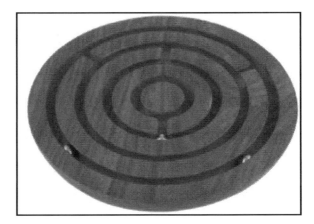

The Spring MVC framework is similar to this Wooden Labyrinth board game at first glance. Instead of the moving the steel ball bearings through various curvy paths and cuts, the Spring MVC framework moves web application requests through various components such as the Front Controller, that is, the dispatcher Servlet, handler mappings, controllers, and view resolvers.

Let's see the request processing flow in the Spring MVC Framework for a web application. The request processing workflow of the Spring Web MVC `DispatcherServlet` is illustrated in the following diagram:

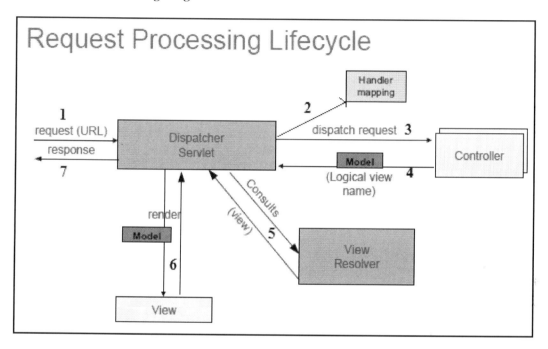

As you already know, the front controller plays a very important role in the Model 2 MVC pattern, because it has the responsibility to handle all incoming requests to the web application, and prepare the response to the browser. In the Spring MVC framework, `org.springframework.web.servlet.DispatcherServlet` plays the role of the Front Controller of the Model 2 MVC pattern. As you can see in the last diagram, this `DispatcherServlet` uses many other components to fulfill its own role. Let's see the step-by-step request processing in the Spring MVC framework:

1. A user clicks on the browser or submits a web form of the application. The request leaves the browser, either with some additional information or with common information. This request lands at Spring's `DispatcherServlet`, which is a simple `servlet` class as other java-based web applications. It is a Front Controller of the Spring MVC framework, and funnels all the incoming requests through the single point. The Spring MVC framework centralizes the request flow control by using this Front Controller.

2. After landing a request at Spring's `DispatcherServlet`, it delegates that request to the Spring MVC controller, that is, application controller. Although, , there may be several controllers in a Spring web application, but each request must be delegated to the specific controller. For that, Spring's `DispatcherServlet` takes help of the handler mappings configured in the web application. Handler mapping decides the particular controller by using the URL and request parameters.

3. Once a particular application controller is decided by Spring's `DispatcherServlet` with the help of the handler mapping configuration, `DispatcherServlet` dispatches that request to the selected controller. This is the actual controller responsible for processing information according to the user's request and its parameters.

4. Spring MVC's controller executes the business logic by using business services of the application, and it creates the model which wraps the information to be carried back to the user, and is displayed in the browser. This model carries information according to the user's request. But this model is not formatted, and we can use any view template technology to render the model information in the browser. That is why Spring MVC's controller also returns a logic view name along with the model. Why does it return a logic view name? This is because Spring MVC's controller is not tied to any specific view technology such as JSP, JSF, Thymeleaf, and so on.

5. Once again, Spring MVC's `DispatcherServlet` takes the help of the view resolver; it is configured in the web application to resolve the view. According to the configured `ViewResolver`, it resolves the actual view name instead of the logic view name. Now `DispatcherServlet` has the view as well to render the model information.

6. Spring MVC's `DispatcherServlet` renders the model to the view, and generates a user-readable format of the model's information.

7. Finally, that information creates a response, and returns it to the user's browser by `DispatcherServlet`.

As you can see, there are several steps and components involved in serving a request of the application. Most of these components are related to the Spring MVC framework, and these components have their own specific responsibility to serve a request.

Till now, you have learned that `DispatcherServlet` is a key component in processing requests with Spring MVC. It is the heart of the Spring Web MVC. It is a front controller that coordinates all request handling activities analogous to Struts `ActionServlet` / JSF `FacesServlet`. It delegates to the web infrastructure beans, and invokes user web components. It is also highly flexible, configurable, and fully customizable. It is very flexible, because all the components used by this servlet are interfaces for all the infrastructure beans. The following table lists some of the involved interfaces provided by the Spring MVC Framework:

Spring MVC Component	Role in request processing
`org.springframework.web.multipart.MultipartResolver`	It handles multipart requests such as file uploads
`org.springframework.web.servlet.LocaleResolver`	It handles locale resolution and modification
`org.springframework.web.servlet.ThemeResolver`	It handles theming resolution and modification

org.springframework.web.servlet.HandlerMapping	It maps all incoming requests to the handler objects.
org.springframework.web.servlet.HandlerAdapter	It is based on the Adapter pattern, and is used for the handler object type to execute the handler
org.springframework.web.servlet.HandlerExceptionResolver	It handles the exceptions thrown during handler execution
org.springframework.web.servlet.ViewResolver	It translates the logical view name to an actual view implementation

The components listed in the preceding table work on the Spring MVC Framework for the request processing life cycle in a web application. In the upcoming section, we'll see how to configure the Spring MVC's main component, that is, DispatcherServlet. We'll also take a closer look at the different ways of implementation and configuration based on either Java or XML.

Configuring DispatcherServlet as the Front Controller

In a Java-based web application, all servlets are defined in the `web.xml` file. It is loaded in a web container at the bootstrap, and maps each servlet to a particular URL pattern. Similarly, the `org.springframework.web.servlet.DispatcherServlet` is the centerpiece of the Spring MVC; it needs to be configured in the same file--`web.xml`, and it is loaded at the bootstrap of the web application. At the time of bootstrapping, `DispatcherServlet` is invoked to create Spring's `org.springframework.web.context.WebApplicationContext` by loading the beans' configuration through Java, XML, or annotation-based. The servlet tries to fetch all the required components from this web application context. It has the responsibility to route the request through all the other components.

 WebApplicationContext is a web version of the `ApplicationContext`, as discussed in previous chapters of this book. It has some additional capabilities necessary for web applications other than the `ApplicationContext`, such as servlet-specific scope request, session, and so on. The `WebApplicationContext` is bound in the `ServletContext`; you can also access it by using the static method of the `RequestContextUtils` class. Let's see the following code snippet for this:
`ApplicationContext webApplicationContext =`
`RequestContextUtils.findWebApplicationContext(request);`

Defined by XML configuration

As you know, `web.xml` is the root file of any web application, placed in the `WEB-INF` directory. It has a servlet specification, and contains all the servlet configuration to be bootstrapped. Let's see the required code of the `DispatcherServlet` configuration in the web application, which is as follows:

```
<web-app version="3.0"
xmlns="http://java.sun.com/xml/ns/javaee"
xmlns:xsi="http://www.w3.org/2001/XMLSchema-instance"
xsi:schemaLocation=http://java.sun.com/xml/ns/javaee
http://java.sun.com/xml/ns/javaee/web-app_3_0.xsd
metadata-complete="true">
  <servlet>
      <servlet-name>bankapp</servlet-name>
      <servlet-
class>org.springframework.web.servlet.DispatcherServlet</servlet-class>
      <load-on-startup>1</load-on-startup>
  </servlet>
  <servlet-mapping>
```

```
        <servlet-name>bankapp</servlet-name>
        <url-pattern>/*</url-pattern>
    </servlet-mapping>
</web-app>
```

The preceding code is the minimum required code to configure the `DispatcherServlet` in a Spring web application using XML-based configuration.

 There is nothing is special in the `web.xml` file; typically, it defines only one servlet configuration very similar to the traditional Java web application. But DispatcherServlet loads a file which contains the spring beans configuration for the application. By default, it loads a file named `[servletname]-servlet.xml` from the WEB-INF directory. In our case, the file name should be `bankapp-servlet.xml` in the WEB-INF directory.

Defined by Java configuration

In this chapter, instead of the XML configuration, we will use Java to configure `DispatcherServlet` in the servlet container for our web application. Servlet 3.0 and later supports java-based bootstrapping, so, we can avoid using the web.xml file. Instead of this, we can create a java class that implements the `javax.servlet.ServletContainerInitializer` interface. Spring MVC provides the `WebApplicationInitializer` interface to ensure that your spring configuration is loaded and initialized in any Servlet 3 container. But the Spring MVC framework makes it even easier by providing an abstract class implementation of the `WebApplicationInitializer` interface. By using this abstract class, you just map your servlet mapping, and provide the root and MVC configuration classes. I, personally, prefer this way of configuration in my web application. The following is the code for this configuration class:

```
package com.packt.patterninspring.chapter10.bankapp.web;

import
org.springframework.web.servlet.support.AbstractAnnotationConfigDispatcherS
ervletInitializer;

import com.packt.patterninspring.chapter10.bankapp.config.AppConfig;
import
com.packt.patterninspring.chapter10.bankapp.web.mvc.SpringMvcConfig;

public class SpringApplicationInitializer extends
AbstractAnnotationConfigDispatcherServletInitializer
{
  // Tell Spring what to use for the Root context: as ApplicationContext
```

```
-  "Root" configuration
      @Override
      protected Class<?>[] getRootConfigClasses() {
          return new Class <?>[]{AppConfig.class};
      }
      // Tell Spring what to use for the DispatcherServlet context:
WebApplicationContext- MVC
      configuration
      @Override
      protected Class<?>[] getServletConfigClasses() {
          return new Class <?>[]{SpringMvcConfig.class};
      }
      // DispatcherServlet mapping, this method responsible for URL pattern
as like in web.xml file
      <url-pattern>/</url-pattern>
      @Override
      protected String[] getServletMappings() {
          return new String[]{"/"};
      }
    }
```

As seen in the preceding code, the `SpringApplicationInitializer` class extends the `AbstractAnnotationConfigDispatcherServletInitializer` class. It asks only the required information from the developer, and all configurations related to the `DispatcherServlet` are configured by this class using the servlet container interfaces. Take a look at the following diagram to understand more about the `AbstractAnnotationConfigDispatcherServletInitializer` class and its implementation to configure the `DispatcherServlet` in the application:

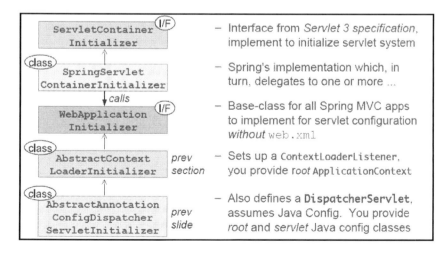

You have seen that the `SpringApplicationInitilizer` class overrides three methods of the `AbstractAnnotationConfigDispatcherServletInitializer` class, that is, `getServletMappings()`, `getServletConfigClasses()`, and `getRootConfigClasses()`. The method `getServletMappings()` defines the servlet mapping-in our application, it's mapped to "/". The method `getServletConfigClasses()` asks `DispatcherServlet` to load its application context with the beans defined in the `SpringMvcConfig` configuration class. This configuration file has bean definitions related to the web components such as controllers, view resolvers, and handler mappings. A Spring web application has another application context, and it is created by `ContextLoaderListener`. So, another method, `getRootConfigClasses()`, loads the other beans such as services, repositories, data-source, and other application beans typically required in the middle-tier and data-tier of the application defined in the `AppConfig` configuration class.

> The Spring Framework provides a listener class--`ContextLoaderListener`. It is responsible for bootstrapping the backend application context.

Let's see the following diagram to understand more about the Spring web application design after starting up the servlet container:

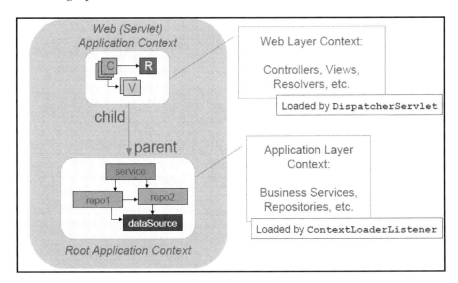

As you can see in the last diagram, the web component beans definitions configuration classes returned by the `getServletConfigClasses()` method are loaded by the `DispatcherServlet`, and the other application beans definition configuration classes returned by the `getRootConfigClasses()` method are loaded by the `ContextLoaderListener`.

 A Java-based web configuration will only work when deploying to a server that supports **Servlet 3.0**, such as **Apache Tomcat 7 or higher.**

Let's see how to enable more features of the Spring MVC Framework in the coming section.

Enabling the Spring MVC

There are many ways to configure the `DispatcherServlet` and other web components. There are many features of the Spring MVC framework which are not enabled by default, such as `HttpMessageConverter`, Support for validating `@Controller` inputs with `@Valid`, and so on. So, we can enable these features by using either a Java-based configuration or XML configuration.

To enable the MVC Java config, add the annotation `@EnableWebMvc` to one of your `@Configuration` classes, as follows:

```
import org.springframework.context.annotation.Configuration;
import org.springframework.web.servlet.config.annotation.EnableWebMvc;
@Configuration
@EnableWebMvc
public class SpringMvcConfig {
}
```

In XML configuration, we can use MVC namespace, there is an `<mvc:annotation-driven>` element that you can use to enable the annotation-driven Spring MVC.

```
<?xml version="1.0" encoding="UTF-8"?>
<beans xmlns="http://www.springframework.org/schema/beans"
xmlns:mvc="http://www.springframework.org/schema/mvc"
xmlns:xsi="http://www.w3.org/2001/XMLSchema-instance"
xsi:schemaLocation="
    http://www.springframework.org/schema/beans
    http://www.springframework.org/schema/beans/spring-beans.xsd
    http://www.springframework.org/schema/mvc
    http://www.springframework.org/schema/mvc/spring-mvc.xsd">
```

```
<mvc:annotation-driven/>

</beans>
```

The Spring MVC advanced feature can be enabled in a Spring web application either by using the @EnableWebMvc annotation, or by using the XML namespace <mvc:annotation-driven/>. The Spring MVC Framework also allows you to customize the default configuration in Java by extending the WebMvcConfigurerAdapter class, or by implementing the WebMvcConfigurer interface. Let's see the modified configuration file after adding a bit more configuration:

```java
package com.packt.patterninspring.chapter10.bankapp.web.mvc;

import org.springframework.context.annotation.Bean;
import org.springframework.context.annotation.ComponentScan;
import org.springframework.context.annotation.Configuration;
import org.springframework.web.servlet.ViewResolver;
import
org.springframework.web.servlet.config.annotation.DefaultServletHandlerConfigurer;
import org.springframework.web.servlet.config.annotation.EnableWebMvc;
import
org.springframework.web.servlet.config.annotation.WebMvcConfigurerAdapter;
import
org.springframework.web.servlet.view.InternalResourceViewResolver;

@Configuration
@ComponentScan(basePackages = {"
com.packt.patterninspring.chapter10.bankapp.web.controller"})
@EnableWebMvc
public class SpringMvcConfig extends WebMvcConfigurerAdapter{
@Bean
public ViewResolver viewResolver(){
    InternalResourceViewResolver viewResolver = new
InternalResourceViewResolver();
    viewResolver.setPrefix("/WEB-INF/view/");
    viewResolver.setSuffix(".jsp");
    return viewResolver;
}
@Override
public void
configureDefaultServletHandling(DefaultServletHandlerConfigurer configurer)
{
    configurer.enable();
}
}
```

As seen in the preceding code, the configuration class `SpringMvcConfig` is annotated with `@Configuration`, `@ComponentScan`, and `@EnableWebMvc`. Here, the `com.packt.patterninspring.chapter10.bankapp.web.controller` package will be scanned for components. This class extends the `WebMvcConfigurerAdapter` class, and overrides the `configureDefaultServletHandling()` method. We have also configured a `ViewResolver` bean.

Till now, you have learned what is the MVC pattern and architecture, and how to set up `DispatcherServlet` and enable the essential Spring MVC components for a Spring web application. In the upcoming section, we'll discuss how to implement controllers in a Spring application, and how these controllers handle web requests.

Implementing controllers

As we have seen in the MVC pattern, controllers are also one of the crucial components of the MVC pattern. They are responsible for executing the actual request, preparing the model, and sending this model along with logical view name to the front controller. In a web application, the controllers work between the web layer and the core application layer. In the Spring MVC framework, controllers are also more like POJO classes with methods; these methods are known as handlers, because these are annotated with the `@RequestMapping` annotation. Let's see how to define controller classes in a Spring web application.

Defining a controller with @Controller

Let's create a controller class for our bank application. `HomeController` is a controller class that handles requests for / and renders the homepage of the bank application:

```
package com.packt.patterninspring.chapter10.bankapp.web.controller;

import org.springframework.stereotype.Controller;
import org.springframework.web.bind.annotation.RequestMapping;
import org.springframework.web.bind.annotation.RequestMethod;

@Controller
public class HomeController {
  @RequestMapping(value = "/", method = RequestMethod.GET)
  public String home (){
     return "home";
  }
}
```

As you can see in the preceding code, the `HomeController` class contains the `home()` method. It is a handler method, because it is annotated with the `@RequestMapping` annotation. It specifies that this method handles all the requests that are mapped to the `/` URL. Another thing to notice is that our controller class, `HomeController`, is also annotated with the `@Controller` annotation. As we know, `@Controller` is a stereotype annotation, and it is also used to create the bean in the Spring IoC container similar to the other Meta annotations of the `@Component` annotation such as `@Service` and `@Repository`. Yes, this annotation specifies any class as the controller, and adds some more capability of Spring MVC to that class. You could also use the `@Component` annotation instead of `@Controller` to create Spring beans in a web application, but in this case, that bean does not have the capability of the Spring MVC framework such as exception handling at web layer, handler mapping, and so on.

Let's take a closer look at the `@RequestMapping` annotation, and also the composed variants of the `@RequestMapping` annotation.

Mapping requests with @RequestMapping

The previously defined `HomeController` class has only one handler method, and this method is annotated with the `@RequestMapping` annotation. Here, I have used two attributes of this annotation--one is value to map the HTTP request to the `/` pattern, and the other attribute is a method for supporting the HTTP GET method. We can define multiple URL mappings with one handler method. Let's see this in the following code snippet:

```
@Controller
public class HomeController {
 @RequestMapping(value = {"/", "/index"}, method = RequestMethod.GET)
 public String home (){
     return "home";
 }
}
```

In the preceding code, the `@RequestMapping` annotation has an array of string values for the value attribute of this annotation. Now, this handler method is mapped with two URL patterns, such as / and /index. The Spring MVC's `@RequestMapping` annotation supports several HTTP methods such as GET, POST, PUT, DELETE, and so on. As of version 4.3, Spring composed `@RequestMapping` variants, and now provides simple methods for the mapping of common HTTP methods, as shown in the following expressions:

```
@RequestMapping + HTTP GET = @GetMapping
@RequestMapping + HTTP POST = @PostMapping
@RequestMapping + HTTP PUT = @PutMapping
@RequestMapping + HTTP DELETE = @DeleteMapping
```

This is the modified version of `HomeController` with composed annotation mappings:

```
@Controller
public class HomeController {
  @GetMapping(value = {"/", "/index"})
  public String home (){
     return "home";
  }
}
```

We can use the `@RequestMapping` annotation at both locations: at the class level, and at the method level. Let's see examples for this:

@RequestMapping at method level

Spring MVC allows you to use the `@RequestMapping` annotation at the method level to make this method as handler method in the Spring web application. Let's see how to use it in the following class:

```
package com.packt.patterninspring.
   chapter10.bankapp.web.controller;
import org.springframework.stereotype.Controller;
import org.springframework.ui.ModelMap;
import org.springframework.web.bind.annotation.RequestMapping;
import org.springframework.web.bind.annotation.RequestMethod;

import com.packt.patterninspring.chapter10.bankapp.model.User;

@Controller
public class HomeController {
 @RequestMapping(value = "/", method = RequestMethod.GET)
 public String home (){
     return "home";
```

```
    }
    @RequestMapping(value = "/create", method = RequestMethod.GET)
    public String create (){
        return "addUser";
    }
    @RequestMapping(value = "/create", method = RequestMethod.POST)
    public String saveUser (User user, ModelMap model){
        model.put("user", user);
        return "addUser";
    }
}
```

As you can see in the preceding code, I have used the `@RequestMapping` annotation with three methods `home()`, `create()`, and `saveUser()`. Here I have also used the attributes "value" and "method" of this annotation. The "value" attribute has the request mapping with request URL and "method" attribute is used to define the HTTP request methods such GET or POST. Mapping rules are, typically, URL-based, and, optionally, use wild cards, as shown here:

```
- /create
- /create/account
- /edit/account
- /listAccounts.htm - Suffix ignored by default.
- /accounts/*
```

In the preceding example, the handler methods have some arguments as well, so we can pass any number of arguments of any type. The Spring MVC will handle these arguments as request parameters. Let's see first how to define `@RequestMapping` at the class level, then we will discuss the request parameters.

@RequestMapping at the class level

The Spring MVC allows you to use the `@RequestMapping` annotation at the class level. This means we can annotate the controller class with `@RequestMapping`, as shown in the following code snippet:

```
package com.packt.patterninspring.chapter10.bankapp.web.controller;

import org.springframework.stereotype.Controller;
import org.springframework.ui.ModelMap;
import org.springframework.web.bind.annotation.RequestMapping;
import org.springframework.web.bind.annotation.RequestMethod;

@Controller
@RequestMapping("/")
```

```
public class HomeController {
  @RequestMapping(method=GET)
  public String home() {
      return "home";
  }
}
```

As you have seen in the preceding code, the `HomeController` class is annotated with the `@RequestMapping` and `@Controller` annotations. But the HTTP method is still defined above the handler methods. Class-level mapping is applied with all the handler methods defined under this controller.

After the Spring MVC configuration, we created a controller class with the handler methods. Let's test this controller before moving ahead with more details. In this book, I haven't use any JUnit test cases, so here, I will just run this web application on the Tomcat container. You can see the output on the browser as follows:

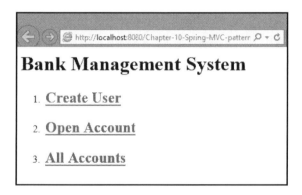

The last image is the homepage of our **Bank Management System** web application.

Before Spring 3.1, the Spring MVC mapped the requests to handler methods using two steps. First, the controller was selected by `DefaultAnnotationHandlerMapping`, and then, the actual method was mapped with the incoming requests by the `AnnotationMethodHandlerAdapter`. But as of Spring 3.1, Spring MVC maps the requests, in one step, directly to the handler methods by using `RequestMappingHandlerMapping`.

In the next section, we'll see how to define the handler methods, and the return type and parameters allowed for the handler methods in Spring MVC.

Defining @RequestMapping handler methods

In the Spring MVC Framework, the `@RequestMapping` handler methods are very flexible in defining signatures. You can pass any number of arguments in any order. These methods support most type of arguments, and are also very flexible in the return type as well. It can have several return types, some of which are listed next:

- Supported method argument types
    - Request or response objects (Servlet API)
    - Session object (Servlet API)
    - `java.util.Locale`
    - `java.util.TimeZone`
    - `java.io.InputStream` / `java.io.Reader`
    - `java.io.OutputStream` / `java.io.Writer`
    - `java.security.Principal`
    - `@PathVariable`
    - `@RequestParam`
    - `@RequestBody`
    - `@RequestPart`
    - `java.util.Map` / `org.springframework.ui.Model` / `org.springframework.ui.ModelMap`
    - `org.springframework.validation.Errors` / `org.springframework.validation.BindingResult`
- Supported method return types:
    - `ModelAndView`
    - `Model`
    - `Map`
    - `View`
    - `String`
    - `void`
    - `HttpEntity<?>` or `ResponseEntity<?>`
    - `HttpHeaders`
    - `Callable<?>`
    - `DeferredResult<?>`

I have listed some of the supported return types and method argument types. It seems that Spring MVC is very flexible and customizable in the nature of defining the request handler methods unlike other MVC frameworks.

In the Spring MVC framework, even the handler method can have any ordering of the arguments, but in case of Errors or `BindingResult` parameters, we have to put these parameters first, followed by the model object for being bound immediately, because the handler method might have any number of model objects, and Spring MVC creates separate instances of the Errors or `BindingResult` for each of them. For example:

Invalid location

```
@PostMapping
public String saveUser(@ModelAttribute ("user") User
user, ModelMap model, BindingResult result){...}
```

Valid location

```
@PostMapping
public String saveUser(@ModelAttribute ("user") User
user, BindingResult result, ModelMap model){...}
```

Let's see how to pass model data to the view layer in the upcoming section.

Passing model data to the view

As of now, we have implemented a very simple `HomeCotroller`, and tested it. But in the web application, we have also passed model data to the view layer. That model data we passed in the model (in a simple word, it is `Map`), and that model is returned by the controller along with logical view name. As you already know, Spring MVC supports several return types of the handler method. Let's see the following example:

```
package com.packt.patterninspring.chapter10.bankapp.web.controller;

import java.util.List;

import org.springframework.beans.factory.annotation.Autowired;
import org.springframework.stereotype.Controller;
import org.springframework.ui.ModelMap;
import org.springframework.web.bind.annotation.GetMapping;
import org.springframework.web.bind.annotation.PostMapping;
```

```
   import com.packt.patterninspring.chapter10.bankapp.model.Account;
   import
com.packt.patterninspring.chapter10.bankapp.service.AccountService;

   @Controller
   public class AccountController {
    @Autowired
    AccountService accountService;
    @GetMapping(value = "/open-account")
    public String openAccountForm (){
        return "account";
    }
    @PostMapping(value = "/open-account")
    public String save (Account account, ModelMap model){
        account = accountService.open(account);
        model.put("account", account);
        return "accountDetails";
    }
    @GetMapping(value = "/all-accounts")
    public String all (ModelMap model){
        List<Account> accounts = accountService.findAllAccounts();
        model.put("accounts", accounts);
        return "accounts";
    }
   }
```

As you can see in the preceding example, the `AccountController` class has three handler methods. Two handler methods return the model data along with the logical view name. But in this example, I am using Spring MVC's `ModelMap`, so, we don't need to forcefully return as logical view, it binds automatically with the response.

Next you'll learn how to accept request parameters.

Accepting request parameters

In a Spring web application, sometimes, we just read the data from the server side like in our example. Reading data for all the accounts was a simple read call, and no request parameter was required. But in case you want to fetch data for a particular account, then you have to pass the account ID with the request parameters. Similarly, for creating a new Account in the bank, you have to pass an account object as a parameter. In Spring MVC, we can accept the request parameters in the following ways:

* Taking query parameters

- Taking request parameters via path variables
- Taking form parameters

Let's look at each of these ways one by one.

Taking query parameters

In a web application, we can fetch the request parameters from the request-the account ID in our example if you want to access the details of a particular account. Let's fetch the account ID from the request parameter using the following code:

```
@Controller
public class AccountController {
  @GetMapping(value = "/account")
  public String getAccountDetails (ModelMap model, HttpServletRequest
request){
      String accountId = request.getParameter("accountId");
      Account account = accountService.findOne(Long.valueOf(accountId));
      model.put("account", account);
      return "accountDetails";
  }
}
```

In the preceding code snippet, I have used the traditional way to access the request parameters. The Spring MVC framework provides an annotation, @RequestParam, to access the request parameters. Let's use the @RequestParam annotation to bind the request parameters to a method parameter in your controller. The following code snippet shows the usage of the @RequestParam annotation. It extracts the parameter from the request, and performs type conversion as well:

```
@Controller
public class AccountController {
  @GetMapping(value = "/account")
  public String getAccountDetails (ModelMap model,
@RequestParam("accountId") long accountId){
      Account account = accountService.findOne(accountId);
      model.put("account", account);
      return "accountDetails ";
  }
}
```

In the preceding code, we access the request parameter by using the `@RequestParam` annotation, and you can also notice that I didn't use the type conversion from `String` to `Long`, it will be done automatically by this annotation. One more thing to note here is that parameters using this annotation are required by default, but Spring allows you to override this behavior by using the `required` attribute of the `@RequestParam` annotation.

```
@Controller
public class AccountController {
  @GetMapping(value = "/account")
  public String getAccountDetails (ModelMap model,
    @RequestParam(name = "accountId") long accountId
    @RequestParam(name = "name", required=false) String name){
    Account account = accountService.findOne(accountId);
    model.put("account", account);
    return " accountDetails ";
  }
}
```

Now let's see how to use path variables to take input as part of the request path.

Taking request parameters via path variables

Spring MVC allows you to pass parameters in the URI instead of passing them through request parameters. The passed values can be extracted from the request URLs. It is based on URI templates. It is not a Spring-specific concept, and is used in many frameworks by using {...} placeholders and the `@PathVariable` annotation. It allows clean URLs without request parameters. The following is an example:

```
@Controller
public class AccountController {
  @GetMapping("/accounts/{accountId}")
  public String show(@PathVariable("accountId") long accountId, Model
model) {
    Account account = accountService.findOne(accountId);
    model.put("account", account);
    return "accountDetails";
  }
  ...
}
```

In the previous handler, the method can handle the request like this:

```
http://localhost:8080/Chapter-10-Spring-MVC-pattern/account?accountId=1000
```

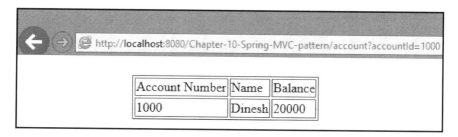

But in the preceding example, the handler method can handle the request such as:

```
http://localhost:8080/Chapter-10-Spring-MVC-pattern/accounts/2000
```

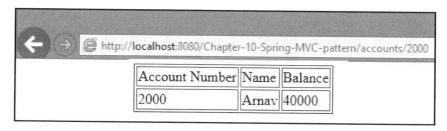

We have seen in the preceding code and images how to pass a value either by using request parameters or using path parameters. Both ways are fine if you are passing small amounts of data on a request. But in some cases, we have to pass a lot of data to the server, such as form submission. Let's see how to write controller methods that handle form submissions.

Processing forms of a web page

As you know, in any web application, we can send and receive data from the server. In a web application, we send the data by filling out forms, and submitting this form to the server. Spring MVC also provides support for form handling of the client end by displaying the form, validating the form data, and submitting this form data.

Basically, Spring MVC handles the form displaying and form processing first. In the Bank management application, you will need to create a new user, and open a new account in the bank, so, let's create a controller class, AccountController, with a single request-handling method for displaying the account open form, as follows:

```
package com.packt.patterninspring.chapter10.bankapp.web.controller;

import org.springframework.stereotype.Controller;
import org.springframework.web.bind.annotation.GetMapping;
```

```
@Controller
public class AccountController {
 @GetMapping(value = "/open-account")
 public String openAccountForm (){
     return "accountForm";
 }
}
```

The `openAccountForm()` method's `@GetMapping` annotation declares that it will handle the HTTP GET requests for /open-account. It's a simple method, taking no input and only returning a logical view named `accountForm`. We have configured `InternalResourceViewResolver`, which means that the JSP at `/WEB-INF/views/accountForm.jsp` will be called on to render the open account form.

Here's the JSP you'll use for now:

```jsp
<%@ taglib prefix = "c" uri = "http://java.sun.com/jsp/jstl/core" %>
<html>
 <head>
     <title>Bank Management System</title>
     <link rel="stylesheet" type="text/css" href="<c:url
value="/resources/style.css" />" >
 </head>
 <body>
     <h1>Open Account Form</h1>
      <form method="post">
      Account Number:<br>
      <input type="text" name="id"><br>
      Account Name:<br>
      <input type="text" name="name"><br>
      Initial Balance:<br>
      <input type="text" name="balance"><br>
      <br>
      <input type="submit" value="Open Account">
      </form>
 </body>
</html>
```

As you can see in the preceding code, we have an open account form. It has some fields such as `AccountId`, `Account Name`, and `Initial Balance`. This JSP page has the `<form>` tag for the form, and this `<form>` tag doesn't have any action parameter. This means that when we submit this form, it will post the form data to the same URI `/open-account` with the `POST` HTTP method call. The following screenshot displays the account form:

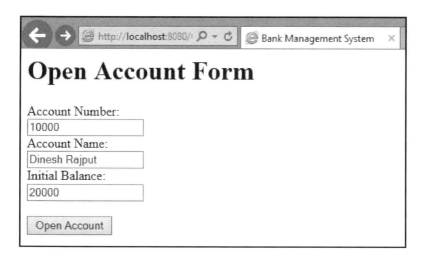

Let's add another method to handle the call for the HTTP POST method with the same URI, /open-account.

Implementing a form handling controller

Let's see the same AccountController class by adding another handler method to handle the HTTP POST request for the URI /open-account in the web application:

```
package com.packt.patterninspring.chapter10.bankapp.web.controller;

import java.util.List;

import org.springframework.beans.factory.annotation.Autowired;
import org.springframework.stereotype.Controller;
import org.springframework.ui.ModelMap;
import org.springframework.web.bind.annotation.GetMapping;
import org.springframework.web.bind.annotation.PathVariable;
import org.springframework.web.bind.annotation.PostMapping;

import com.packt.patterninspring.chapter10.bankapp.model.Account;
import
com.packt.patterninspring.chapter10.bankapp.service.AccountService;

@Controller
 public class AccountController {
    @Autowired
    AccountService accountService;
    @GetMapping(value = "/open-account")
```

```
        public String openAccountForm (){
          return "accountForm";
        }
        @PostMapping(value = "/open-account")
        public String save (Account account){
          accountService.open(account);
          return "redirect:/accounts/"+account.getId();
        }
        @GetMapping(value = "/accounts/{accountId}")
        public String getAccountDetails (ModelMap model, @PathVariable Long
accountId){
          Account account = accountService.findOne(accountId);
          model.put("account", account);
          return "accountDetails";
        }
    }
```

As you can see in the preceding code, we have added two more handler methods in the AccountController method, and also injected the service AccountService with this controller to save the account details in the database. Whenever we process the POST request from the open account form, the controller accepts the account form data, and saves it to the database by using the injected account service. It will accept the account form data as an Account object. You may also notice here that after processing the form data using the HTTP POST method, the handler method redirects to the account details page. It is also a better practice to redirect after POST submission to prevent accidentally submitting the form twice. The following screen is displayed after submission of the request:

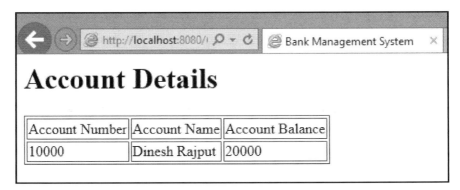

As you can see in the preceding output on the browser, this page is rendered after submitting the account form. Because we have added one request handler method, this handler method handles the request, and renders another web page including the account details. The following JSP page is rendered as the view of the preceding output:

```
<%@ taglib prefix = "c" uri = "http://java.sun.com/jsp/jstl/core" %>
<html>
 <head>
    <title>Bank Management System</title>
    <link rel="stylesheet" type="text/css" href="<c:url
value="/resources/style.css" />" >
 </head>
 <body>
    <h1>${message} Account Details</h1>
      <c:if test="${not empty account }">
        <table border="1">
            <tr>
                <td>Account Number</td>
                <td>Account Name</td>
                <td>Account Balance</td>
            </tr>
            <tr>
                <td>${account.id }</td>
                <td>${account.name }</td>
                <td>${account.balance }</td>
            </tr>
        </table>
      </c:if>
 </body>
</html>
```

In this last code, the handler method sends the Account object to the model, and also returns the logical view name. This JSP page renders the Account object taken from the response.

One thing to be noticed here is that the Account object has ID, name, and balance properties, which will be populated from the request parameters of the same name as the field name in the account form. If any object property name matches the field name of the HTML form, then this property will be initialized with a NULL value.

Data binding with Command Design pattern

Encapsulate a request as an object, thereby letting you parameterize clients with different requests, queue or log requests, and support undoable operations.
- GOF Design Pattern

You learned about the Command Design pattern in Chapter 3, *Consideration of Structural and Behavioral Patterns*. It is a part of the Behavioral pattern family of the GOF pattern. It is a very simple data-driven pattern. It allows you to encapsulate your request data into an object, and pass that object as a command to the invoker method, and that method returns the command as another object to the caller.

Spring MVC implements the Command Design pattern to bind the request data from the web form as an Object, and passes that object to the request handler method in the controller class. Here, we will explore how to use this pattern to bind the request data to the Object, and also explore the benefits and possibilities of using data binding. In the following class, the Account java bean is a simple object with three properties--id, name, and balance:

```
package com.packt.patterninspring.chapter10.bankapp.model;

public class Account{
 Long id;
 Long balance;
 String name;
 public Long getId() {
     return id;
 }
 public void setId(Long id) {
     this.id = id;
 }
 public Long getBalance() {
     return balance;
 }
 public void setBalance(Long balance) {
      this.balance = balance;
 }
 public String getName() {
     return name;
 }
 public void setName(String name) {
     this.name = name;
 }
 @Override
 public String toString() {
```

```
            return "Account [id=" + id + ", balance=" + balance + ", name=" +
    name + "]";
        }
    }
```

Either we submit the web form with the input text fields' names the same as the Object properties' name, or we receive the request as `http://localhost:8080/Chapter-10-Spring-MVC-pattern/account?id=10000`. In both cases, behind the scenes, Spring calls the setter methods of the Account class to bind the request data or web form data to the object. Spring also allows you to bind indexed collections such as List, Map, and others.

We can also customize data binding. Spring provides these two ways to customize data binding:

- **Global Customization**: It customizes the data-binding behavior across the web application for a particular Command Object
- **Per Controller Customization**: It customizes the data-binding behavior per controller class for a particular Command Object

Here, I will discuss only the per controller customization. Let's see the following code snippet for customizing data binding for the `Account` object:

```
    package com.packt.patterninspring.chapter10.bankapp.web.controller;

    . . . .
    . . . .
    @Controller
    public class AccountController {
     @Autowired
     AccountService accountService;
     . . . .
     . . . .
     @InitBinder
     public void initBinder(WebDataBinder binder) {
         binder.initDirectFieldAccess();
         binder.setDisallowedFields("id");
         binder.setRequiredFields("name", "balance");
     }
     . . . .
     . . . .
    }
```

As you can see in the preceding code, `AccountController` has a `initBinder(WebDataBinder binder)` annotated with the `@InitBinder` annotation. This method must have a void return type, and have an `org.springframework.web.bind.WebDataBinder` as a method argument. The `WebDataBinder` object has several methods; we have used some them in the preceding code. `WebDataBinder` is used to customize the data binding.

Using @ModelAttributes for customizing data binding

Spring MVC provides one more annotation, `@ModelAttributes`, for binding data to the `Command` object. It is another way to bind the data and to customize the data binding. This annotation allows you to control the creation of the `Command` object. In a Spring MVC application, this annotation can be used on a method and on method arguments. Let's see the following examples:

- Using `@ModelAttribute` on methods

    We can use the `ModelAttribute` annotation on methods to create an object to be used in our form, as follows:

    ```
    package com.packt.patterninspring.chapter10.bankapp.web.controller;
    . . . .
    . . . .
    @Controller
    public class AccountController {
      . . . .
      @ModelAttribute
      public Account account () {
        return new Account();
      }
      . . . .
    }
    ```

- Using `@ModelAttribute` on method arguments

We can also use this annotation on a method argument. In this case, the handler method's arguments are looked up from the model object. If these are not available in the model, then they are created by using the default constructor:

    ```
    package com.packt.patterninspring.chapter10.bankapp.web.controller;
    . . . .
    ```

```
....
@Controller
public class AccountController {
  ...
  @PostMapping(value = "/open-account")
  public String save (@ModelAttribute("account") Account account){
      accountService.open(account);
      return "redirect:/accounts/"+account.getId();
  }
  ....
}
```

As you can see in the last code snippet, the `@ModelAttribute` annotation is used on the method argument. This means that the `Account` object fetches from the model object. If it is not there, it will be created by using the default constructor.

 When the `@ModelAttribute` annotation is put on a method, this method will be called before the request handling method is called.

Till now, we have seen how Spring MVC handles requests and request parameters either in the traditional way or by using the `@RequestParam`, `@PathVariable` annotations. We have also seen how to process the form web page and handle the `POST` request with the form data binding to an object in the controller layers. Now let's move to see how to validate if the submitted form data is valid or invalid for the business.

Validating forms input parameters

In a web application, validation of the web form data is very important, because end users can submit any thing. Suppose in an application, a user submits the account form by filling in the account name, then it could create the new account in the bank with account holder name. So, we have to ensure the validity of the form data before creating the new record in the database. You do not need to handle the validation logic in the handler method. Spring provides support for the JSR-303 API. As of Spring 3.0, Spring MVC supports this Java Validation API. There isn't much configuration required to configure the Java Validation API in your Spring web application-you just add the implementation of this API in your application class path such as Hibernate Validator.

The Java Validation API has several annotations to validate the properties of the Command object. We can place constraints on the value of the properties of the Command object. In this chapter, I have not explored all these annotations, but let's see the following examples with some of these annotations:

```
package com.packt.patterninspring.chapter10.bankapp.model;

import javax.validation.constraints.NotNull;
import javax.validation.constraints.Size;

public class Account{
 // Not null
 @NotNull
 Long id;
 // Not null
 @NotNull
 Long balance;
 // Not null, from 5 to 30 characters
 @NotNull
 @Size(min=2, max=30)
 String name;
 public Long getId() {
     return id;
 }
 public void setId(Long id) {
     this.id = id;
 }
 public Long getBalance() {
     return balance;
 }
 public void setBalance(Long balance) {
     this.balance = balance;
 }
 public String getName() {
     return name;
 }
 public void setName(String name) {
     this.name = name;
 }
 @Override
 public String toString() {
     return "Account [id=" + id + ", balance=" + balance + ", name=" +
name + "]";
 }
}
```

As you can see in the preceding code, the properties of the Account class are now annotated with @NotNull to ensure that the value must not be null, and some properties are also annotated with the @Size annotation to ensure the count of characters between the minimum and maximum lengths.

Only annotating the properties of the Account object is not enough. We have to annotate the save() method argument of the AccountController class as follows:

```
package com.packt.patterninspring.chapter10.bankapp.web.controller;
....

....
@Controller
public class AccountController {
 ....
  @PostMapping(value = "/open-account")
  public String save (@Valid @ModelAttribute("account") Account account,
Errors errors){
      if (errors.hasErrors()) {
          return "accountForm";
      }
      accountService.open(account);
      return "redirect:/accounts/"+account.getId();
  }
  ....
  }
```

As you can see in the preceding code, the Account parameter is now annotated with @Valid to indicate to Spring that the command object has validation constraints that should be enforced. Let's see the output when we submit the web open account form while filling invalid data:

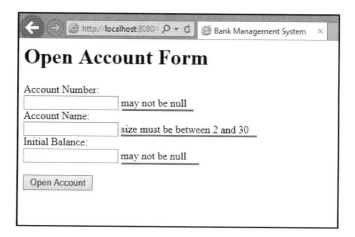

As I had submitted this form without data, it has been redirected to the same page with validation errors. Spring also allows you to customize these validation messages by configuring these messages into the properties file.

As of now, in this chapter, you have learned about the controller component of the MVC pattern. You also learned how to create and configure in a web application. Let's explore another component of the MVC pattern, view, in the upcoming section.

Implementing View in the MVC pattern

View is the most important component of the MVC pattern. The controller returns the model to the front controller along with the logical view name. The front controller resolves to the actual view by using the configured view resolver. Spring MVC provides several view resolvers to support multiple view technologies, such as JSP, Velocity, FreeMarker, JSF, Tiles, Thymeleaf, and so on. You have to configure the view resolver according to the view technology that you use in your web application. Take a look at the following figure to understand more about the view pattern in Spring MVC:

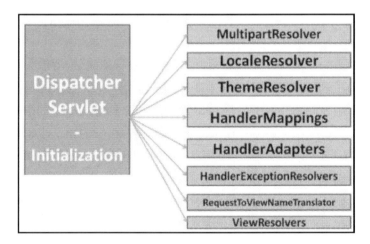

As you can see in the diagram, Spring MVC's Front Controller has several view resolvers according to the different view technologies. But in this chapter, we will use only JSP as the view technology, and so, we will explore only the JSP-related view resolver, `InternalResourveViewResolver`.

A View renders the web output. There are many built-in views available for JSPs, XSLT, templating approaches (Velocity, FreeMarker), and others. Spring MVC also has view support classes for creating PDFs, Excel spreadsheets, and so on.

Controllers, typically, return a *logical view name* in String MVC, but Spring's ViewResolvers select a View based on the view name. Let's see how to configure the ViewResolver in a Spring MVC application.

Defining ViewResolver in the Spring MVC

In Spring MVC, the DispatcherServlet delegates to a ViewResolver to obtain the View implementation based on the view name. The default ViewResolver treats the view name as a web application-relative file path, that is, a JSP--/WEB-INF/views/account.jsp. We can override this default by registering a ViewResolver bean with the DispatcherServlet. In our web application, we have used InternalResourceViewResolver, because it is related to the JSP view, but there are several other options available in Spring MVC, as mentioned in the previous section.

Implement the View

The following code renders the view in the MVC pattern:

accountDetails.jsp:

```
<%@ taglib prefix = "c" uri = "http://java.sun.com/jsp/jstl/core" %>
<html>
  <head>
      <title>Bank Management System</title>
      <link rel="stylesheet" type="text/css" href="<c:url
value="/resources/style.css" />" >
  </head>
<body>
      <h1>${message} Account Details</h1>
        <c:if test="${not empty account }">
            <table border="1">
                <tr>
                        <td>Account Number</td>
                        <td>Account Name</td>
                        <td>Account Balance</td>
                </tr>
                <tr>
                        <td>${account.id }</td>
                        <td>${account.name }</td>
```

```
                    <td>${account.balance }</td>
                </tr>
            </table>
        </c:if>
    </body>
</html>
```

As you can see in the preceding code, Spring MVC renders this view when the controller will be returned `accountDetails` as the logical view name. But how is it resolved by Spring MVC? Let's see the configuration of the `ViewResolver` in the Spring configuration file.

Register ViewResolver with Spring MVC

Let's register the JSP-related `ViewResolver`, that is, configure `InternalResourceViewResolver` in the Spring web application, as follows:

```java
package com.packt.patterninspring.chapter10.bankapp.web.mvc;

import org.springframework.context.annotation.Bean;
import org.springframework.context.annotation.ComponentScan;
import org.springframework.context.annotation.Configuration;
import org.springframework.web.servlet.ViewResolver;
import org.springframework.web.servlet.config.annotation.EnableWebMvc;
import org.springframework.web.servlet.config.annotation.WebMvcConfigurerAdapter;
import org.springframework.web.servlet.view.InternalResourceViewResolver;

@Configuration
@ComponentScan(basePackages =
{"com.packt.patterninspring.chapter10.bankapp.web.controller"})
@EnableWebMvc
public class SpringMvcConfig extends WebMvcConfigurerAdapter{
    ....
      @Bean
       public ViewResolver viewResolver(){
       InternalResourceViewResolver viewResolver = new
InternalResourceViewResolver();
      viewResolver.setPrefix("/WEB-INF/views/");
      viewResolver.setSuffix(".jsp");
      return viewResolver;
   }
    ....
   }
```

As in the preceding code, suppose the controller returns with the logical view name, `accountDetails`. All the JSP files for views are placed in the `/WEB-INF/views/` directory of the web application. The `accountDetails.jsp` view file for account details. As per the preceding configuration file, the actual view name is derived by adding the prefix `/WEB-INF/views/` and the postfix `.jsp` to the logical view name returned by the application controller. If the application controller returns `accountDetails` as the logical view name, then `ViewResolver` changes it to the physical by adding a prefix and postfix to the logical view name; finally, it is changed to `/WEB-INF/views/accountDetails.jsp` in the our application. The following diagram illustrates how Spring MVC's Front Controller resolves the view in a Spring web application:

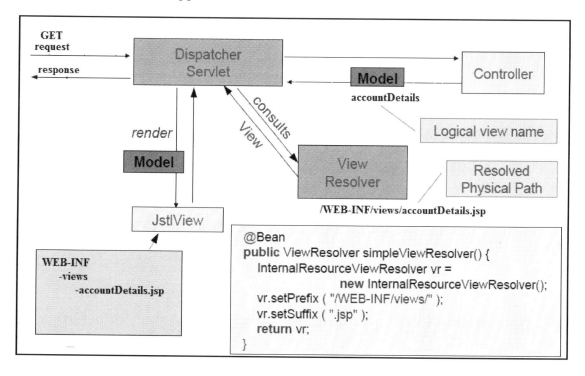

This last diagram illustrates the whole picture of the Spring MVC request flow with all the components (**Model**, **View**, and **Controllers**) of the MVC pattern, and the Front controller pattern. Any request, either HTTP GET or POST, lands at the Front Controller first, which is, actually, the DispatcherServlet in Spring MVC. The controllers in a Spring web application are responsible for generating and updating the **Model**, and the **Model** is another component of the MVC pattern. Finally, the controller returns that model along with the logical view name to the DispatcherServlet. It consults with the configured view resolver, and resolves the physical path of the view. The **View** is another component of the MVC pattern.

In the next section, we'll elaborate on the View Helper pattern, and how Spring support the pattern in a Spring web application.

The View Helper pattern

The View Helper pattern separates the static view, such as JSP, from the processing of the business model data. The View Helper pattern is used in the presentation layer by adapting the model data and the View components. The View Helper can format the model data according to the business requirement, but it cannot generate model data for the business. The following diagram illustrates the View Helper pattern:

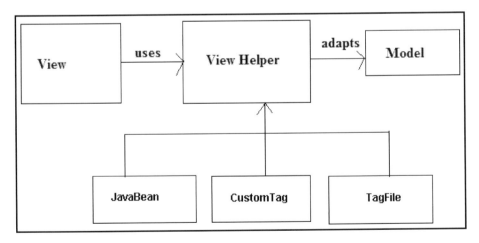

We know that View is the a static and formatted component of the MVC pattern, but sometimes, we need some business processing the presentation layer. If you are using JSPs, then you could use a scriptlet for the business processing at the the view layer, but using a scriptlet is not a best practice, because it promotes tight coupling between the view and business logic. But some View Helper classes based on the View Helper pattern take over that responsibility of business processing at the presentation layer. Some of the technologies based on the View Helper pattern areas follows:

- The JavaBeans `View` helper
- The tag `LibraryView` helper
  - Using JSTL tags
  - Using spring tags
  - Using third-party tag Library

The following tag libraries are used in our web application in this chapter:

```
<%@ taglib prefix = "c" uri = "http://java.sun.com/jsp/jstl/core" %>
<c:if test="${not empty account }">
  ....
  ....
</c:if>

<%@ taglib prefix="form" uri="http://www.springframework.org/tags/form"
%>
<form:form method="post" commandName="account">
  ....
  ...
</form:form>
```

As you can see in the preceding code, I have used the JSTL tag library for the check not empty account in the model, and the Spring tag library to create the open account form in the web application.

In the next section, you'll learn about the Composite View pattern, and how Spring MVC supports it to implement it in the web application.

Composite View pattern using Apache tile view resolver

In a web application, the View is one of the most important components. Developing this component is not as easy as seems. It is very complicated to maintain, and a daunting task. Whenever we create the view for a web application, we always focus on the reusability of the view components. We can define some static templates that can be reused in other view pages in the same web application. According to the Composite Design pattern of the GOF pattern, we compose sub-view components for a particular view component. The Composite View pattern promotes reusability of views, and is easy to maintain due to the multiple sub-views instead of creating a large and complicated view. The following diagram illustrates the Composite View pattern:

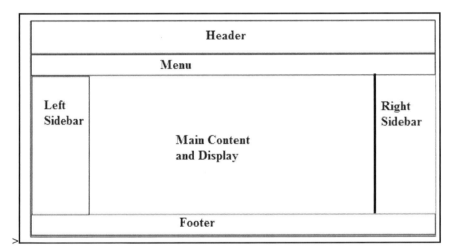

As you can see in the previous diagram, we can create multiple sub-views to create the view in a web application, and these sub-views will be reused across the web application.

Spring MVC provides support for implementation of the Composite View pattern through frameworks such as SiteMesh and Apache tiles. Here we will explore Apache Tiles with a Spring MVC application. Let's see how to configure the Apache Tiles `ViewResolver`.

Configuring a Tiles ViewResolver

Let's configure Apache Tiles in the Spring MVC application. In order to configure it, we have to configure two beans in the Spring configuration file as follows:

```
package com.packt.patterninspring.chapter10.bankapp.web.mvc;
.....
@Configuration
@ComponentScan(basePackages =
{"com.packt.patterninspring.chapter10.bankapp.web.controller"})
@EnableWebMvc
public class SpringMvcConfig extends WebMvcConfigurerAdapter{
.....
@Bean
public TilesConfigurer tilesConfigurer() {
    TilesConfigurer tiles = new TilesConfigurer();
    tiles.setDefinitions(new String[] {
        "/WEB-INF/layout/tiles.xml"
    });
    tiles.setCheckRefresh(true);
    return tiles;
}
@Bean
public ViewResolver viewResolver() {
    return new TilesViewResolver();
}
  ...
}
```

In the preceding configuration file, we configured two beans, `TilesConfigurer` and the `TilesViewResolver` bean. The first bean, `TilesConfigurer`, has the responsibility to locate and load tile definitions, and, generally, coordinate Tiles. The second bean, `TilesViewResolver`, is responsible for resolving logical view names to tile definitions. The XML file `tiles.xml` has the tile definitions in the application. Let's see the following code for the tiles configuration file:

```
<tiles-definitions>
   <definition name="base.definition" template="/WEB-
INF/views/mainTemplate.jsp">
      <put-attribute name="title" value=""/>
      <put-attribute name="header" value="/WEB-INF/views/header.jsp"/>
      <put-attribute name="menu" value="/WEB-INF/views/menu.jsp"/>
      <put-attribute name="body" value=""/>
      <put-attribute name="footer" value="/WEB-INF/views/footer.jsp"/>
   </definition>
   <definition extends="base.definition" name="openAccountForm">
      <put-attribute name="title" value="Account Open Form"/>
```

```
        <put-attribute name="body" value="/WEB-INF/views/accountForm.jsp"/>
      </definition>
      <definition extends="base.definition" name="accountsList">
        <put-attribute name="title" value="Employees List"/>
        <put-attribute name="body" value="/WEB-INF/views/accounts.jsp"/>
      </definition>
      ...
      ...
    </tiles-definitions>
```

In the preceding code, the `<tiles-definitions>` element has multiple `<definition>` elements. Each `<definition>` element defines a tile, and each tile references a JSP template. Some `<definition>` elements extend the base tile definition, because the base tile definition has the common layout for all the views in the web application.

Let's see the base definition template, that is, `mainTemplate.jsp`:

```
<%@ taglib uri="http://www.springframework.org/tags" prefix="s" %>
<%@ taglib uri="http://tiles.apache.org/tags-tiles" prefix="t" %>
<%@ page session="false" %>
<html>
  <head>
    <title>
      <tiles:insertAttribute name="title" ignore="true"/>
    </title>
  </head>
  <body>
    <table border="1" cellpadding="2" cellspacing="2" align="left">
        <tr>
            <td colspan="2" align="center">
                <tiles:insertAttribute name="header"/>
            </td>
        </tr>
        <tr>
            <td>
                <tiles:insertAttribute name="menu"/>
            </td>
            <td>
                <tiles:insertAttribute name="body"/>
            </td>
        </tr>
        <tr>
            <td colspan="2"  align="center">
                <tiles:insertAttribute name="footer"/>
            </td>
        </tr>
    </table>
```

```
        </body>
    </html>
```

In this preceding JSP file, I have used the `<tiles:insertAttribute>` JSP tag from the `tiles` tag library to insert other templates.

Let's now see some best practices used to design and develop a web application.

Best practices for web application design

The following are some of the best practices that must be considered while designing and developing a web application:

- Spring MVC is the best choice to design and develop a web application because of the Spring DI pattern and the very flexible MVC pattern with Spring. Spring's `DispatcherServlet`, too, is very flexible and customizable.
- In any web application using the MVC pattern, the front controller should be generic and as lightweight as possible.
- It is important to maintain a clear separation of concerns across the layers of the web application. Separating layers improves the clean design of the application.
- If an application layer has too many dependencies with the other layers, as a best approach, introduce another layer to reduce the dependency of that layer.
- Never inject a DAO object to the controllers in the web application; always inject a services object to the controller. The DAO objects must be injected with the service layers so that the service layer talks to the data access layer, and the presentation layer talks to the service layer.
- Application layers such service, DAO, and presentation layers must be pluggable, and must not be bound with the implementation, that is, using interfaces reduces the actual coupling to concrete implementations, as we know that loosely coupled layered applications are easier to test and maintain.
- It is strongly recommended to place JSP files in the WEB-INF directory, because this location is not accessed by any client.
- Always specify the name of the command object in the JSP file.
- JSP files must not have any business logic and business processing. For such a requirement, we strongly recommend the use of View helper classes such as tags, libraries, JSTL, and so on.

- Remove the programming logic from template-based views like JSP.
- Create reusable components that can be used to combine model data across views.
- Each component of the MVC pattern must have a consistent behavior for which the MVC introduced it. This means that the controller should follow the Single Responsibility Principle. Controllers are responsible only for delegating business logic invocation and view selection.
- Finally, be consistent with naming of the configuration files. For example, web beans such as controllers, interceptors, and view resolvers must be defined in separate configuration files. Other application beans such as services, repositories, and so on must be defined into another, separate file. Similarly for security concerns.

Summary

In this chapter, you've seen how the Spring Framework allows you to develop a flexible and loosely coupled web-based application. Spring employs annotations for near-POJO development model in your web application. You learned that with Spring MVC, you can create a web-based application by developing controllers that handle requests, and these controllers are very easy to test. In this chapter, we covered the MVC pattern, including its origins and what problems it solves. The Spring Framework has implemented MVC patterns, which means that for any web application, there are three components--Model, View, and Controller.

Spring MVC implements the Application Controller and Front Controller patterns. Spring's dispatcher servlet (`org.springframework.web.servlet.DispatcherServlet`) works as a Front Controller in a web-based application. This dispatcher or front controller routes all requests to the application controller by using handler mapping. In Spring MVC, the controller classes have extremely flexible request handler methods. And these handler methods handle all the requests of a web application. There several ways, as we explained in this chapter, to handle request parameters. The `@RequestParam` annotation is one of the ways to handle request parameters, and it is also very easy to test without using the http request object in test cases.

In this chapter, we explored the request processing workflow, and discussed all the components which play a role in this workflow. The `DispatcherServlet` can be considered the main component in Spring MVC; it plays the role of a front controller in Spring MVC. Another main component is the view resolver, which has the responsibility to render the model data to any view template such JSP, Thymeleaf, FreeMarker, velocity, pdf, xml and so on depending om the configured view resolver in the web application. Spring MVC provides support for several view technologies, but, in this chapter, we briefly looked at how to write views for your controllers using JSPs. We can also add consistent layouts to your views using Apache tiles.

And finally, we covered the web application architecture, and discussed the different layers in a web application such as domain, user interface, web, service, and data access. We created a small bank management web application, and deployed it to the tomcat server.

11
Implementing Reactive Design Patterns

In this chapter, we will explore one of the most important features of the Spring 5 Framework, which is reactive pattern programming. The Spring 5 Framework introduced this new feature with the Spring web reactive module. We will discuss this module in this chapter. Before that, let's have a look at reactive patterns. What is the reactive pattern, and why is it growing more popular nowadays? I will start my discussion on reactive pattern with the following statement made by **Satya Nadella**, CEO, Microsoft Corporation:

> *Every business out there now is a software company, is a digital company.*

The topics we will cover here are as follows:

- Why reactive pattern?
- The reactive pattern principles
- Blocking calls
- Non-blocking calls
- Back-pressure
- Implementing the reactive pattern using the Spring Framework
- The Spring web reactive module

Understanding application requirement over the years

If you go back 10 to 15 years, there were very few internet users, and far less online portals for end users compared to what we have today. Nowadays, we cannot think of a life without a computer or without any online system. In short, we have become extremely dependent on computers and online computing for personal as well as business use. Every business model is moving towards digitalization. The Prime Minister of India, Mr. Narendra Damodardas Modi has launched a Digital India campaign to ensure that the Government's services are made available to citizens electronically by improved online infrastructure, increasing internet connectivity, and by making the country digitally empowered in the field of technology.

All this implies that the number of internet users is increasing dramatically. According to the Ericsson Mobility Report,

> *The Internet of Things (IoT) is expected to surpass mobile phones as the largest category of connected devices in 2018.*

There has been a tremendous growth of mobile internet users, and there is no sign of that slowing down anytime soon. In these sectors, by definition, the server side has to handle millions of connected devices concurrently. The following table compares the infrastructure and application requirements today with the requirement from 10 years back:

Requirements	Now	Ten years ago
Server nodes	More than 1000 nodes required.	Ten nodes were enough.
Response times	Takes milliseconds to serve requests, and send back responses.	Took seconds to response.
Maintenance downtimes	Currently, there is no or zero maintenance downtime required.	Took hours of maintenance downtime.
Data volume	Data for the current application that increased to TBs from PBs.	Data was in GBs.

You can see the differences in the requirement of resources in the preceding table. These requirements have increased, because we now expect responses immediately, within the second. At the same time, the complexity of tasks given to computers have also increased. These tasks are not just pure computation in a mathematical sense, but also in requesting the responses to be distilled from enormous amounts of data. So, now we have to focus the performance of such systems by designing a single computer in the form of multi-core CPUs, possibly, combined in multi-socket servers. The first thing on our minds is to make the system responsive. It is the first of the reactive traits-responsiveness. We will explore more of this in this chapter, along with the following topics:

- Why reactive pattern
- Reactive pattern principles
- Blocking calls
- Non-blocking calls
- Back-pressure
- Implementing reactive pattern using the Spring Framework
- Spring Web reactive module
- Implementing reactive at server side
- Implementing reactive at client side
- Request and response body type conversion

This chapter will teach you how to make a system responsive in the face of any variable load, partial outages, program failure, and more. Nowadays, systems are distributed across different nodes to efficiently serve requests.

Let's look at the aforementioned topics in detail.

Understanding the reactive pattern

Today, the modern applications must be more robust, more resilient, more flexible, and better positioned to meet the requirements of the organizations, because, in the recent couple of years, the requirements for applications have changed dramatically. As we have seen in the last table, 10 to 15 years ago, a large application had 10 server nodes, the response time taken to serve a request was in seconds, we required a couple of hours of downtime for maintenance and deployment, and the data was in gigabytes. But today, an application requires thousands of server nodes, because it is accessed by multiple channels such as mobile devices. The server responses are expected within milliseconds, and the downtime for deployment and maintenance is near to 0%. Data has been increased from terabytes to petabytes.

Ten-year old systems cannot fulfill the requirements of today's applications; we need a system that can fulfill all user's requirements either at the application level or the system level, which means we need a responsive system. Responsiveness is one of the properties of the reactive pattern. We want a system that must be responsive, resilient, elastic, and message-driven. We know these systems as reactive systems. These systems are more flexible, loosely-coupled, and scalable.

A system must react to failure and stay available, that is, it should be resilient, and the system must react to variable load conditions, and not be overloaded. The system should react to events--event-driven or message-driven. If all these properties are associated with a system, then it will be responsive, that is, if a system reacts to its users, it is responsive. To create a reactive system, we must focus on the system level and application level. Let's see first the all reactive traits.

The reactive pattern traits

The following are the principles of the Reactive pattern:

- **Responsive**: This is the goal of each application today.
- **Resilient**: This is required to make an application responsive.
- **Scalable**: This is also required to make an application responsive; without resilience and scalability, it is impossible to achieve responsiveness.
- **Message-driven**: A message-driven architecture is the base of a scalable and resilient application, and ultimately, it makes a system responsive. Message-driven either based on the event-driven or actor-based programming model.

The preceding points mentioned are core principles of the reactive pattern. Let's explore each principle of the reactive pattern in detail, and understand why all of them must be applied together in order to make a reactive system with quality software for a modern context application, which is able to handle millions of parallel requests in milliseconds without any failure. Let's first understand these principles with the following diagram:

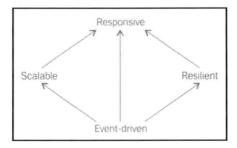

As you can see in the preceding diagram, to make a system reactive, we need scalability and resilience. To make a system scalable and resilient, we need an event-driven or message-driven architecture of the application. Ultimately, these principles, scalability, resilience, and event-driven architecture make a system responsive to the client. Let's see these properties in detail.

Responsiveness

When we say that a system or an application is responsive, it means that the application or system responds quickly to all users in a given time in all conditions, and that is in good condition as well as bad. It ensures a consistent positive user experience.

Responsiveness is required for a system for usability and utility. A responsive system means that up on system failure, either because of an external system or a spike in traffic, the failures are detected quickly, and dealt with effectively in a short time without the users knowing of the failure. An end user must be able to interact with the system by providing rapid and consistent response times. A user must not face any failure during interaction with the system, and it must deliver a consistent quality of service to the user. That consistent behavior solves the failures and builds end-user confidence in the system. Quickness and a positive user experience under various conditions make a system responsive. It depends on the two other traits of a reactive application or system, that is, resilience and scalability. Another trait, that is, event-driven or message-driven architecture, provides the overall foundation for a responsive system. The following diagram illustrates a responsive system:

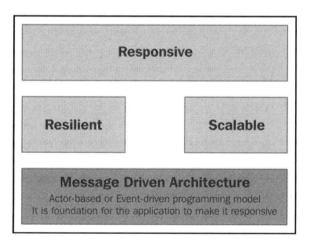

As you can see in the preceding diagram, a responsive system depends on resilient and scalability of the system, and these depend on its event-driven architecture. Let's look at the other traits of a reactive application.

Resilience

When we design and develop a system, we have consider all conditions--good and bad. If we consider only the good conditions, then we tend to implement a system that may fail after just a few days. A major application failure results in downtime and data loss and damages your application's reputation in the market.

So, we have to focus on every condition to ensure the responsiveness of the application under all conditions. Such a system or application is known as a resilient system.

Every system must be resilient to ensure responsiveness. If a system is not resilient, it will be unresponsive after a failure. So, a system must be responsive in the face of failure as well. In the whole system, failure can exist in any component of the application or system. So, each component in the system must be isolated from each other so that at the time of failure of a component, we can recover it without compromising the system as a whole. Recovery of an individual component is achieved by replication. If a system is resilient, then it must have replication, containment, isolation, and delegation. Take a look at the following diagram, which illustrates the resilient traits of a reactive application or system:

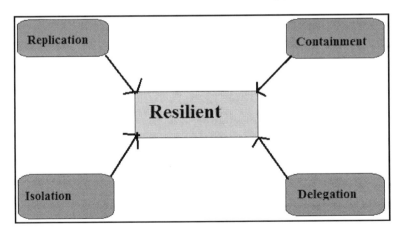

As you can see in the preceding diagram, resilience is achieved by replication, containment, isolation, and delegation. Let's discuss these points in detail:

- **Replication**: This ensures high-availability, where necessary, at the time of component failure.
- **Isolation**: This means that the failure of each component must be isolated, which is achieved by decoupling the components as much as possible. Isolation is needed for a system to self-heal. If your system has isolation in place, then you can easily measure the performance of each component, and check the memory and CPU usage. Moreover, the failure of one component won't impact the responsiveness of the overall system or application.
- **Containment**: The result of decoupling is containment of the failure. It helps avoid failure in the system as a whole.
- **Delegation**: After failure, the recovery of each component is delegated to another component. It is possible only when our system is composable.

Modern applications not only depend on the internal infrastructure but are also integrated with other web services via network protocols. So, our applications must be resilient at their core in order to stay responsive under a variety of real-world in the opposite conditions. Our applications must not only be resilient at the application level but also at the system level.

Let's see another principle of the reactive pattern.

Scalable

Resiliency and scalability together make a system consistently responsive. A scalable system or an elastic system can easily be upgraded under a varying workload. A reactive system can be made scalable on demand by increasing and decreasing the resources allocated to service these inputs. It supports multiple scaling algorithms by providing relevant live performance for the scalability of the application. We can achieve scalability by using cost-effective software and cheap commodity hardware (for example, the Cloud).

An application is scalable if it can be extended according to its usage, in the following ways:

- **scale-up**: It makes use of parallelism in multi-core systems.
- **scale-out**: It makes use of multi-server nodes. Location transparency and resilience are important for this.

Minimizing the shared mutable state is very important for scalability.

 Elasticity and Scalability are both the same! Scalability is all about the efficient use of resources already available, while elasticity is all about adding new resources to your application on demand when the needs of the system changed. So, eventually, the system can be made responsive anyway--by either using the existing resources of the system or by adding new resources to the system.

Let's see the final foundation of the resilient and scalability of the reactive pattern, that is, message-driven architecture.

Message-driven architecture

A message-driven architecture is the base of a responsive application. A message-driven application can be an event-driven and actor-based application. It can also be a combination of both architectures--event-driven and actor-based architecture.

In event-driven architecture, events and event observers play the main role. Events happen, but are not directed to a specific address; event listeners listen to these events, and take actions. But in message-driven architecture, the messages have a proper direction to the destination. Let's look at the following diagram that illustrates message-driven and event-driven architectures:

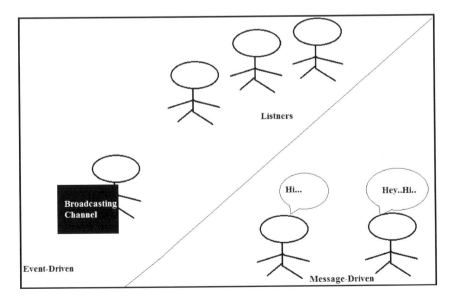

As you can see in the preceding diagram, in event-driven architecture, if an event happens, then listeners listen to it. But in the message-driven one, one generated message communication has an addressable recipient and a single purpose.

Asynchronous message-driven architecture acts as the foundation for a reactive system by establishing limitations between the components. It ensures loose coupling, isolation, and location transparency. Isolation between components fully depends on the loose coupling between them. And isolations and loose coupling develop the base of resilience and elasticity.

A large system has multiple components. These components either have smaller applications, or they may have reactive properties. This means that the reactive design principles have to apply at all levels of the scale to make a large system composable.

Traditionally, large systems are composed of multiple threads which communicate with a shared synchronized state. It tends to have strong coupling and is hard to compose, and it also tends to block stage. But, for now, all large systems are composed of loosely coupled event handlers. And events can be handled asynchronously without blocking.

Let's look at the blocking and non-blocking programming models.

In very simple terms, reactive programming is all about non-blocking applications that are asynchronous and event-driven, and require a small number of threads to scale vertically rather than horizontally.

Blocking calls

In a system, a call may be holding the resources while other calls wait for the same resources. These resources are released when the other one finishes using them.

Let's come to the technical words--actually, blocking a call means some operations in the application or system that take a longer time to complete, such as file I/O operations and database access using blocking drives. The following is a diagram of blocking calls for the JDBC operation in a system:

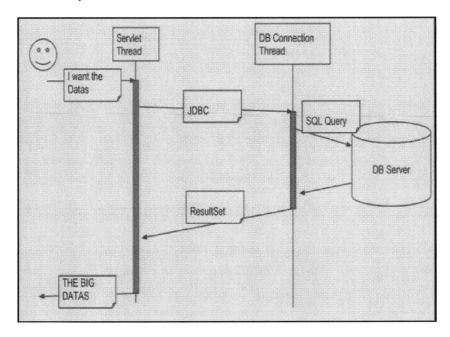

As you can see in the preceding diagram, the blocking operations, shown here in red, are the ones where the user calls the servlet to fetch data, then that moves to the JDBC and DB connection with the DB server. Until that time, the current thread waits for the result set from the DB server. If the DB server has latency, then this wait time can increase. That means that thread execution depends on the DB server latency.

Let's look at how to make this a non-blocking execution.

Non-blocking calls

Non-blocking execution of a program means that a thread competes for a resource without waiting for it. A non-blocking API for the resources allows calling the resources without waiting for the blocked call such as database access and network calls. If the resources are not available at the time of calling, then it moves to other work rather than waiting for the blocked resources. The system is notified when the blocked resources are available.

Take a look at the following diagram that shows the JDBC connection to access data without the blocking thread execution:

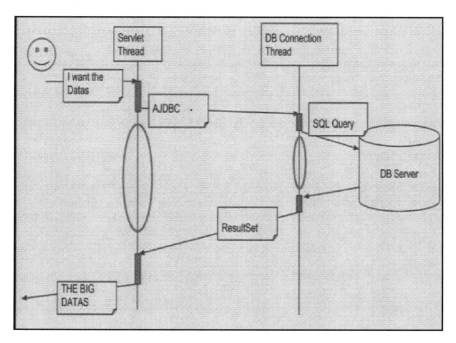

As you can see in the preceding diagram, thread execution does not wait for the result set from the DB server. The thread makes the DB connection and SQL statement for the DB server. If the DB server has latency in the response, then the thread moves on to do other work rather than be blocked waiting for the resource to become available.

Back-pressure

A reactive application is never given up in overload conditions. Back-pressure is a key aspect of a reactive application. It is a mechanism to ensure that the reactive application doesn't overwhelm the consumers. It tests aspects for the reactive application. It tests the system response gracefully under any load.

The back-pressure mechanism ensures that the system is resilient under load. In a back-pressure condition, the system makes itself scalable by applying other resources to help distribute the load.

Until now, we have seen the reactive pattern principles; these are mandatory to make a system responsive in the blue sky or grey sky. Let's see, in the upcoming section how Spring 5 implements reactive programming.

Implementing reactive with the Spring 5 Framework

The most highlighted feature of the latest version of the Spring Framework is the new reactive stack web framework. Reactive is the update that takes us to the future. This area of technology is gaining popularity with every passing day, which is the reason why Spring Framework 5.0 has been launched with the capability of reactive programming. This addition makes the latest version of the Spring Framework convenient for event-loop style processing, which enables scaling with a small number of threads.

The Spring 5 Framework implements the reactive programming pattern by using the reactor internally for its own reactive support. A reactor is a Reactive Stream implementation that extends the basic Reactive Streams. Twitter has been implemented as a reactive passed by using Reactive Streams.

Reactive Streams

Reactive Streams provide a protocol or rule for asynchronous stream processing with non-blocking back-pressure. This standard is also adopted by Java 9 in the form of `java.util.concurrent.Flow`. Reactive Streams is composed of four simple Java interfaces. These interfaces are `Publisher`, `Subscriber`, `Subscription`, and `Processor`. But the main goal of the Reactive Streams is handling the backpressure. As discussed earlier, backpressure is a process that allows a receiver to ask about a data quantity from the emitter.

You can use the following Maven dependency for adding Reactive Streams in your application development:

```
<dependency>
  <groupId>org.reactivestreams</groupId>
  <artifactId>reactive-streams</artifactId>
  <version>1.0.1</version>
```

```
</dependency>
<dependency>
    <groupId>org.reactivestreams</groupId>
    <artifactId>reactive-streams-tck</artifactId>
    <version>1.0.1</version>
</dependency>
```

The preceding Maven dependency code adds the required libraries for the Reactive Streams in your application. In the upcoming section, we'll see how Spring implements Reactive Streams in the web module of Spring and the Spring MVC Framework.

Spring Web reactive module

As of Spring 5.0 Framework, Spring has introduced a new module for reactive programming--the spring-web-reactive module. It is based on Reactive Streams. Basically, this module uses the Spring MVC module with reactive programming, so, you can still use the Spring MVC module for your web application either separately or with the spring-web-reactive module.

This new module in the Spring 5.0 Framework contains support for the Reactive-web-functional- based programming model. It also supports the Annotation-based programming model. The Spring-web-reactive module contains support for reactive HTTP and WebSocket clients to call the reactive server application. It also enables the reactive web client to make a connection with a reactive HTTP connection with a reactive web application.

The following diagram shows a Spring-web-reactive module with its components that give reactive behavior to the Spring web application:

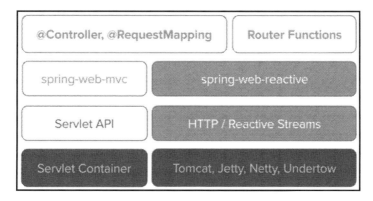

As you can see in the preceding diagram, there are two parallel modules--one for the traditional Spring MVC framework, and the other for the Spring-reactive web modules. On the left side in the diagram are the Spring-MVC-related components such as the @MVC controllers, **spring-web-mvc module**, **Servlet API module**, and **Servlet Container.** On the right side in the diagram are the spring-web-reactive related components such as the Router Functions, spring-web-reactive module, HTTP/Reactive Streams, Reactive version of Tomcat, and so on. **Spring-web-reactive** related components such as the **Router Functions**, **spring-web-reactive module**, **HTTP/Reactive Streams**, Reactive version of Tomcat, and so on.

In the preceding diagram, you must focus on the placement of the modules. Each module on the same level has comparisons between the traditional Spring MVC and Spring-web-reactive modules. These comparisons are given as follows:

- In the Spring web reactive modules, the Router functions are similar to the @MVC controllers in the Spring MVC modules such as the @Controller, @RestController, and @RequestMapping annotations.
- The Spring-web-reactive module is parallel to the Spring-web-MVC modules.
- In the traditional Spring MVC Framework, we use the Servlet API for the HttpServletRequest and HttpServletResponse in the servlet container. But in the Spring-web-reactive framework, we use HTTP/Reactive Streams, which creates HttpServerRequest and HttpServerResponse under the reactive support of the tomcat server.
- We can user Servlet Container for the traditional Spring MVC Framework, but a reactive-supported server is required for the Spring-web-reactive application. Spring provides support for Tomcat, Jetty, Netty, and Undertow.

In Chapter 10, *Implementing MVC Pattern in a Web Application using Spring*, you learned how to implement a web application using the Spring MVC module. Let's now see how to implement a reactive web application by using the Spring web reactive module.

Implementing a reactive web application at the server side

Spring reactive web modules support both programming models--Annotation-based or the Functional-based programming model. Let's see how these models work on the server side:

- **Annotations-based programming model**: It is based on MVC annotations such as `@Controller`, `@RestController`, `@RequestMapping`, and many more. Annotations are supported by the Spring MVC framework for server-side programming for a web application.
- **Functional programming model:** It is a new paradigm of programming supported by the Spring 5 Framework. It is based on the Java 8 Lambda style routing and handling. Scala also provides the functional programming paradigm.

The following are the Maven dependencies that we have to add for a reactive web application based on Spring Boot:

```xml
<parent>
    <groupId>org.springframework.boot</groupId>
    <artifactId>spring-boot-starter-parent</artifactId>
    <version>2.0.0.M3</version>
    <relativePath/> <!-- lookup parent from repository -->
</parent>

<properties>
    <project.build.sourceEncoding>UTF-
     8</project.build.sourceEncoding>
    <project.reporting.outputEncoding>UTF
     -8</project.reporting.outputEncoding>
    <java.version>1.8</java.version>
</properties>

<dependencies>
    <dependency>
        <groupId>org.springframework.boot</groupId>
        <artifactId>spring-boot-starter-webflux</artifactId>
    </dependency>

    <dependency>
        <groupId>org.springframework.boot</groupId>
        <artifactId>spring-boot-starter-test</artifactId>
        <scope>test</scope>
    </dependency>
    <dependency>
        <groupId>io.projectreactor</groupId>
```

```
            <artifactId>reactor-test</artifactId>
            <scope>test</scope>
        </dependency>
    </dependencies>
```

As you can see in the preceding Maven configuration file for dependencies, we have added the `spring-boot-starter-webflux` and `reactor-test` dependencies to the application.

Let's create a reactive web application based on the Annotation-based programming model.

The Annotation-based programming model

You can use the same annotations that you have used in `Chapter 10`, *Implementing MVC pattern in a Web Application with Spring*. Annotations such as `@Controller` and `@RestController` of Spring MVC are also supported on the reactive side. There is no difference till now between the traditional Spring MVC and Spring web with reactive module. The actual difference starts after the `@Controller` annotation configuration declaration, that is, when we go to the internal working of the Spring MVC, starting with `HandlerMapping` and `HandlerAdapter`.

The main difference between the traditional Spring MVC and Spring web reactive comes into play in the request-handling mechanism. Spring MVC without reactive handles the requests using the blocking `HttpServletRequest` and the `HttpServletResponse` interfaces of the Servlet API, but the Spring web reactive framework is non-blocking, and operates on the reactive `ServerHttpRequest` and `ServerHttpResponse` rather than on `HttpServletRequest` and `HttpServletResponse`.

Let's see the following example with a reactive controller:

```
package com.packt.patterninspring.chapter11.
    reactivewebapp.controller;

import org.reactivestreams.Publisher;
import org.springframework.beans.factory.annotation.Autowired;
import org.springframework.web.bind.annotation.GetMapping;
import org.springframework.web.bind.annotation.PathVariable;
import org.springframework.web.bind.annotation.PostMapping;
import org.springframework.web.bind.annotation.RequestBody;
import org.springframework.web.bind.annotation.RestController;

import com.packt.patterninspring.chapter11.
    reactivewebapp.model.Account;
import  com.packt.patterninspring.chapter11.
    reactivewebapp.repository.AccountRepository;
```

```
import reactor.core.publisher.Flux;
import reactor.core.publisher.Mono;

@RestController
public class AccountController {
  @Autowired
  private AccountRepository repository;
  @GetMapping(value = "/account")
  public Flux<Account> findAll() {
    return repository.findAll().map(a -> new
      Account(a.getId(), a.getName(),
        a.getBalance(), a.getBranch())));
  }
  @GetMapping(value = "/account/{id}")
  public Mono<Account> findById(@PathVariable("id") Long id) {
    return repository.findById(id)
      .map(a -> new Account(a.getId(), a.getName(), a.getBalance(),
        a.getBranch()));
  }
  @PostMapping("/account")
  public Mono<Account> create(@RequestBody
    Publisher<Account> accountStream) {
    return repository
      .save(Mono.from(accountStream)
      .map(a -> new Account(a.getId(), a.getName(), a.getBalance(),
        a.getBranch()))))
      .map(a -> new Account(a.getId(), a.getName(), a.getBalance(),
        a.getBranch()));
  }
}
```

As you can see in the preceding Controller code of `AccountController.java`, I have used the same Spring MVC annotations such as `@RestController` to declare a controller class, and `@GetMapping` and `@PostMapping` are used to create the request handler methods for the `GET` and `POST` request methods respectively.

Let's focus on the return types of the handler methods. These methods return values as **Mono** and **Flux** types. These are types of the reactive steams provided by the reactor framework. Also, the handler method takes the request body using the Publisher type.

Reactor is a Java Framework from the Pivotal open-source team. It builds directly on Reactive Streams, so there is no need for a bridge. The Reactor IO project provides wrappers around low-level network runtimes like Netty and Aeron. Reactor is a "4th Generation" library according to David Karnok's Generations of Reactive classification.

Let's look at the same controller class using the functional programming model to handle requests.

The functional programming model

The functional programming model uses the API that has functional interfaces such as `RouterFunction` and `HandlerFunction`. It uses Java 8 Lambda style programming with routing and request handling instead of the Spring MVC annotations. They are simple, but powerful, building blocks for creating web applications.

The following is an example of functional request handling:

```
package com.packt.patterninspring.chapter11.web.reactive.function;

import static org.springframework.http.MediaType.APPLICATION_JSON;
import static org.springframework.web.reactive.
   function.BodyInserters.fromObject;

import org.springframework.web.reactive.
   function.server.ServerRequest;
import org.springframework.web.reactive.
   function.server.ServerResponse;

import com.packt.patterninspring.chapter11.
   web.reactive.model.Account;
import com.packt.patterninspring.chapter11.
   web.reactive.repository.AccountRepository;

import reactor.core.publisher.Flux;
import reactor.core.publisher.Mono;

public class AccountHandler {

  private final AccountRepository repository;

  public AccountHandler(AccountRepository repository) {
     this.repository = repository;
  }

  public Mono<ServerResponse> findById(ServerRequest request) {
    Long accountId = Long.valueOf(request.pathVariable("id"));
    Mono<ServerResponse> notFound =
      ServerResponse.notFound().build();
    Mono<Account> accountMono =
     this.repository.findById(accountId);
    return accountMono
```

```
      .flatMap(account ->    ServerResponse.ok().contentType
      (APPLICATION_JSON).body(
         fromObject(account)))
      .switchIfEmpty(notFound);
   }
   public Mono<ServerResponse> findAll(ServerRequest request) {
    Flux<Account> accounts = this.repository.findAll();
    return ServerResponse.ok().contentType
    (APPLICATION_JSON).body(accounts,
      Account.class);
   }
   public Mono<ServerResponse> create(ServerRequest request) {
     Mono<Account> account = request.bodyToMono(Account.class);
     return   ServerResponse.ok().build(this.
     repository.save(account));
   }
 }
}
```

In the preceding code, the class file, `AccountHandler.java`, is based on the functional reactive programming model. Here, I have used the reactor framework to handle the request. Two functional interfaces, `ServerRequest` and `ServerResponse`, are used to handle requests and to generate responses.

Let's see the Repositories classes of this application. The following `AccountRepository` and `AccountRepositoryImpl` classes are the same for both type of applications- Annotation-based and the functional-based programming model.

Let's create an interface `AccountRepository.java` class as follows:

```
package com.packt.patterninspring.chapter11.
   reactivewebapp.repository;
import com.packt.patterninspring.chapter11.
   reactivewebapp.model.Account;

import reactor.core.publisher.Flux;
import reactor.core.publisher.Mono;

public interface AccountRepository {
   Mono<Account> findById(Long id);
   Flux<Account> findAll();
   Mono<Void> save(Mono<Account> account);
}
```

The preceding code is an interface, let's implements this interface with the
`AccountRepositoryImpl.java` class as following:

```
package com.packt.patterninspring.chapter11.
  web.reactive.repository;

import java.util.Map;
import java.util.concurrent.ConcurrentHashMap;

import org.springframework.stereotype.Repository;

import com.packt.patterninspring.chapter11.web.
  reactive.model.Account;

import reactor.core.publisher.Flux;
import reactor.core.publisher.Mono;

@Repository
public class AccountRepositoryImpl implements AccountRepository {
  private final Map<Long, Account> accountMap = new
  ConcurrentHashMap<>();
  public AccountRepositoryImpl() {
    this.accountMap.put(10001, new Account(10001,
    "Dinesh Rajput", 500001,
      "Sector-1"));
    this.accountMap.put(20001, new Account(20001,
    "Anamika Rajput", 600001,
      "Sector-2"));
    this.accountMap.put(30001, new Account(30001,
    "Arnav Rajput", 700001,
      "Sector-3"));
    this.accountMap.put(40001, new Account(40001,
   "Adesh Rajput", 800001,
      "Sector-4"));
  }
  @Override
  public Mono<Account> findById(Long id) {
    return Mono.justOrEmpty(this.accountMap.get(id));
  }

  @Override
  public Flux<Account> findAll() {
    return Flux.fromIterable(this.accountMap.values());
  }

  @Override
  public Mono<Void> save(Mono<Account> account) {
    return account.doOnNext(a -> {
```

```
        accountMap.put(a.getId(), a);
        System.out.format("Saved %s with id %d%n", a, a.getId());
    }).thenEmpty(Mono.empty());
    // return accountMono;
  }
}
```

As you can see in the preceding code, we created the `AccountRepository` class. This class has only three methods: `findById()`, `findAll()`, and `save()`. We implemented these methods according to the business requirements. In this repository class, I have, especially, used the Flux and Mono react types to make it a reactive-based application.

Let's create the server for the functional-based programming model. In Annotation-based programming, we use the simple tomcat container to deploy the web application. But for this functional-based programming, we have to create a Server class to start the Tomcat server or Reactor server, as follows:

```
package com.packt.patterninspring.chapter11.web.reactive.function;

//Imports here

public class Server {

  public static final String HOST = "localhost";
  public static final int TOMCAT_PORT = 8080;
  public static final int REACTOR_PORT = 8181;
  //main method here, download code for GITHUB
  public RouterFunction<ServerResponse> routingFunction() {
    AccountRepository repository = new AccountRepositoryImpl();
    AccountHandler handler = new AccountHandler(repository);

    return nest(path("/account"), nest(accept(APPLICATION_JSON),
      route(GET("/{id}"), handler::findById)
      .andRoute(method(HttpMethod.GET), handler::findAll)
      ).andRoute(POST("/").and(contentType
      (APPLICATION_JSON)), handler::create));
  }

  public void startReactorServer() throws InterruptedException {
    RouterFunction<ServerResponse> route = routingFunction();
    HttpHandler httpHandler = toHttpHandler(route);

    ReactorHttpHandlerAdapter adapter = new
      ReactorHttpHandlerAdapter(httpHandler);
    HttpServer server = HttpServer.create(HOST, REACTOR_PORT);
    server.newHandler(adapter).block();
  }
```

```
public void startTomcatServer() throws LifecycleException {
    RouterFunction<?> route = routingFunction();
    HttpHandler httpHandler = toHttpHandler(route);

    Tomcat tomcatServer = new Tomcat();
    tomcatServer.setHostname(HOST);
    tomcatServer.setPort(TOMCAT_PORT);
    Context rootContext = tomcatServer.addContext("",
        System.getProperty("java.io.tmpdir"));
    ServletHttpHandlerAdapter servlet = new
        ServletHttpHandlerAdapter(httpHandler);
    Tomcat.addServlet(rootContext, "httpHandlerServlet", servlet);
    rootContext.addServletMapping("/", "httpHandlerServlet");
    tomcatServer.start();
  }
}
```

As you can see in the preceding `Server.java` class file, I have added both, the Tomcat and Reactor servers. The Tomcat server uses port 8080, but the Reactor server uses the port `8181`.

This `Server.java` class has three methods. The first method, `routingFunction()`, is responsible for handling client requests by using the `AccountHandler` class. It depends on the `AccountRepository` class. The second method, `startReactorServer()`, is responsible for starting the Reactor server by using the `ReactorHttpHandlerAdapter` class of the reactor server. This class takes an object of the `HttpHandler` class as a constructor argument to create the request handler mapping. Similarly, the third method, `startTomcatServer()`, is responsible for starting the Tomcat server. And it is bound to the `HttpHandler` object through a reactor adapter class, `ServletHttpHandlerAdapter`.

You can run this server class file as a Java application, and see the output on the browser by typing the URL, `http://localhost:8080/account/`:

You can also type the same URL with port 8181 for the Reactor server, as follows, and you will get the same output:

```
http://localhost:8181/account/
```

In this section, you learned how to create a reactive web application using the Spring-web-reactive module. We created the web application by using both the programming paradigms: Annotation-based and Functional-based.

In the next section, we'll discuss client-side code, and how a client accesses the reactive web application.

Implementing a Reactive Client-Side application

The Spring 5 Framework introduces a functional and reactive WebClient. It is a fully non-blocking and reactive web client, and an alternative to `RestTemplate`. It creates the network input and output in the form of reactive `ClientHttpRequest` and `ClientHttpRespones`. It creates the body of the request and response in the form of `Flux<DataBuffer>` instead of `InputStream` and `OutputStream`.

Let's see the code for the web client, which creates a `Client.java` class:

```java
package com.packt.patterninspring.chapter11.web.reactive.function;

//Imports here

public class Client {

  private ExchangeFunction exchange = ExchangeFunctions.create(new
    ReactorClientHttpConnector());

  public void findAllAccounts() {
    URI uri = URI.create(String.format("http://%s:%d/account",
    Server.HOST,
      Server.TOMCAT_PORT));
    ClientRequest request = ClientRequest.method(HttpMethod.GET,
    uri).build();

    Flux<Account> account = exchange.exchange(request)
    .flatMapMany(response -> response.bodyToFlux(Account.class));

     Mono<List<Account>> accountList = account.collectList();
     System.out.println(accountList.block());
  }

  public void createAccount() {
    URI uri = URI.create(String.format("http://%s:%d/account",
    Server.HOST,
       Server.TOMCAT_PORT));
    Account jack = new Account(50001, "Arnav Rajput", 5000001,
    "Sector-5");

    ClientRequest request = ClientRequest.method(HttpMethod.POST,
    uri)
```

```
        .body(BodyInserters.fromObject(jack)).build();

    Mono<ClientResponse> response = exchange.exchange(request);

    System.out.println(response.block().statusCode());
    }
}
```

The preceding class, `Client.java`, is a web client class for `Server.java`. It has two methods. The first method is `findAllAccounts()`. It fetches all accounts from the account repository. It uses the `org.springframework.web.reactive.function.client`. The `ClientRequest` interface to create a request to the `http://localhost:8080/account/` URI with the GET http method. By using the `org.springframework.web.reactive.function.client`. The `ExchangeFunction` interface, it calls the server, and fetches the result as the JSON format. Similarly, the other method, `createAccount()`, creates a new account in the server by using the URI with the POST method `http://localhost:8080/account/`.

Let's run the Client class as a Java application and see the output on the console, which is as follows:

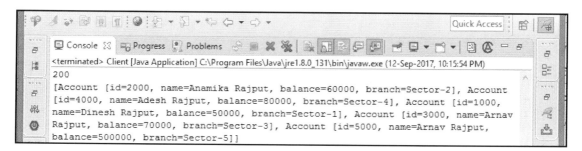

It creates a new record and fetch all five record in the form of JSON list.

The `AsyncRestTemplate` also supports non-blocking interactions. The main difference is that it can't support non-blocking streaming, for example, Twitter one, because, fundamentally, it's still based and relies on `InputStream` and `OutputStream`.

In the next section, we'll talk about the request and response body parameters in a reactive web application.

Request and response body conversion

In `Chapter 10`, *Implementing MVC Pattern in a Web Application with Spring*, we discussed message conversion for the request body and response body either from Java to JSON, or from JSON to Java object, and many more. Similarly, conversion is also required in the case of a Reactive web application, . The spring core module provides reactive Encoder and Decoder to enable the serialization of a Flux of bytes to and from the typed objects.

Let's see the following example for request body type conversions. Developers do not need to forcefully do type conversion--the Spring Framework automatically converts it for you in both types of approaches: Annotation-based programming, and functional-based programming.

- **Account account**: This means that the account object is deserialized before the controller is called without blocking.
- **Mono<Account> account**: This means that `AccountController` can use the Mono to declare logic. The account object is first deserialized, and then this logic is executed.
- **Flux<Account> accounts**: This means that `AccountController` can use Flux in case of the input streaming scenario.
- **Single<Account> account**: This is very similar to the Mono, but here the Controller uses RxJava.
- **Observable<Account> accounts**: This is also very similar to Flux, but in this case, the Controller uses input streaming with RxJava.

In the preceding list, you saw the Spring Framework for type conversion in the reactive programing model. Let's see the following return types in the example for the response body:

- **Account**: This serializes without blocking the given Account; implies a synchronous, non-blocking controller method.
- **void**: This is specific to the annotation-based programming model. Request handling completes when the method returns; this implies a synchronous, non-blocking controller method.
- **Mono<Account>**: This serializes without blocking the given Account when the Mono completes.
- **Mono<Void>**: This implies that request handling completes when the Mono completes.

- **Flux<Account>**: This is used in the streaming scenario, possibly, the SSE depends on the requested content type.
- **Flux<ServerSentEvent>**: This enables SSE streaming.
- **Single<Account>**: The same, but uses RxJava.
- **Observable<Account>**: The same, but uses the RxJava Observable type.
- **Flowable<Account>**: The same, but uses the RxJava 2 Flowable type.

In the preceding list, you have seen the return types of the handler methods. The Spring Framework does type conversions in the reactive programing model.

Summary

In this chapter, you learned about the Reactive pattern and its principles. It is not a new innovation in programming--it is a very old concept, but it very fits in very well with the demands of modern applications.

Reactive programming has four principles: responsiveness, resilience, elasticity, and message-driven architecture. Responsiveness means a system must be responsive in all conditions: odd conditions and even conditions.

The Spring 5 Framework provides support for the reactive programming model by using the Reactor framework and reactive stream. Spring has introduced new a reactive web module, that is, spring-web-reactive. It provides the reactive programming approach to a web application by either using Spring MVC's annotations, such as `@Controller`, `@RestController`, and `@RequestMapping`, or by using the functional programming approach using the Java 8 Lambda expression.

In this chapter, we created a web application by using the spring web reactive modules. The code for this application is available on GitHub. In the next chapter, you will learn about implementation of concurrency patterns.

12
Implementing Concurrency Patterns

In `Chapter 11`, *Implementing Reactive Design Patterns*, we discussed the Reactive Design Pattern and how it fulfills the requirements of today's applications. Spring 5 Framework has introduced the Reactive Web Application Modules for the web application. In this chapter, we will explore some of the Concurrency Design Patterns and how these patterns solve the common problems of the multithreaded application. Spring 5 Framework's reactive modules also provide the solution for the multithreaded application.

If you are a software engineer or are in the process of becoming one, you must be aware of the term *concurrency*. In geometric properties, concurrent circles or shapes are those shapes that have a common center point. These shapes can differ in dimensions but have a common center or midpoint.

The concept is similar in terms of software programming as well. The term *concurrent programming* in the technical or programming means the ability of a program to carry out multiple computations in parallel and also the capability of a program to handle multiple external activities taking place in a single time interval.

As we are talking in terms of software engineering and programming, concurrency patterns are those design patterns that help in dealing with multi-threaded programming models. Some of the concurrency patterns are as follows:

- Handling concurrency with concurrency patterns
- Active object pattern
- Monitor object pattern
- Half-Sync/Half-Async patterns
- Leader/followers pattern

- Thread-specific storage
- Reactor pattern
- Best practices for concurrency module

Let's now explore each of these five concurrency design patterns in depth.

Active object pattern

The active object type of concurrency design pattern differentiates/distinguishes the method execution from the method invocation. The job of this pattern is the enhancement of concurrency along with simplification in the synchronized access to objects that reside in separate and distinguishable threads of control. It is used for dealing with the multiple client requests that arrive all at once, and also for improving the quality of the service. Let's see the following diagrams, which illustrates the active object design pattern in the concurrency and multithread-based application:

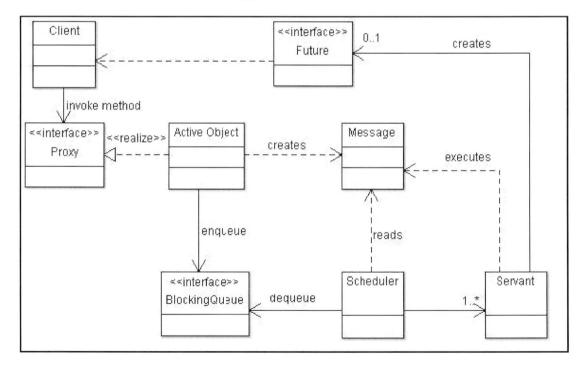

As you can see in the preceding diagram, the following components of this concurrency design pattern:

- **Proxy**: This is the active object that is visible to the client. The proxy advertises its interface.
- **Servant**: There is a method that is defined in the interface of the proxy. The servant is the provider of its implementation.
- **Activation list**: This is a serialized list that contains method request objects that the proxy inserts. This list allows the servant to run concurrently.

So, how does this design pattern work? Well, the answer to this is that every concurrent object belongs to or resides in a separate thread of control. This is also independent of the thread of control of the client. This invokes one of its methods, which means that both the method execution and method invocation take place in separate threads of control. However, the client sees this process as an ordinary method. In order for the proxy to pass the requests of the client to the servant at runtime, both must be run in separate threads.

In this design pattern, what the proxy does after receiving a request is that it sets up a method request object and inserts it in an activation list. This method carries out two jobs; holds the method request objects and keeps track of on which method request it can execute. Request parameters and any other information are contained in the method request object for executing the desired method later. This activation list in return helps the proxy and the servant to run concurrently.

Let's see another concurrency design pattern in the upcoming section, which is the monitor object pattern.

Monitor object pattern

The monitor object pattern is another concurrency design pattern that helps in the execution of multi-threaded programs. It is a design pattern implemented to make sure that at a single time interval, only one method runs in a single object, and for this purpose, it synchronizes concurrent method execution.

Unlike the active object design pattern, the monitor object pattern does not have a separate thread of control. Every request received is executed in the thread of control of the client itself, and until the time the method returns, the access is blocked. At a single time interval, a single synchronized method can be executed in one monitor.

The following solutions are offered by the monitor object pattern:

- The synchronization boundaries are defined by the interface of the object, and it also makes sure that a single method is active in a single object.
- It must be ensured that all the objects keep a check on every method that needs synchronization and serialize them transparently without letting the client know. Operations, on the other hand, are mutually exclusive, but they are invoked like ordinary method calls. Wait and signal primitives are used for the realization of condition synchronization.
- To prevent the deadlock and use the concurrency mechanisms available, other clients must be allowed to access the object when the method of the object blocks during execution.
- The invariants must always hold when the thread of control is interrupted voluntarily by the method.

Let's see the following diagram, which illustrates more about the monitor object design pattern in the concurrency application:

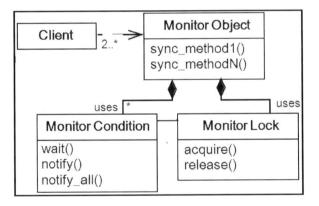

In this preceding diagram, the client object calls the monitor object that has several synchronized methods and the monitor object associated with the monitor conditions and monitor locks. Let's explore each component of this concurrency design pattern as follows:

- **Monitor object**: This component exposes the methods that are synchronized to the clients
- **Synchronized methods**: The thread-safe functions that are exported by the interface of the object are implemented by these methods
- **Monitor conditions**: This component along with the monitor lock decides whether the synchronized method should resume its processing or suspend it

The active object and the monitor object patterns are the branches of design patterns of concurrency.

Now, the other type of concurrency patterns that we will discuss are the branches of architectural patterns for concurrency.

Half-Sync/Half-Async patterns

The job of Half-Sync and Half-Async is to distinguish between the two types of processing called asynchronous and synchronous, for the simplification of the program without hindering its performance.

The two layers intercommunicating are introduced for both asynchronous and synchronous services for the purpose of processing with a queuing layer in between.

Every concurrent system contains both asynchronous and synchronous services. To enable these services to communicate with each other, the Half-Sync/Half-Async pattern decomposes the services in the system into layers. Using the queuing layer, both these services pass messages to each other for intercommunication.

Let's see the following diagram that illustrates these design patterns:

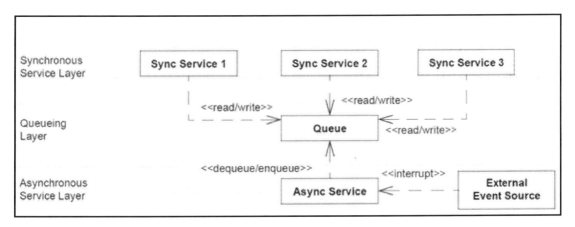

As you can see in the preceding diagram, there are three layers--**Synchronous Service Layer**, **Queuing Layer**, and **Asynchronous Service Layer**. Synchronous layer contains the services that are working synchronously to the queue at the **Queuing Layer**, and this query performs asynchronously using Asynchronous services at the **Asynchronous Service Layer**. These Asynchronous Services at this layer are using the external event-based resources.

As you can see in the preceding diagram, there are three layers included here. Let's look at these layers:

- **Synchronous Task Layer**: The tasks in this layer are active objects. High-level input and output operations are carried by these tasks, which transfer the data synchronously towards the queuing layer.
- **Queuing Layer**: This layer provides the synchronization and buffering required between the synchronous and asynchronous task layers.
- **Asynchronous Task Layer**: The events from the external sources are handled by the tasks present in this layer. These tasks do not contain a separate thread of control.

We have discussed the Half-Sync and Half-Async design patterns of the concurrency pattern. Let's move to another concurrency pattern, that is, the leader/follower Pattern.

Leader/follower pattern

Detection, demultiplexing, dispatching, and processing of service requests in the event sources is carried out in an efficient way in a concurrency model, in which many multiple threads process one by one to use the set on event sources. Another replacement for the Half-Sync/Half-Async is the leader/follower pattern. This pattern can be used instead of the Half-Sync/Half-Async and active object patterns for improvement in the performance. The condition of using this is that there must be neither ordering nor synchronization constraints while processing multiple threads of requests:

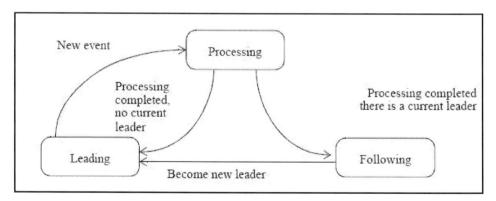

The focused job of this pattern is to process multiple events concurrently or simultaneously. Due to concurrency-related overheads, it might not be possible to connect a separate thread with each single socket handle. The highlighted feature of this design is that by using this pattern, demultiplexing the associations between threads and event source becomes possible. When the events arrive on the event sources, this pattern builds up a pool of threads. This is done to share a set of event sources efficiently. These event sources demultiplex the arriving events turn by turn. Also, the events are synchronously dispatched to application services for processing. Out of the pool of threads structured by the leader/follower pattern, only a single thread waits for the occurrence of the event; other threads queue up waiting. A follower is promoted as the leader when a thread detects an event. It then processes the thread and dispatches the event to the application handler.

In this type of pattern, processing threads can be run concurrently, but only one thread is allowed to wait for the upcoming new events.

Let's see another concurrency-based design pattern in the upcoming section.

Reactor pattern

The reactor pattern is used to handle service requests that are received concurrently by a service handler from a single or multiple input sources. The received service requests are then demultiplexed by the service handler and dispatched to the associated request handlers. All the reactor systems are commonly found in single threads, but they are also said to exist in a multi-threaded environment.

The key benefit of using this pattern is that the application components can be divided into multiple parts such as modular or reusable. Furthermore, this allows simple coarse-grain concurrency without the additional complexity of multiple threads to the system.

Let's see the following diagram about the reactor design pattern:

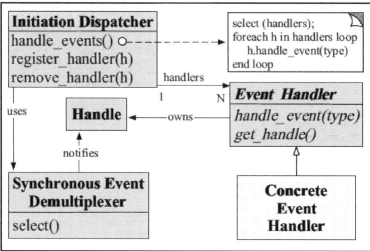

As you can see in the preceding diagram, the dispatcher uses the demultiplexer to notify handler and the handler performs the actual work to be done with an I/O event. A reactor responds to I/O events by dispatching the appropriate handler. Handlers perform non-blocking actions. The preceding diagram has the following components of this design pattern:

- **Resources:** These are the resources through which input is provided or output is consumed.
- **Synchronous event demultiplexer:** This blocks all resources via an event loop. When there is a possibility that a synchronous operation will start, the resource is sent to the dispatcher through the demultiplexer without blocking.
- **Dispatcher:** The registering or unregistering of request handler is handled by this component. Resources are dispatched to the respective request handler through the dispatcher.
- **Request Handler:** This handles the request dispatched by the dispatcher.

Now, we are moving on to our next and the last concurrency pattern that is the thread-specific storage pattern.

Thread-specific storage pattern

A single logical global access point can be used to retrieve an object local to the thread. This concurrency design pattern allows multiple threads to carry this function out. This is done without incurring locking overhead on each access to the object. Sometimes, this particular pattern can be viewed as an antithesis among all the concurrency design patterns. This is due to the fact that several complexities are addressed by the thread-specific storage by prevention of sharing of the available resources among the threads.

The method appears to be invoked on an ordinary object by the application thread. Actually, it is invoked on a thread-specific object. A single thread-specific object proxy can be used by multiple application threads for accessing the unique thread-specific objects associated to each of them. The proxy to distinguish between the thread-specific object it encapsulates uses the application thread identifier.

Best practices for concurrency module

Here is a list of considerations that a programmer must look into when carrying out concurrency. Let's look at the following best practices to consider when you to get a chance to work with the concurrent application module.

- **Obtaining an executor**: The Executor Framework for obtaining an executor supplies the executors utility class. Various types of executors offer specific thread executions policies. Here are three examples:
  - **ExecutorService newCachedThreadPool()**: This creates a thread pool using the previously constructed threads if available. The performance of the programs that make use of the short-lived asynchronous tasks is enhanced using this type of thread pool.
  - **ExecutorService newSingleThreadExecutor()**: A worker thread that is operating in an unbounded queue is used here to create an executor. In this type, the tasks are added to the queue that is then executed one by one. In case, this thread fails during the execution, a new thread will be created and replace the failed thread so that the tasks can be executed without interruption.

- **ExecutorService newFixedThreadPool(int nThreads)**: A fixed number of threads that are operating in a shared unbounded queue are reused in this case for the creation of a thread pool. At threads, the tasks are being actively processed. While all the threads in the pool are active and new tasks are submitted, the tasks will be added in the queue until a thread becomes available for the processing of the new task. If before the shutdown of the executor, the thread fails, a new thread will be created for carrying out the execution of the task. Note that these thread pools exist only when the executor is active or on.

- **Use of cooperative synchronized constructs**: It is recommended to use cooperative synchronized constructs when possible.

- **No unnecessary lengthy tasks and oversubscription**: Lengthy tasks are known to cause deadlock, starvation, and even prevent other tasks from functioning properly. Larger tasks can be broken down into smaller tasks for proper performance. Oversubscription is also a way to avoid the deadlock, starvation, and so on. Using this, more threads than the available number of threads can be created. This is highly efficient when a lengthy task contains a lot of latency.

- **Use of concurrent memory-management functions**: If in a situation, ensuing concurrent memory management functions can be used, it is highly recommended to use it. These can be used when objects with a short lifetime are used. The functions such as `Allot` and `Free` are used to free memory and allocate, without memory barriers or using locks.

- **Use of RAII to manage the lifetime of concurrency objects**: RAII is the abbreviation for **Resource Acquisition Is Initialization**. This is an efficient way to manage the lifetime of a concurrency object.

This was all about the concurrency and it's design patterns that can be used to handle and implement concurrency. These are the most common five design patterns for concurrency programs. Also, some of the best practices for carrying out concurrency modules were discussed. Hope this was an informative a piece and helped you understand how concurrency patterns work!

Summary

In this chapter, you learned several concurrency design patterns and also saw the use cases of these patterns. In this book, I have covered only the basic of the concurrency design patterns. We have included the active object, monitor object, Half-Sync/Half-Async, leader/followers, thread-specific storage, and reactor patterns. These all are the part of the concurrency design patterns in the multithreaded environment of the application. We also discussed some best practices consideration to use the concurrency design pattern in the application.

Index

33671065R00219

Made in the USA
Lexington, KY
13 March 2019